INTERNATIONAL PERSPECTIVES ON ORGANIZATIONAL BEHAVIOR AND HUMAN RESOURCE MANAGEMENT

INTERNATIONAL PERSPECTIVES ON ORGANIZATIONAL BEHAVIOR AND HUMAN RESOURCE MANAGEMENT

THIRD EDITION

BETTY JANE PUNNETT

M.E.Sharpe
Armonk, New York
London, England

The EuroSlavic fonts used to create this work are © 1986–2012 Payne Loving Trust.
EuroSlavic is available from Linguist's Software, Inc.,
www.linguistsoftware.com, P.O. Box 580, Edmonds, WA 98020-0580 USA
tel (425) 775-1130.

Library of Congress Cataloging-in-Publication Data

Punnett, Betty Jane.
  International perspectives on organizational behavior and human resource management / by
Betty Jane Punnett. — 3rd ed.
    p. cm.
  Includes bibliographical references and index.
  ISBN 978-0-7656-3107-7 (hardcover : alk. paper) — ISBN 978-0-7656-3108-4 (pbk. : alk. paper)

1. Organizational behavior—Cross-cultural studies. 2. Corporate culture—Cross-cultural studies.
3. Industrial relations—Cross-cultural studies. 4. Communication in management—Cross-
cultural studies. 5. Intercultural communication. 6. Personnel management—Cross-cultural
studies. 7. International business enterprises—Personnel management—Cross-cultural studies.
I. Title.

  HD58.7.P86 2012
  658′.049—dc23   2012016254

Printed in the United States of America

The paper used in this publication meets the minimum requirements of
American National Standard for Information Sciences
Permanence of Paper for Printed Library Materials,
ANSI Z 39.48-1984.

IBT (c)   10   9   8   7   6   5   4   3   2   1
IBT (p)   10   9   8   7   6   5   4   3   2   1

For the family, with love—
Don, Amanda, Justin
Megan, Dax, Abigail, Mya, Olivia

Contents

Preface   xiii

1. The Management World in the Twenty-First Century   3
   Overview of the Book   5
   The Meaning of Globalization for Managers   7
   Understanding Attitudes to Globalization   8
   The Future of Globalization   11
   Cross-National Convergence and Divergence   14
   The World Beyond 2010   17
   References   19

2. The Cultural Environment   20
   Introduction   20
   Defining Culture   22
   Cultural Values   23
      Values   23
      Needs   24
      Attitudes   24
      Norms   25
   Cultural Value Models   25
      Kluckhohn and Strodtbeck's Value Orientation Model   25
      The Kluckhohn and Strodtbeck Model in International
         Management   27
      Hofstede's Value Survey Model   29
      Limitations of the Value Survey Model   31
      Using the Value Survey Model in International Management   32
      Country Clusters   34
      Smith and Peterson (1988) Event Management Approach   40
      Alternative Cultural Models   46
   Ethnocentrism and Parochialism   47
   Variation Within Cultures   48

Beyond National Culture   50
   Understanding Subcultures   50
   Understanding Overlapping Cultures   51
The Importance of Cultural Values for International Managers   52
Summary and Conclusions   53
References   54

3. The Political and Regulatory Environment   56
Introduction   56
Political Systems   58
Government, Business, and Society   63
   Government View of Business   64
   View of Foreign Business   65
   View of the Home Country   68
Types of Political Risk   69
   Forced Divestment   70
   Unwelcome Regulations   71
   Interference in Operations   72
Assessment and Management of Political Risk   72
   Sources of Information   73
   Factors Affecting Political Risk   74
   Defensive Political Risk Management   76
   Integrative Political Risk Management   77
   Managerial Choices   78
Summary and Conclusions   79
References   80

**4. The Role of History and Geography in International
      Management**   81
Introduction   81
   History and Culture   83
   Geography and Culture   83
   History and Behavior   84
   Geography and Behavior   84
Understanding History and Geography   85
   History, Values, and Behavior   85
   Geography, Values, and Behavior   86
   Influences on Language, Religion, and Economics   89
   Ways of Seeing the World   91

Managing Internationally: The Role of History and Geography   94
    International Trade and Investment   95
    Regional Economic Linkages   98
    International Strategy   100
    Current Events   102
Summary and Conclusions   103
Notes   104
References   104

5. Language and Religion in International Management   105
Introduction   105
Language   105
Linguistic Diversity   109
    The Impact of Homogeneity   109
    The Impact of Heterogeneity   109
    National Languages   110
    Linguistic Hierarchies   110
    Linguistic Change   112
Managing Language Differences   113
    Learning New Languages   113
    Translation and Interpretation   113
Religion   116
    The Expression of Religion   117
Major Religions of the World   118
    Buddhism   118
    Christianity   120
    Hinduism   121
    Islam   122
    Other Religious Beliefs   123
Summary and Conclusions   123
Note   124
References   124

**6. Economic Development and the Management
of Organizational Behavior and Human Resources**   125
Introduction   125
Understanding Development Issues   127
Definitions of Development   128
    Developed Countries   129
    Developing Countries   129
Characteristics of Developing Countries   132

The Impact of Level of Development 134
Demography and Development 136
Culture and Development 140
Politics and Development 144
Summary and Conclusions 148
References 148

7. Motivation in a Cross-National Context 150
Introduction 150
North American Theories of Motivation 151
The Role of Needs in Motivation 152
The Role of Equity in Motivation 157
The Role of Rewards in Motivation 158
The Role of Goals and Expectations in Motivation 161
The Role of Delegation and Participation in Motivation 164
Is Motivation Universal or Culture Bound? 165
Summary and Conclusions 168
Note 168
References 168

8. Leadership in a Cross-National Context 170
Introduction 170
Theories of Leadership 171
Supports/Substitutes for Leadership 178
Charismatic and Transformational Leadership and
    the GLOBE Project 179
Path/Goal Clarification 181
Variation in Leadership Concepts 182
Some Cultural Interactions 186
Summary and Conclusions 190
References 191

**9. Cross-National Dimensions of Communication and
    Negotiation** 193
Introduction 193
The Communication Flow 194
Communication Is a Process 195
Communication Includes Purposive and Expressive
    Messages 195
Communication Is Made Up of Multi-Unit Signals 195
Communication Depends on the Context for Its Meaning 196

Communication Depends on the Competence of the
    Communicators   197
Barriers to Cross-National Communication Competence   198
    Ignorance of Rules of Communication   198
    Perceptual Biases   201
    Faulty Attributions   203
    Stereotypes   204
Negotiations in International Contexts   205
    The Negotiation Process   206
    Negotiating Norms in Selected Countries   211
Summary and Conclusions   215
References   216

10. Human Resource Choices in a Cross-National Context   218
Introduction   218
Groups of Employees in International Firms   218
Employee Groups: Benefits and Drawbacks   220
    Parent Country Nationals (PCNs)   220
    Host Country Nationals (HCNs)   222
    Third Country Nationals (TCNs)   224
    Staffing and the International Product Life Cycle   228
    Foreign Guest Workers   229
    Organizational Structure and International HRM Choices   231
Selection and Training of International Managers   233
    The Training Process   237
    Compensation and Benefits   238
    Promotion, Career Development, Retirement   240
Summary and Conclusions   241
References   241

11. Managing the Expatriate Experience   242
Introduction   242
Special Issues Associated with Expatriates   243
Expatriate Adjustment   244
    The Cycle of Culture Shock and Cross-Cultural Adjustment 246
    Determinants of Expatriate Adjustment   247
Cross-Cultural Training   252
    Approaches to Cross-Cultural Training   252
    Appropriate Training   256
Dual-Career Couples   257
Summary and Conclusions   261
References   261

12. Special Issues in International Human Resource Management   263
   Introduction   263
   The Role of Women in Business Around the World   264
      Some Examples of Women's Role in Business   267
      The Meaning of Equality   271
   Women as Managers in Different Countries   272
      The Role of Women as Managers in Selected Locations   273
   Women as International Managers   275
   Other Personal Characteristics   278
   Ethics in International Management Decisions   279
      Universal Versus Culturally Contingent   283
   Climate Change: The New Ethical Issue   283
   Summary and Conclusions   284
   References   285

Index   287
About the Author   301

Preface

Globalization of the business world has become an accepted fact of the twenty-first century. In turn, this means that managers must have a global perspective and be able to function effectively as international managers. This need was the impetus for my undertaking this book. Although globalization and international management are both realities, the business world has largely overlooked the need to understand how cross-national differences affect management. The focus of international business discussions is often on economics, finance, trade, and investment—that is, the forces that drive the internationalization of businesses. Less often do we see discussions of the human face of managing in different countries, and managing people of varying national backgrounds. Yet, it is often the ability to manage across national differences that leads to success in international business.

For the global business world, 2011 and 2012 were eventful years. Among other events of interest to international managers:

- The European Union and the euro were under severe stress because of imbalances in various countries.
- The "Arab Spring" continued to affect countries in North Africa and the Middle East, with changes in government and a major conflict in Syria.
- Iran continued to develop its nuclear capability and was largely shunned by much of the Western world.
- Citizens around the world demonstrated against extremes of wealth and poverty, in what was called initially the "Occupy Wall Street" movement.
- China continued to be the main supplier of manufactured products for the rest of the world, but even China's growth slowed in response to lower demand from the developed countries of the world.

Studies and books that have looked at national differences and their impact on management have focused largely on cultural differences. Cultural differences are a very important component of cross-national differences, and they are a core aspect of the discussions in this book; however, as the events outlined previously illustrate, there are other aspects of nations that also affect management. The approach in this book is, therefore, to address a variety of national characteristics (culture, politics and regulations, history and geography, language and religion, and economic development) and explore how they are likely to affect management. In addition, chapters address the issues of motivation, leadership, communication, and negotiation from a cross-national perspective, and consider human resource choices, the expatriate experience, and special international management issues relating to women, personal characteristics, and ethics.

There is relatively little research and literature that directly addresses the question of how national characteristics affect management. This book draws on the existing research and literature, but it also relies substantially on real examples and on identifying conceptual or theoretical propositions about the relationship between certain national characteristics, behavior, and effective management. Much of what is presented in the book is intended to be thought-provoking and to encourage managers, and soon-to-be managers, to think about the issues they encounter cross-nationally. The book explores a variety of cross-national differences and provides a basis for managers to understand and deal with the differences they encounter.

I was encouraged to write the first edition of this book by a number of colleagues, as well as by my students. My students particularly commented that the material I covered in class went beyond the traditional cross-cultural and international management information in ways that they found helpful. The first and second editions of the book have been well received, and this has encouraged me to put in the time and effort to complete this third edition. Writing the third edition has been an interesting experience. I began thinking it would be easy—I would update a few numbers and add a few new examples. In reality, I found that there was much to be updated. While this meant the task was more time consuming than I had envisioned, I was also pleased to find that there was a substantial body of new material to be incorporated into the third edition. It seems that the importance of understanding a variety of cross-national differences and how they affect management is now more mainstream than when I wrote the first edition of the book. There is a burgeoning interest in management in developing countries that did not exist earlier, and this has spurred interest in cross-national issues and how these affect management in a global business environment.

There is a companion book, *Experiencing International Business and Management*, which many people find a good addition to the classroom. This book consists of a variety of exercises and cases that encourage student involvement and add an interesting dimension to classes. Interestingly, this book, originally written twenty years ago, has changed little over the years, in comparison to the *International Perspectives on Organizational Behavior and Human Resource Management.* This is probably because the exercises that simulate reality and involve students remain relatively constant, while the theory and concepts dealing with cross-national issues are continually evolving.

My aim in this third edition has been to continue to keep the language simple and straightforward so that students as well as practicing managers will find the book readable and easy to understand. At the same time, the book covers complex concepts and incorporates up-to-date and mainstream academic research. Examples are used throughout the text to illustrate the concepts and theories, and to ensure that the material is both lively and practical.

If I have achieved my aims, both students and instructors will like using this text. People learn best when they enjoy what they are doing, so if you like the text, I believe it will be a good learning tool. At the same time, I recognize that there will always be substantial room for improvement, and I welcome and look forward to your comments.

Many people have contributed to this book, including my former professors, academic colleagues, and students who have read and commented on early drafts of chapters. My husband, Don, has carefully and painstakingly read each draft of all chapters and helped me to improve them and ensure that they are accurate and readable. I have enjoyed working with the people at M.E. Sharpe, Inc., particularly the editor, Harry Briggs, who provided enthusiastic support for the first and second editions, and encouragement to complete the third edition. I want to thank all those who have contributed to completing the book.

INTERNATIONAL PERSPECTIVES ON ORGANIZATIONAL BEHAVIOR AND HUMAN RESOURCE MANAGEMENT

1

The Management World in the
Twenty-First Century

About four thousand years ago, the technologically advanced Minoan civilization flourished on the Greek island of Crete. This society had amenities like flush toilets and drainage and road systems, which still function today. The Minoans also had a well-developed system of foreign trade and investment. Around 1450 B.C.E., for reasons that are unclear today, most of their infrastructure was destroyed and the civilization returned to a much less advanced level of technology, with little foreign trade or investment.

The Minoan experience reminds us that the world can change suddenly and dramatically. There is no question today that the effects of environmental changes, often referred to as climate change or global warming, could have an equally dramatic impact on our world. The world's very dependence on the Internet and electronic communication could cause major problems if the Internet were shut down for an appreciable time. These changes might mean that well-thought-out plans made today become essentially meaningless in the future. While we cannot plan for unexpected discontinuities, an effective international manager makes a conscious effort to be aware of changes occurring around the world. This book is about managing businesses that operate across national boundaries. The particular focus of the book is on organizational behavior and human resource management. These aspects of management are crucial in international companies because people in different locations are different. International managers need to deal with these differences effectively. There are many stories about managers making mistakes or failing internationally because they assumed that "their way was best," yet they could not function effectively in a foreign environment. For example:

- "In the facilitation of a national program in St. Lucia, the leadership practice developed was congruent with the top-down hierarchical leadership system, involving little information sharing or empowerment of subordinates. This style emerged in spite of efforts on the part of the consultants to flatten the hierarchy and share the power. It appeared that leaders and subordinates supported and felt more comfortable with the clearly defined hierarchy. This comfort is not present with a Caribbean manager in my Canadian company. In St. Lucia this style worked because it was accepted. In Canada it is not working and 'tricksters' continually try to undermine the manager's authority. The more this happens the less she trusts them and accordingly her dictatorial stance increases" (Punnett and Greenidge 2009).

- It was reported in the 1980s that North American managers negotiating with the Japanese often found the Japanese predilection for silence disconcerting. Some Americans and Canadians, seeking to fill the silence, would apparently agree to unnecessary concessions. The Japanese were simply considering the situation (although it is also believed that they learned to use silence effectively to their advantage). The North Americans were not getting the best deal they could because they did not understand the communication context.

- A Nepalese academic visiting a Canadian colleague commented that she was surprised to find that Canadians were very religious. The Canadian was surprised at the comment because Canadians do not generally see themselves in this light. Further discussions revealed that it was Halloween and all the houses, shops, and gas stations were decorated with ghosts and carved pumpkins that the Nepalese visitor saw as evidence of religious devotion. Of course, the custom is based on religious traditions, but these have largely disappeared from Canadian thinking.

- According to Mercer's *2008/2009 Benefits Survey for Expatriates and Globally Mobile Employees*, the number of expatriates had almost doubled in the preceding three years (Mercer 2008). Companies continued to report that a number of expatriates are "failures"; that is, they return early or do not perform well on assignments abroad. Studies suggest that a major reason for failure is an inability to adjust to the new cultural environment, on the part of either the expatriate or their spouse and family. Expatriates are costly to companies, and their success or failure is important to the company's effectiveness; thus, high levels of failure are a concern for international companies, as well as host countries seeking international investment and local employment.

These cases illustrate the importance of understanding the environment in different countries. Effective managers are ones who pay attention to the variations across national borders and adjust to and manage these variations. The objective of this book is to provide managers with ways to understand, adjust to, and manage cross-national variations.

This first chapter provides an overview of the business world at the beginning of the twenty-first century. It considers the concept of globalization and different views of globalization by examining some economic events and trends around the world. This discussion illustrates the international nature of business today and, through this, the need for managers to focus on understanding organizational behavior and managing human resources cross-nationally. The chapter concludes by discussing the forces for convergence and divergence in today's business environment and sets the stage for the topics covered in the subsequent chapters.

Overview of the Book

Cross-national distinctions exist for many reasons. Cultural values can vary greatly from country to country. One focus of this book will be culture—that is, cultural values, cultural similarities and differences, and the role of culture in behavior. Culture is not, however, the only variable that makes countries different and that affects behavior and human resource choices cross-nationally. This book will also consider the role of politics and regulations, history and geography, language and religion, and economics and demographics. Culture will be introduced and covered in chapter 2; the other topics will be covered in chapters 3 to 6. These are all related to culture, but each has its own impact on management, and it is important to look at this impact. These chapters provide a description of the cross-national environment in which international firms operate. Chapters 7 to 9 consider the impact of this environment on specific aspects of management, motivation, leadership, and communication and negotiation. They explore the links between culture, politics, and other environmental factors and organizational behavior. Chapters 10 and 11 consider human resource issues, including cross-national workforce choices and managing expatriates. The final chapter, chapter 12, focuses on special issues, especially gender, race, and religion internationally, as well as ethical issues for international managers, including issues of universality and contingency in decisions that have an ethical dimension.

Throughout the book, sophisticated concepts and theories are explored, but every attempt is made to discuss these in plain and understandable language. Research is reported, wherever possible, to support the contentions put forward. There is little research, however, that specifically links such variables as cultural values or political systems to behavior and human resource management, so these discussions are often based on logically reasoning what relationships can be expected. It is important to note, as well, that the majority of research on organizational behavior and human resource management has focused on North America, Europe, and Japan

(Thomas 1996), the three countries that account for much of the world's trade and investment. This means that there is relatively little research to draw on when other parts of the world are discussed. For example, Das and colleagues (2009) found that research papers published in mainstream economics journals were linked to level of development. They found that countries with the lowest incomes and weakest economies received the least attention in the literature—over a twenty-year period they identified 4 papers on Barundi and more than 37,000 on the United States. Similarly, in management, Baruch (2001) commented that examinations of management have focused on locations in the industrialized world, particularly North America and Western Europe, resulting in management theories that are biased. Bruton (2010) said that there was limited research on the poorer countries of the world, and identified only a small number of articles dealing with issues associated with poor countries in the past two decades.

Other parts of the world are becoming increasingly relevant to international firms, as markets as well as supply sources and locations for operations, and this book does include substantial reference to these "forgotten locations" as Thomas (1996) called them. More recently, countries such as Mexico have received more research attention than in the past, probably reflecting their growing business importance to the United States. In addition, the BRICS countries (Brazil, Russia, India, China, and South Africa) have recently become of interest to researchers because of the increasing importance of their economies in the world. Other countries and regions, such as the Caribbean and the Middle East, have indigenous researchers who conduct management research locally, but this is not widely available to managers in other parts of the world. The advent of the Internet has increased the number of global research teams looking at a variety of management issues, and we can expect that in the future, management research will be more all-encompassing.

The 2008 G8 (eight rich countries) meeting in Davos, Switzerland, illustrated the global concern over the lack of input from a wide array of important countries, large and small, into economic decisions that affect everyone in the world. Traditionally the G8 group has consisted of the richest countries of the world, and they have met annually to discuss global economic issues. In 2008, the rest of the world questioned this tradition. Similar concerns have been raised about the legitimacy of the Security Council of the United Nations. The recent round of World Trade Organization talks—the Doha round—has continued slowly, largely because the poorer countries of the world would not simply agree to the demands of the wealthier countries. These developments all suggest that managers will need to be knowledgeable about a wider array of countries in the future than they have been in the past.

The Meaning of Globalization for Managers

Globalization is no longer a buzzword or considered a fad; it is now an accepted fact of the business world. Virtually every business and management publication, whether academic or popular, includes discussions of the global nature of the business world and the spread of global trade and investment. Essentially, globalization refers to growth of trade and investment, accompanied by the growth in international businesses and the integration of economies around the world. The globalization concept is based on a number of relatively simple premises, which continue to hold true and accelerate:

- Technological developments have increased the ease and speed of international communication and travel.
- Increased communication and travel have made the world seem smaller.
- A smaller world means that people are more aware of events outside of their home country and are more likely to travel to other countries.
- Increased awareness and travel result in a better understanding of foreign opportunities.
- A better understanding of opportunities leads to increases in international trade and investment and the number of businesses operating across national borders.
- These increases mean that the economies around the world are more closely integrated.
- The World Trade Organization (WTO) continues to encourage global free trade, and many regional trade agreements have been signed in the past five years, all leading to increases in trade and investment.

Managers at the beginning of the twenty-first century are faced with the reality of globalization. Whether they are in a major, global organization or a small, domestic one, whether operating from the U.S. superpower base or from a tiny island state in the Pacific, globalization is the reality of their business environment. The impact in 2008 of the subprime loans in the United States was clearly felt around the world, as it was discovered that questionable loans had been bought by investors from Australia to Zanzibar. Although globalization can be described as a reality, some people question whether there are real benefits to globalization. More developed countries have continued to experience low levels of growth, or recession, including high levels of unemployment, through to 2012. Developing countries have fared better, but these countries have been affected by the slow growth in the more developed countries.

Managers must be conscious that markets, supplies, investors, locations, partners, competitors, and so on can exist anywhere in the world. Successful businesses will exploit opportunities wherever they are and will be ready for the threats from wherever they come. This can be described as having a "global philosophy"—seeing the world as the place to do business and making decisions in this context. Even where a company's strategy is to remain essentially local, this should be a conscious strategy, having considered the global possibilities. Successful managers in this environment need to understand the similarities and differences across national boundaries in order to exploit the opportunities and deal with the threats. For example:

- Consumers in Africa may want a different kind of Internet access from consumers in the United States. In some locations, speed is valued; in others unrestricted access is more important.
- Suppliers in Europe may provide different credit terms from suppliers in Latin America. In some countries liberal credit terms are the norm (payment in six months); in others payment in advance is expected.
- Negotiations in the People's Republic of China (PRC) will be different from negotiations in Canada. Some people negotiate from extreme points and expect each side to give concessions; others begin where they expect to end and do not give concessions.
- Motivating employees in Nigeria will be different from motivating employees in Japan. In some cultures, people like to work individually and are motivated by individual rewards; in other cultures, people prefer to work closely with their peers and look for group recognition and rewards.

The objective of this book is to give readers a thorough understanding of the factors that are important in managing across national boundaries, particularly those factors that influence people's behavior and human resource choices. We begin in the following section by considering different attitudes toward globalization.

Understanding Attitudes to Globalization

The phenomenon of globalization arouses passionate responses, both positive and negative, from different groups. These different responses are briefly described here.

During the 1980s and the 1990s, there were significant efforts to promote global free trade and investment, with the general belief that freer trade and investment would be good for the world economy. It was believed that developing countries, as well as developed ones, would benefit from globalization. Institutions such as the World Bank and regional development banks saw

globalization as an essential part of economic, political, and social development throughout the world. The World Trade Organization was established
at the beginning of 1995 with the mandate to carry forward the work of the
General Agreement on Tariffs and Trade (GATT), which had negotiated freer
trade among its members during a series of negotiating rounds beginning in
the 1950s.

During the early 1990s, there were reasons to feel that globalization was
working. The economic success of Singapore; the rapid economic growth
in the "Asian Tigers" (as the Asian countries that grew rapidly were called,
including Indonesia, the Philippines, South Korea, Taiwan, and Thailand);
the industrializing of such countries as Brazil and Mexico; and a variety of
other positive economic events around the world suggested that the results
of globalization were indeed good for development in poorer countries, as
well as in richer ones. During the 1990s, the United States experienced one
of its most sustained periods of growth as well, and there was much talk of
a "new economy" based on globalization, which was immune to economic
shocks and recession.

Unfortunately, this brave new world was not a reality. The Seattle
meetings of the WTO in the 1990s (referred to as "the battle in Seattle" or
the "Seattle debacle") turned into a fiasco, with anti-globalization groups
demonstrating against globalization on all fronts—from animal rights to
environmental concerns, poverty alleviation, and jobs for Americans. The
anti-globalization forces have not coalesced into a coherent whole because
they represent such diverse and often contradictory views, but the vehe-
mence of their protests makes it clear that globalization is not a panacea
for the world's problems. In addition, the Asian Tigers suffered major economic setbacks in the late 1990s; and in 2002, Argentina's economy, which
had been one of the stars of the 1990s, crashed when the country could no
longer maintain its currency at par with the U.S. dollar.

Further problems occurred in the economies of Japan, Europe, and the
United States—often referred to as the "triad" that for much of the second half
of the twentieth century has dominated international trade and investment.
The Japanese economy went into a severe period of recession and deflation
later in the 1990s, and in 2001, the U.S. economy turned downward as did
the European. In turn, the rest of the world was negatively affected by the
economic situation in the triad. The terrorist attacks in the United States
in September 2001 exacerbated this already negative economic situation.
The early years of the twenty-first century included the major war in Iraq
that dominated U.S. attention, high oil prices that affected all of the world,
concerns about climate change, and major economic problems in 2008.
More recently, developed countries around the world have experienced slow

growth, or in some cases no growth. In 2012, several countries in the European Union experienced serious economic problems (Greece, for example, suffered its third consecutive year of negative economic growth; and many European countries were experiencing high unemployment rates, especially among young people). These problems have led to significant cutbacks in government spending in the affected countries. Perhaps most important is that many people are rethinking the benefits of the European Union and its common currency, the euro.

Inevitably, the pendulum swung away from praise for globalization to a belief that it was actually the cause of the economic woes of the early twenty-first century. This is no more the reality than the brave new world was. It is an economic fact that periods of faster growth are followed by periods of slower growth, and that downturns occur following upturns in economic activity. The problems that such Asian countries as Japan have faced may have more to do with systems that needed to be restructured than with free trade and investment (e.g., the close ownership linkages between banks and corporations and government/business ties may result in inefficiencies). Argentina's problems appeared to be associated with the choice to link its currency to the U.S. dollar when trade and investment imbalances made it impossible to maintain the Argentine currency at this level. Argentina's economy grew at about 7.5 percent in 2010 and is currently described as a stable economy in 2012.

The reality is that globalization is neither a panacea nor a demon. Economically, it can be demonstrated that a move from no trade to free trade, and similarly a move to freer trade, benefits all trading partners; thus, globalization should provide benefits for all participants. The benefits are not necessarily shared equally, however, and some partners will likely benefit more than others. Those who benefit most will like globalization; those who benefit least will not. Within a given country, as well, some segments will benefit while others will be hurt. Those who benefit will want globalization; those who are hurt will want protection. Similarly, free trade and investment often require restructuring, which can be painful in any country, and possibly devastating for countries whose economies are already fragile.

The differing impact of globalization can be seen in the disparity between the developed and developing countries, as the following statistics illustrated (United Nations 2000):

- The richest 20 percent of the world have 86 percent of the world's gross domestic product (GDP), the middle 60 percent have 13 percent, and the poorest 20 percent, only 1 percent.
- Gross national product (GNP) per capita in the developed world is $22,785; in the developing world it is $5,725.

- Disparity between rich and poor countries is growing. Comparisons of GNP per capita of the top 20 percent with the bottom 20 percent over the past two centuries show a dramatic increase. The ratio in 1820 was 3:1; in 1870, 7:1; in 1913, 11:1; in 1960, 30:1; in 1990, 60:1; and in 1997, 74:1.

There is no question that during the twentieth century, the rich were growing richer, and the poor were not catching up; people in developing countries feel disadvantaged by this disparity. Advocates for the developing world point to this disparity as evidence that globalization has not helped the poorer 80 percent of the world. In contrast, advocates of globalization argue that incomes in the poorer countries have been increasing, and that these countries do not trade as much as the richer ones, and therefore cannot expect to have benefited as much. This argument says more trade and investment are needed, not less. Notably, the recession of 2008 onward affected the rich countries more than it did the poorer countries and there is a new interest in the developing countries. The situation in the People's Republic of China (PRC) is instructive. The PRC has become the supplier of inexpensive manufactured products for most of the world. The PRC lacks some needed resources, however, and has been investing substantially in countries in Africa and Latin America, where the resources are available. This has pushed economic growth in the PRC as well as in the countries where it invests.

In the context of managing across national boundaries, the important issue for managers is that they understand the arguments for and against globalization rather than seeking to prove or disprove them. Managers in international companies are likely to find themselves having to deal with people who have both positive and negative views of globalization. These managers are, by default, the human face of globalization. The current concerns with the results of globalization mean that international firms will be examined more closely today than a decade ago, and management's decisions and activities will often be carefully scrutinized. Making appropriate human resource choices and paying attention to behavioral issues will be critical to success in this environment.

The Future of Globalization

An article in the *Economist* entitled "Steel the Prize" (2006, 64) discussed the takeover battle between Tata, an Indian steel conglomerate, and CSN, a Brazilian Steelmaker, for Corus, the Anglo-Dutch company that absorbed British Steel. This may be a harbinger of the face of the future—two giant companies from developing countries fighting over a developed-country asset. The Indian company Tata has emerged as a pioneer in automotive innovation and China's car makers continue to copy cars from traditional automakers. Chinese-owned businesses are investing around the world, Dubai is establishing itself as a global financial center, and companies small and large from developing countries around the world are now investing in the developed world. The *Economist* ("India's Foreign Takeover Spree" 2012) reported that India's cross-border takeovers during the previous decade were worth US$129 billion. This seems a huge sum, but is only about 1.5 percent of the total, similar to Brazil and Russia, and well below China, whose share, including Hong Kong, was about 6.2 percent. Early in 2012, an interesting new development in the international business world was under way—Myanmar (formerly Burma) was liberalizing, both politically and from a business perspective, and prospective business was reported in the media as anxious to take advantage of this new opportunity. After years of repression, it is not clear how complete or lasting this liberalization in Myanmar will be, but it certainly illustrates the constantly changing nature of international business opportunities and challenges.

What literature there is on management interactions between developing and developed countries implicitly assumes that managers from developed countries will be adapting to the environment in developing countries. The reverse may be more and more the reality of the management challenges of the twenty-first century.

Earlier, a "Special Report on Globalization" appeared in a 2002 issue of the *Economist*. The article discussed the downturn in the world's big economies, and many emerging ones, and the consequent stagnation in cross-border flows of goods and capital that underlie economic integration. The article looked further at the impact of the September 11 attacks on the World Trade Center, exposing the dark side of global interconnectedness. Finally, it raised the question of Argentina's collapse after it had removed trade barriers and made itself open for business internationally. Some critics were quick to say that this was the end of the global era. The *Economist* argued otherwise and found little evidence that there was likely to be an extended slowdown in global economic integration, suggesting that new rounds of trade talks were likely to continue. The article drew attention to the fact that "globalization is not, and never was, global" (66) (as mentioned earlier, a relatively small number of countries account for a large proportion of trade and investment).

Not surprisingly, the economic slowdown in the developed countries has had a negative impact on trade and investment. During slow economic times, there is less consumption and production, and this affects domestic and international trade and investment. The 9/11 terrorist attacks also had an impact that slowed international trade and investment, resulting in less international travel for businesspeople and tourists, higher costs for services such as insurance and security, and closer scrutiny of international financial transactions. More recent concerns with climate change and the impact of one's carbon footprint are also likely to have a significant impact on trade and investment, affecting both the direction and the focus of global movements of goods, services, capital, and human resources.

According to a report in 2008, foreign direct investment (FDI) inflows were US$640 billion in 1998, three times the US$174 billion of 1988. By 2006 international investment had grown to over 1.2 trillion U.S. dollars (www.unglobalcompact.org, accessed February 14, 2008). According to www.unctad.com (accessed March 4, 2012), like other economic activities, FDI has been going through dramatic changes since the end of 2008. The ongoing economic and financial crisis has resulted in decreased investment and expansion abroad. Faltering profits, reduced access to financial resources, declining market opportunities, as well as the risk of a possible worsening of the current global economic downturn, are the obvious causes for a fall in FDI flows. The report notes, however, that companies are more optimistic about the future, and FDI is expected to start rising again.

In recent years there has also been a dramatic increase in commerce between developing countries; it has doubled from about 8 percent of world trade in 1990 to over 16 percent in 2007, and the share of developing countries' exports to developing countries increased from 29 percent in 1990 to 47 percent in 2008 (Broadman 2011). A substantial portion of this has been Chinese and Indian investments in Africa. According to Broadman, many observers believe that Chinese and Indian firms dominate Africa's economies, but this is incorrect, because 90 percent of the stock of FDI originated from developed countries; however, Chinese and Indian investments have dominated African inward FDI in recent years.

The BRICS countries have emerged as an important force globally. The acronym "BRIC" was originally coined to encapsulate the fast growing economies of Brazil, Russia, India, and China. It later evolved into a formal grouping that held policy meetings, and South Africa joined the group. In March 2012, BRICS held a meeting where they discussed the formation of a bank for developing/emerging countries, which would essentially rival the World Bank, and counter the influence of the more developed world in international financial institutions. Whether this idea will ever become a reality, only time will tell, but these discussions suggest a shift in the balance of economic power in the world. The G20, a bloc of developing nations established at the WTO Ministerial Conference, is also a force to be considered. The G20 accounts for about 60 percent of the world's population.

These numbers suggest a continuing trend toward globalization and continued increases in trade and investment. We do not know whether or not this will change. Today managers in international companies clearly have to be alert at all times to what is happening in their environment. The underlying forces contributing to globalization (such as technology that improves global communication and travel) are continuing to advance, and this suggests that globalization will persist and probably accelerate. The statement at the beginning of the chapter, referring to Crete four millennia ago, is a reminder, however, of how the business world can change. During periods where change is anticipated, as it is today, it is especially important that the right people are in the right place, and that behavioral interactions are managed well. Today's business environment is one where attention to cross-national issues, appropriate human resource choices, and effective management of people are essential.

Cross-National Convergence and Divergence

Globalization, and the forces that lead to global integration, also lead to a certain degree of convergence in behaviors around the world. Some observers have argued that people are becoming more and more alike, and that cross-national differences are not as important today as they were, say, fifty years ago. Thirty years ago, Levitt (1983) wrote, "a powerful force drives the world toward a converging commonality." More travel and easier communication certainly means that people everywhere are much more aware of what is happening in other parts of the world. Much of the media is now global, so that the people of Afghanistan can know what is happening in the United States and can see the lifestyles of the people there. Movies made in India are shown around the world, as are American movies. Jeans and t-shirts have become the preferred dress for young people almost everywhere; a Middle Eastern businessman is as likely to wear a Western suit as traditional Middle Eastern robes; an African professor in Canada will wear traditional dress one day and gray flannels with a blue blazer the next. Chinese restaurants abound in New York and London, and Kentucky Fried Chicken and McDonald's are found around the world from Beijing to Tokyo to Moscow. These examples are evidence of the spread of different cultural and national characteristics globally. The spread of the Internet and access to the Internet, combined with the spread of cell phone access, has had a dramatic influence on people's attitudes, allowing users from virtually anywhere to share their opinions with others around the world. Even where countries limit their citizens' access to the Internet or cell phones, as is the case in countries such as the People's Republic of China or Myanmar, people find ways around these restrictions.

The growth in firms operating cross-nationally also contributes to the convergence of attitudes, values, and behaviors. Managers, when they operate in different countries, naturally take aspects of their home culture with them, and some of this will be appealing to those with whom they work and will be adopted by them. Some international firms make efforts to standardize policies and procedures throughout the nations in which they operate. These firms often try to develop a corporate culture that is common to all their diverse locations. The activities of individual managers, as well as the efforts of firms, can be expected to result in a certain degree of convergence across nations.

Shared worldwide concerns, such as climate change, also suggest a potential convergence of values. If cultural values develop in response to perceived survival needs, then global concerns that are not defined by national boundaries may lead to global solutions and shared values. Similarly, regional economic integration, as exemplified by the European Union (EU), is also a force for convergence of values. These regions seek to standardize a variety of practices, and this standardization, in turn, is likely to influence cultural values.

In contrast to the convergence arguments, many people believe that cross-national differences continue and are as important, if not more so, today. For example, managers in the English-speaking Caribbean were asked what advice they would give to a foreign manager coming to the region (Punnett 2002). Overwhelmingly, they responded that things were done differently, and that the foreign manager would need to spend the time to learn how things were done in the region. Discussing marketing issues in earlier stages of globalization, Terpstra (1982) said, "it is the international differences in buyer behavior, rather than the similarities, which pose stumbling blocks to successful international marketing. Thus the differences must receive disproportionate attention." The same can be said for differences in people's behavior more generally. The terrorist attacks of September 11, 2001, brought home these differences for many people in the United States. The idea that there were people elsewhere who so hated the United States, and all it stands for, that they would take their own lives along with those of thousands of others, was simply unbelievable. Consider the many disputes around the world today, from Afghanistan to Zimbabwe, that are based on an "us" versus "them" mentality; these certainly illustrate that cross-national and cross-cultural differences have by no means disappeared. Continuing ethnic and tribal problems in places like Iraq, Gaza, Kenya, and countries around the world make it clear that we are not all the same.

If you take the London subway or walk down the street in Toronto, you cannot help but notice the many languages that are spoken, the various forms of dress that are worn, the different greetings that are used, the assortment of foods prepared by different groups. Italian communities in Toronto are still very Italian, Chinese communities in New York still very Chinese, and West Indian communities in London very West Indian. If people retain their national and cultural characteristics when they immigrate and live in a mixed society, they will surely retain them at home. The evidence of cross-national and cross-cultural divergence, or distinctiveness, is as compelling as the evidence of convergence.

Ease of communication and travel can possibly have a divergent effect instead of a convergent one. Extensive exposure to foreigners and foreign media may increase awareness of the home values, which may be seen as particularly "good" in contrast to foreign values. A sense of domination by foreigners can result in a determination to maintain one's own value system. Canadians, for example, feel that they are very influenced by the United States and react by being more Canadian; a decade ago, some people in the United States were concerned about the Japanese influence and reacted by perceiving Japanese ways as negative.

The collapse of the Soviet Union suggests that strong cultural value differences can be maintained by groups within a union, in spite of efforts to eliminate these differences. Similarly, French Canadians wish to be recognized as a distinct society within Canada, and Native American groups argue for self-government based on cultural uniqueness.

An interesting view has been put forward by Kotkin in connection with the World Values Survey in the *Economist* ("Schumpeter" 2012). He argues that the world can be divided into big cultural zones, including the Confucian zone and the English-speaking zone. In each of these zones people hold common values. These common values appear to positively affect trade and investment. Describing the common values as "tribal loyalties," the *Economist* explained that tribal loyalty fosters trust, and cultural affinity supercharges communication. At the same time, the *Economist* says that the lines between different cultural zones are often blurred, with countries pulled in different directions.

It could also be argued that the activities of multinational and global companies can contribute to divergence. Some of these companies provide products or services specifically developed for particular countries or regions, and some adapt their business decisions to fit the needs of different locations. This sensitivity to cultural differences can in effect perpetuate the differences.

The reality of the world is both convergence and divergence, and arguments for both are quite reasonable. Perhaps one can conclude that convergence will occur in some aspects of culture and divergence in others; that is, in some ways, people are becoming more similar, but in many ways, they retain their distinctiveness. For marketing or production decisions, it may be appropriate to look for the similarities and standardize approaches where possible. However, the managers who motivate those with whom they work, who provide leadership, communicate effectively, and make good human resource choices, are more likely to focus on the differences, as awareness of these is likely to be critical in achieving desired performance. Differences in behavior are important in all firms, even domestic ones, and managers in the United States may find that Mexican Americans differ from Chinese Americans, and it may be beneficial to pay attention to these differences by treating certain groups of employees in special ways.

Managers in international firms must always expect and be ready to deal with differences, and it is especially critical for them if they are the foreigners or work with others from different national/cultural backgrounds. A quiz used in a Canadian class in Ontario says, "You are in Japan, with two colleagues from Quebec, negotiating with a team of six Japanese managers," and asks how many foreigners there are (personal correspondence with Professor Lorna Wright currently with York University, formerly with Queen's University). There were always a few students whose answer was "six," illustrating that we do not always recognize that we are the foreigners when we are outside our home country. In many ways, managers in international firms, when they are outside their home country, are like ambassadors, and thus they should be particularly cognizant of their own behavior, as well as their interactions with others. International managers should be aware of the forces leading to both convergence and divergence and in specific situations consider their likely impact.

The Internet may potentially be a force for both convergence and divergence because it provides an opportunity for people around the world to communicate easily with each other. This increased communication means that people can easily learn about each other, and this is likely to contribute to converging values. At the same time, it can be argued that the Internet allows small numbers of people who share a particular view to communicate with each other and develop divergent value systems. The Internet continues to change and evolve, and the final impact of the Internet on cultural values remains to be identified by future researchers.

The World Beyond 2010

The world today seems, in many ways, a world of extremes. There are very large business enterprises that dominate the news (in 2010, the Ponzi schemes of Bernard Madoff and Alan Stanford captured people's attention and many were concerned with news of huge bonuses paid to executives in the financial industry), but at the same time the vast majority of businesses—even international ones—are small or medium-sized. There are a small number of individuals who are incredibly wealthy (multibillionaires are now discussed in place of millionaires), yet much of the world remains agonizingly poor. The superpower United States and its allies fight wars with high-technology equipment, such as drones, while people are hacked to death with homemade machetes in parts of Africa. The Internet and instant communication are accepted as a part of life in North America and Europe, but millions of people in Africa live without clean drinking water or electricity. The human genome project promises longer and better lives, but the HIV/AIDS epidemic is widespread in many parts of the world. Religious divides seem wider than ever: the Israel–Palestine conflict has continued with little expectation of change, religious terrorist attacks in Iraq were motivated by Islamic extremists, Christians and Muslims clashed in Nigeria, Hindus and Muslims killed each other in India, and people still discussed whether the United States should consider "waterboarding" as torture. The "Arab Spring" has led to major changes, with countries such as Tunisia, Egypt, and Libya overthrowing leaders who had been in power for almost half a century, but the situation has remained in a state of flux with no one sure of what the outcome will be.

The world no longer worries about the millennium year (a major concern only fifteen years ago). This earlier worry illustrates both global and local issues. Because essentially all existing computers had been manufactured with the largely Western time frame, the change from one millennium to the next could have affected computers around the world. At the same time, the year 2000 or 2001 only has significance in the Christian calendar. It represents about two thousand years since the beginning of the Christian religion. Christians are a major group in the world, but Muslims, Sikhs, Buddhists, Jews, and members of other religions are equally a part of the world, and for them there is nothing magical about two millennia after Christ's appearance. A much bigger concern today is climate change. It has become clearer to ordinary people of the world that our climate appears to be changing. While climate is a long-term phenomenon, and short-term changes may be short-lived, ask almost anyone, anywhere and they will likely say "our weather has not been the same in recent years." Some places are colder, some warmer, some dryer, some wetter. It is not clear what the end result will be for a particular location. Climate change leads to many challenges, and it also leads to new international opportunities.

International managers function in this world of extremes and differences. It is vital that they be aware of the reality of the world, in all its many guises, and take the time and make the effort to learn about other countries. This book is intended to provide a beginning for such understanding and learning. While this book covers many of the issues that are critical to international managers, and provides information on a variety of countries, it can only point the way; readers will want to identify particular issues and particular countries for further study. Fortunately, there are a wide variety of sources available for the interested reader.

References

Baruch, Y. 2001. "Global or North American? A Geographical Based Comparative Analysis of Publications in Top Management Journals." *International Journal of Cross Cultural Management* 1(1): 109–126.

Broadman, H.G. 2011. "The Backstory of China and India's Growing Investment and Trade with Africa." *Columbia FDI Perspectives*, no. 34, February 17. Vale: Colorado.

Bruton, G.D. 2010. "Business and the World's Poorest Billion: The Need for an Expanded Examination by Management Scholars." *Academy of Management Perspectives* 24(3): 6–10.

Das, J., Q.T. Do, K. Shaines, and S. Srinivasan. 2009. "U.S. and Them: The Geography of Academic Research." *Policy Research Working Paper 5152*. Washington, DC: World Bank.

"India's Foreign Takeover Spree." 2012. *Economist* (March 3–9): 75–76.

Levitt, T. 1983. "The Globalization of Markets." *Harvard Business Review* (May–June): 2–11.

Mercer. 2008. "Expatriate Employee Numbers Double as Companies See Increased Value in Expatriate Assignments." Press release, October 27. http://www.mercer.com/press-releases/1326180 (accessed March 4, 2012).

Punnett, B.J. 2002. "Report on Interviews with Managers in the English-speaking Caribbean." Paper presented to the St. Vincent and the Grenadines Chamber of Industry and Commerce, Kingstown, St. Vincent, February.

Punnett, B.J., and D. Greenidge. 2009. "Culture, Myth and Leadership in the Caribbean." In *Cultural Mythology and Global Leadership*, ed. E.H. Kessler and D.J. Wong-MingJi, 65–78. London: Edward Elgar.

"Schumpeter: The Power of Tribes." 2012. *Economist* (January 28–February 3): 68.

"Special Report on Globalization." 2002. *Economist* (February 2–8): 65–68.

"Steel the Prize." 2006. *Economist* (November 25): 64.

Terpstra, V. 1982. *The Cultural Environment of International Business*. Cincinnati, OH: Southwestern.

Thomas, A. 1996. "A Call for Management Research in the Forgotten Locations." In *Handbook for International Management Research,* ed. B.J. Punnett and O. Shenkar, 485–506. Boston: Blackwell.

United Nations. 2000. "Entering the 21st Century." *World Development Report.* Oxford: Oxford University Press.

2

The Cultural Environment

Introduction

This chapter discusses firms doing business across national borders and the role of culture in effective management of these firms. Exhibit 2.1 outlines relationships between a variety of variables and organizational effectiveness.

The major focus in this chapter is on three central items: (1) national culture; (2) cultural values; and (3) individual and group needs, attitudes, and norms.

Exhibit 2.1 identifies national culture as emanating from *societal* variables (not necessarily restricted by national boundaries) such as language, religion, and history, as well as *national* variables (which are clearly associated with national boundaries) such as government, laws and regulations, geography, and economic conditions. National culture is also seen as being influenced by current events both within the country and in the world at large. National culture is, thus, relatively stable but does change over time in response to circumstances.

National culture is depicted as playing a fundamental role in forming cultural values. In turn, these values interact with the needs, attitudes, and norms of individuals and groups and result in behaviors that contribute to organizational effectiveness, or lack thereof. Additional influences are the values derived from the corporate culture and the individual's professional (or trade) culture; thus individuals and groups within an organization can be expected to share some values, but they can also be expected to differ with respect to others.

The organization's effectiveness will increase to the extent that the factors influencing behavior are understood by managers. An international firm's performance is likely to be enhanced when systems are in place that are congruent with the various influences that determine behaviors.

While it is clearly impossible to understand all of the factors influencing behavior, national cultures and attendant values appear to be an important starting point. A focus on national culture has been questioned by some scholars. Their concern is that the idea that nations and cultures may be coterminous is incorrect and, thus, thinking in these terms is misleading. It is certainly

Exhibit 2.1   **Relationships to Organizational Effectiveness**

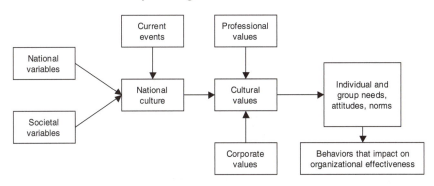

the case that nations and cultures are not the same; nevertheless, it seems appropriate from an international organization's viewpoint to consider national cultures, as the following illustrates.

Organizations are usually legal entities that exist within a defined national legal framework; that is, their activities are legally constrained by national requirements, rather than cultural ones. This means that international firms identify their activities with national boundaries. Human resource laws and other similar considerations encourage firms to take a national perspective. For example, the workforce in a particular location is predominantly a national workforce, and labor mobility within a country is usually greater than between countries. This means that management systems need to be designed with the national character of the workforce in mind. Governments encourage this through legislation; usually, laws and regulations regarding employees encompass all citizens of a country and do not apply differentially to different cultural groups (there are a few notable contradictions to this, such as the differential application of Shariah law in Nigeria to Muslims and non-Muslims). In contrast, laws and regulations may differ quite dramatically from country to country—for example, holidays and legislated benefits are substantially different even in Canada and the United States. The firm has to function within this system; therefore, it is appropriate to begin its cultural analysis at the national culture level.

Exhibit 2.1 serves as a guide for this chapter: First, a focus on the meaning of cultural values, defining various terms and looking at their associations; second, examining four cultural value models that can be applied at the national level and their impact on effective management; and last, considering a variety of additional issues—stereotyping, variation within nations, overlapping cultures, and environmental forces leading to convergence or divergence of cultures in different national locations.

Defining Culture

Culture is a concept that is familiar to most people. It is difficult, however, to specify what is meant by the concept. For example, two anthropologists (Kroeber and Kluckhohn 1952) catalogued 164 separate and distinct definitions of the word "culture." Culture can refer to a shared, commonly held body of general beliefs and values that define what is right for one group (Kluckhohn and Strodtbeck 1961; Lane and DiStefano 1988), or to socially elitist concepts, including refinement of mind, tastes, and manners (Heller 1988).

The word apparently originates with the Latin *cultura,* which is related to *cultus,* which can be translated as cult or worship. Members of a cult believe in specific ways of doing things and thus develop a culture that enshrines those beliefs. I use the term "culture" in this sense. The following definition, proposed by Terpstra and David, delineates what is meant by the word "culture" in the international management context: "Culture is a learned, shared, compelling, interrelated set of symbols whose meaning provides a set of orientations for members of a society. These orientations, taken together, provide solutions to problems that all societies must solve if they are to remain viable" (Terpstra and David 1985, 5).

There are several elements of this definition that are important in our understanding of the relationship between cultural issues and international management:

- Culture is learned—this means that it is not innate; people are socialized from childhood to learn the rules and norms of their culture. It also means that when one goes to another culture, it is possible to learn the new culture.
- Culture is shared—this means that the focus is on those things that are shared by members of a particular group rather than on individual differences; as such, it means that it is possible to study and identify group patterns.
- Culture is compelling—this means that specific behavior is determined by culture without individuals being aware of the influence of their culture; as such, it means that it is important to understand culture in order to understand behavior.
- Culture is an interrelated set—this means that while various facets of culture can be examined in isolation, these should be understood in the context of the whole; as such, it means that a culture needs to be studied as a complete entity.
- Culture provides orientation to people—this means that members of a particular group generally react in the same way to a given stimulus; as such, it means that understanding a culture can help in determining how group members might react in various situations.

An interesting approach to culture links the use of the hoe versus the plow to the current role of women in society. The argument is that where the hoe was dominant, women were able to perform in the fields and expected to participate in the active workforce; where the plow became the norm, women were not able to perform physically, and they were not expected to participate in the active workforce. There is some evidence that these cultural preferences continue in the current expectations of the roles of men and women in different cultural groups. Because culture is so fundamental to society, it influences people's behaviors in critical ways. Effective management depends, at least in part, on ensuring that people behave in ways that are appropriate for the organization. This means that understanding culture is important for managers. Where cultural differences exist they may need to be accommodated to achieve desired behavior and results. This is easier in theory than it is in reality. Each of us is influenced by our own culture, and people are inevitably somewhat ethnocentric, as discussed later.

Cultural Values

Values are useful in explaining and understanding cultural similarities and differences in behavior; thus, understanding values and their cultural basis is helpful to international managers. If international managers understand how values can vary from culture to culture, they are more likely to accept and interpret correctly behavioral differences. This acceptance and correct interpretation, in turn, enable managers to interact effectively with others whose values and behaviors are unfamiliar.

It is helpful to define the concept of cultural values, as well as to distinguish it from and relate it to other concepts. This serves to delineate the domain of cultural values, and to underscore their importance to international managers. The following discussion begins with cultural values, then examines needs, attitudes, and norms. These latter concepts are all similar to that of cultural values, but each contributes somewhat differently to behavior.

Values

Values have been described as enduring beliefs that specific modes of conduct or end states of existence are socially preferable to their opposites (Rokeach 1973); a value system is seen as a relatively permanent perceptual framework that influences an individual's behavior (England 1978). Values establish the standards by which the importance of everything in society is judged. Throughout these definitions, the important issue for international management appears to be the role of social values in behavior.

In a general sense, values and norms are societal, while needs and attitudes are individual. Values interact with needs, attributes, and norms, as the following explains.

Needs

Needs are described as forces motivating an individual to act in a certain way; once satisfied, needs no longer have an impact on behavior. For example, a need for food motivates people to seek food; once people have eaten, they normally no longer seek food (unless motivated by other needs). Cultural values interact with individual needs because they influence how people choose to satisfy their needs.

It is generally accepted that two of the most basic and universal human needs are the need for food and the need for sex, yet satisfaction of these needs differs because of societal values. In most societies the value of human life precludes cannibalism. Societies often have accepted times for eating, and even when people are hungry, they observe these time frames. Similarly, social customs regarding sexual partners limit satisfaction of sexual needs.

Many societies practice restrictions regarding food, often associated with religious rituals. During Lent, Christians may forgo favorite foods or limit their intake of meat. During the month of Ramadan, Muslims fast completely during daylight hours. Some sects eat no meat, some do not allow beef, others prohibit shellfish or pork, and still others proscribe certain combinations of foods. Individual needs are put aside to observe these restrictions.

Many societies also have customs regarding the timing and selection of sexual partners. Some societies allow men to have multiple wives; others have group marriages where any partner may have sex with any other. In some locations marriages are arranged for girls at birth and they must remain virgins until marriage; in others men and women select their own sexual and marriage partners. As with food, individual needs are often put aside to observe these customs.

Attitudes

Attitudes are described as a tendency to respond favorably or unfavorably to objects or situations based on beliefs about them. Societal values influence what we respond favorably to and what we view with disfavor.

In a business setting, dress can mean quite different things depending on what the society values and how different types of dress are interpreted. If wearing a suit and tie indicates a conservative business perspective and conservatism is valued, this would result in a favorable attitude to someone in this attire. Elsewhere, if innovation in business was more highly valued, and wearing a brightly colored t-shirt and jeans was seen as indicating an innovative perspective, this might be viewed positively. Similarly, in some societies males with long hair are seen negatively, while in others long hair represents virtue.

Norms

Norms prescribe or proscribe specific behaviors in specific situations and result in standardized, distinctive ways of behaving. These behaviors are seen as normal (thus the word "norm") and appropriate. A typical U.S. norm involves eating with the fork in the right hand, and this seems acceptable and normal to people who have lived in the United States for extended periods. People in many other countries hold their forks in the left hand, and in other places forks are not used at all. For those accustomed to using the right hand for a fork, the reverse can be quite uncomfortable, and using chopsticks in place of a fork is almost impossible for some people. Similarly, for those used to a fork in the left hand or chopsticks, the U.S. norm is uncomfortable.

Norms probably originated from values, but they no longer clearly represent these. The U.S. norm of eating with the fork in the right hand would not be described as a "societal value"; it is simply the accepted way of behaving in the United States.

Cultural Value Models

There are a variety of cultural value models that have been developed by scholars in different fields. I have selected four for discussion here to give a sense of the models available for managers. These particular models were identified because they have been presented widely in the international management literature. Each model is described and its limitations noted, then the model is related to some aspect of management. This discussion is very simplistic and in no way comprehensive. It is intended only to illustrate the potential for practical applications of cultural models in the international business setting.

Kluckhohn and Strodtbeck's Value Orientation Model

The anthropologists Kluckhohn and Strodtbeck (1961) explained cultural similarities and differences in terms of basic problems that all human societies face. Cultural differences develop because of varying ways of coping with these problems—different societies adopt different solutions. This model has been used by a number of international management authors and provides a means of assessing national culture that many people find helpful.

Consider the various solutions that societies have developed for the six problem areas identified by these two anthropologists.

Relationship to Nature: Subjugation, Harmony, and Mastery

Societies that view themselves as subjugated to nature view life as essentially preordained; people are not masters of their own destinies, and trying to change the inevitable is futile. Societies that view themselves as living in harmony with nature believe that people must alter their behavior to accommodate nature. Societies that view themselves as able to master nature think in terms of the supremacy of the human race and harnessing the forces of nature.

Time Orientation: Past, Present, and Future

Societies that are oriented toward the past look for solutions in the past: What would our forefathers have done? Societies that are present-oriented consider the immediate effects of their actions: What will happen if I do this? Societies that are future-oriented look to the long-term results of today's events: What will happen to future generations if we do these things today?

Basic Human Nature: Evil or Good, Changeable

Societies that believe that people are primarily evil focus on controlling the behavior of people through specified codes of conduct and sanctions for wrongdoing. Societies that believe that people are essentially good exhibit trust and rely on verbal agreements. Societies that see people as changeable and capable of both good and evil focus on means to modify behavior, encourage desired behavior, and discourage behaviors that are not desirable.

Activity Orientation: Being, Doing, Containing and Controlling

Societies that are primarily "being"-oriented are emotional; people react spontaneously based on what they feel at the time. Those that are "doing"-oriented are constantly striving to achieve; people are driven by a need to accomplish difficult tasks. Those that are concerned with containing and controlling focus on moderation and orderliness; people seek to achieve a balance in life and in society.

Human Relationships: Individualistic, Lineal, Co-Lineal

Societies that are primarily individualistic believe that individuals should be independent and take responsibility for their own actions. Those that are lineal are concerned with the family line and the power structure that underlies a hierarchy. Those that are co-lineal are group-oriented and emphasize group interactions and actions.

Space: Private, Public

Societies that see space as private will partition space for individual or small group use. Societies that see space as public have few divisions and use space for interchangeable purposes. Anglo societies are relatively private in terms of their view of space, and organizations in the United States or the United Kingdom will generally have offices for one or a few persons; within shared offices each person will have a clearly defined space. In Japan, where space is viewed as public, offices are open, with employees sharing desks as well as such resources as telephones, pens, pads, and so on. Interestingly, people who see space as private find ways of identifying their space through the use of photographs, personal mementos, and so on, while people who see space as public do not typically do this. In addition to these different views of space, people have a sense of personal space, and the degree of personal space that is comfortable varies from place to place. Latin Americans, for example, like to be very close when conversing; North Americans tend to stand about an arm's length apart, and the Japanese prefer to maintain a greater distance.

The Kluckhohn and Strodtbeck Model in International Management

These value orientations can be related to effective management practices in different locations. The following suggestions illustrate how these orientations may be related to management:

1. In a society that believes humans are subjugated by nature, planning would be futile, because the future is preordained.
2. In a society that is present-oriented, rewards would be closely tied to current performance.
3. In a society that believes in the basic goodness of human beings, participative management is likely to be the normal approach.
4. In a society that is primarily being-oriented, decisions are likely to be intuitive with less concern for logic.

5. In a society that is lineal and hierarchical, organization structures are likely to reflect this in formal, authority-based hierarchy.

Understanding these aspects of culture can provide international managers with insights into people's behavior in foreign locations and allow these managers to adapt their own style and adjust their organization's practices to accommodate the differences. Consider the following possibilities:

• In a society that thinks in terms of mastery over nature, technology is likely to be admired and people are willing to work toward production goals and objectives set by management. In a society that emphasizes harmony with nature, technology may be accepted but there will be concern over the impact of technology on nature, and goals and objectives will be acceptable if they relate both to productivity and the environment. In a society that sees itself as subject to nature, mastery of technology may be viewed with caution and specific goals and objectives disliked.

• In a past-oriented society, market research will focus on the past and consumer tastes will not be expected to change dramatically or quickly. Sales efforts emphasize past quality, performance, and so on, and use familiar approaches. In a present-oriented society, market research will focus on what is current and identify products and services with immediate practical benefits. Sales efforts will emphasize these immediate benefits and use topical references and up-to-date approaches. In a future-oriented society, market research will be concerned with expectations of the future and will try to identify tomorrow's tastes and needs. Sales efforts will emphasize the long-term benefits of products and services and use futuristic references and images.

• If the society believes that all people are basically good, then managers will expect that people working for a firm intend to do their best and contribute to the organization's effectiveness. If errors occur, they will be explained as occurring in spite of people's efforts. If people are believed to be basically evil, managers will not expect people to work hard on their own. Errors will be explained in terms of individual human error and disassociated from the firm. If people are seen as changeable and a mixture of good and evil, the selection of the best people to work in the firm might be emphasized. Errors can be admitted readily and the actions taken to correct and avoid them in the future explained.

• In a being-oriented society, people are spontaneous and react emotionally. Accounting and financial systems need to be relatively flexible to allow for alternative ways of carrying out necessary activities. Policies and procedures will be general and provide guidelines rather than specific and detailed instructions. In a containing and controlling society, the emphasis will be on logic. Systems are rationally designed and explained assuming that people will comply with logical systems. Policies and procedures will be complex and include both qualitative and quantitative guidelines and instructions. In a doing-oriented society, the concern is for activity and accomplishment. Systems will be pragmatic, emphasizing expected results. Policies and procedures will be relatively simple and described in operational, active terms.

• In a society that is primarily individualistic, the individual person will be the focus of management activities. This will be true of decision making, leadership, work design, rewards, and so forth. In a society that is lineal, the hierarchy of power and authority will be important in all management activities. Leadership is associated with the level in the organization that is accompanied by power and authority. Vertical differentiation will be stressed, and decisions, work design, and rewards will conform to the hierarchical structure. In a society that is co-lineal, group activities are normal and preferred. The group becomes the focus in terms of decisions, leadership, work design, and rewards.

• In a society where space is private, offices will be divided so that people have private spaces. Public spaces such as conference rooms will be clearly identified, and systems for booking use of these rooms will be in place. Meetings will often take place behind closed doors. Where societal attitudes view space as public, offices will be open, with people using whatever space is available, and using desks and other amenities interchangeably. Managers and employees will work together in close proximity, and meetings will take place in public.

Hofstede's Value Survey Model

The value survey model (VSM), introduced by Hofstede (1980), has been widely discussed in international management literature, and it appears to provide information of relevance from a managerial point of view. The model proposed four dimensions of culture, and a fifth dimension was later added based on research in the Far East (Chinese Culture Connection 1987). The five dimensions are as follows.

Individualism

Individualism (IDV) is the degree to which individual decision making and action are accepted and encouraged by the society. Where IDV is high, the society emphasizes the role of the individual; where IDV is low, the society emphasizes the role of the group. Some societies view individualism positively and see it as the basis for creativity and achievement; others view it with disapproval and see it as disruptive to group harmony and cooperation.

Uncertainty Avoidance

Uncertainty avoidance index (UAI) is the degree to which a society is willing to accept and deal with uncertainty. Where UAI is high, the society is concerned with certainty and security, and seeks to reduce uncertainty; where UAI is low, the society is comfortable with a high degree of uncertainty and is open to the unknown. Some societies view certainty as important, and people prefer functioning without worrying about the consequences of uncertainty; others view uncertainty as providing excitement and opportunities for innovation and change.

Power Distance

Power distance index (PDI) is the degree to which power differences are accepted and sanctioned by a society. Where PDI is high, the society believes that there should be a well-defined hierarchy in which everyone has a rightful place; where PDI is low, the prevalent belief is that all people should have equal rights and the opportunity to change their position in the society. Some societies view a well-ordered distribution of power as contributing to a well-managed society because each person knows what his/her position is, and people are, in fact, protected by this order. Where PDI is low, people view power as corrupting and believe that those with less power will inevitably suffer at the hands of those with more.

Masculinity

Masculinity (MAS) is the degree to which traditional male values are important to a society. Traditional male values incorporate assertiveness, performance, ambition, achievement, and material possessions, while traditional female values focus on the quality of life, the environment, nurturing, and concern for the less fortunate. In societies that are high on MAS, sex roles are clearly differentiated and men are dominant; if MAS is low, sex roles are more fluid and feminine values predominate throughout. Some societies see the traditional male values as being necessary for survival; that is, men must be aggressive and women must be protected. Others view both sexes as equal contributors to society, and they believe that the traditional value of dominance by men is destructive.

Confucian Dynamism

Confucian Dynamism (CD) is a complex dimension based on beliefs of the Chinese philosopher Confucius. The dimension incorporates ideas of time and activity. Here, for simplicity, CD is defined as a time orientation only—taking a long-term or short-term view. A society that is high on CD has a long time horizon and looks to the future. A society that is low on CD has a shorter time horizon and is more concerned with events in the present and immediate future.

The extremes of each of these indices have been described. Most countries are not at the extreme, but may be moderately high or moderately low; thus, effective management practices will not usually reflect an extreme tendency. An examination of profiles of selected countries shows the variety that is possible when considering these five dimensions. Some examples illustrate how these might influence management practices:

- New Zealand society is individualistic, does not avoid uncertainty, and believes in equality and traditional male values. This would suggest that organizational structures will be relatively flat, with individuals making decisions on their own and competing for scarce resources.
- Italian society is individualistic, avoids uncertainty, and believes in equality (within the confines of sex distinctions) and traditional male values. This would suggest a similar structure, but a reliance on gathering information for decisions and an emphasis on job security and seniority are important components of the management system.
- Singaporean society is collectivist, does not avoid uncertainty, believes in power distinctions, and is relatively low on masculinity. This suggests a paternalistic leadership system, with the leader expressing concern for subordinates and the quality of life, but without undue concern for job security.
- Japanese society is relatively collectivist but also high on uncertainty avoidance as well as masculinity, and relatively high on power distance. This would suggest a system that seeks consensus among group members but is competitive and has clear distinctions in terms of power; job security would be stressed and jobs allocated on the basis of gender.
- Asian countries are generally high on CD and collectivism. This would suggest a concern for the good of the group or society in the future.

Limitations of the Value Survey Model

Hofstede reports scores from 1 to 100 for each country in his sample. The scores reported by Hofstede are based on employees within one organization, a large U.S. multinational company. Certain types of individuals are attracted to such an organization, and this is reflected in these scores. These scores should not, therefore, be interpreted as an accurate description of the national culture as a whole; rather, they should be seen as an indication of the similarities and differences that one might expect to find among employees in this type of organization in different countries.

In addition, these scores represent a central tendency in a particular population, but there is likely to be a wide array of values in any country; organizations and industries will attract and retain individuals with value systems that fit into the organizational culture. For example, a study of fast-food restaurant managers in Canada and the United States revealed a very low level of individualism combined with no uncertainty avoidance and high power distance and masculinity (Punnett and Withane 1990). This is quite dissimilar from the Canadian and U.S. value profile presented by Hofstede, but it appears to match the needs of an industry where people must work in close coordination, where there is little job security, and where there are clear distinctions of power and a great deal of competition.

Researchers have also expressed concerns regarding the survey instrument used in Hofstede's research, and the validity of the measure has been questioned. Researchers question whether the country scores provided are representative of the normal population and whether the important cultural variables are the ones being measured. These concerns should all be kept in mind when interpreting the results of Hofstede's study. From a practical perspective, the cultural variables described by the model are intuitively appealing because of their apparent relationship to the management process.

Using the Value Survey Model in International Management

The management process is often described as consisting of planning, organizing, staffing, directing, and controlling. These aspects of the management process probably occur in some form in all enterprises, but that form may differ depending on the environment. In particular, the cultural values that are typical of a particular society can influence what is effective in terms of the management process. Consider some extremes of the Hofstede dimensions as they might relate to aspects of the management process.

Where individualism is high, individual input is sought from those individuals who have particular knowledge or expertise. Superiors are expected to make day-to-day decisions and communicate these to subordinates who are expected to carry them out. Input may be sought from subordinates or others who will be affected by decisions, or who have particular knowledge or expertise. Individuals may disagree with particular decisions, but will generally go along with them if the majority agrees or if the decision has been made by a person in a position of power.

Individuals are given specific responsibility for completing tasks and achieving goals and objectives. The individual is expected to make the necessary decisions to carry through a given assignment. Management by objectives (MBO) is a popular approach in individualistic societies, because MBO incorporates the idea of top management setting strategic directions, lower levels developing action plans to achieve these, and individuals accepting and working toward individual goals.

Where collectivism is high, organizational plans are formulated on the basis of the larger societal direction, with input from all organizational members. The overall direction of the organization is discussed and agreed to throughout the organization. Decisions are made collectively, with all affected parties participating in the process. Disagreements are dealt with throughout the process and consensus from all members is sought. Tasks and assignments are carried out by groups. There is pressure from the group for conformance to acceptable standards. When decisions need to be made, they are made by the group as a whole. The quality circle approach is popular, because it incorporates the idea of bottom-up decision making, consensus among members, and group involvement.

Where UAI is high, uncertainty can be avoided by having group members share responsibility for planning and decisions, or, alternatively, by having one person in a position of power take responsibility. The advice of experts is likely to be important in formulating plans and making decisions. Planning provides security and is well accepted. Plans are likely to be detailed and complex, incorporating priorities and contingencies. Specific plans provide direction and little ambiguity. Strategic planning is as long-term as it is practical. Checks and balances ensure that performance is at the planned level and allow for correction before a major departure occurs. Decisions are reached slowly. If responsibility is shared, then group agreement is important to the planning process. If a powerful individual makes the decisions, then these are imparted to subordinates as absolutes. In any case, disagreement is discouraged.

Where UAI is low, planning is flexible and relatively short-term. Uncertainty is seen as inevitable, and the organization must therefore be able to change direction quickly. Planning is accepted as providing guidance but not constraints. Formal planning is most likely to take place at top levels and be, at least partially, based on a subjective evaluation of opportunities. Personal preferences are likely to be evident in strategic directions. A certain amount of risk taking will be encouraged. Individuals are likely to accept the risk of individual decision making, and the need for making quick decisions will be stressed.

Where PDI is high, planning and decision making are done at the top. Input is accepted from those in powerful positions, but no input is expected from those at lower levels. Long-term plans are kept secret. Operational decisions are made on a daily basis by superiors, and work assigned to subordinates. All decisions are referred to the superior, and subordinates are discouraged from taking the initiative and making decisions. Subordinates accept assigned work and carry out tasks as instructed. Those in positions of power are respected; those in inferior positions expect that more powerful individuals will take responsibility for decision making.

Where PDI is low, everyone is seen as being capable of contributing to the planning process, and input from a variety of organizational levels is sought in developing strategic plans. Decision making in general is participative, and long-term plans are likely to be shared among organizational members. Operational decisions incorporate the views of those who must carry them out. The people involved in particular tasks are expected to make the routine decisions necessary to complete the task, and decisions are referred to the superior only when they involve unusual circumstances. Power differences exist, but are minimized, and friendly relationships between superiors and subordinates are the norm.

Where traditional MAS values predominate, strategic plans emphasize specific, measurable advances by the organization (e.g., increases in market share, profitability); these are difficult but believed to be achievable, and results are observable. Strategic choices are made at the top level. Operational decisions focus on task accomplishment, and tasks are undertaken by those people considered most likely to perform at the desired level. Certain tasks are seen as more suitable for males, others for females. In some cases, responsibility for different types of decisions is delegated on the basis of gender.

Where traditional feminine values predominate, strategic plans take into account the environment, the quality of working life, and concern for the less fortunate. Profitability and market share goals and objectives, for example, are defined within this context. Operational decisions focus on satisfaction with work and development of a congenial and nurturing work environment. Task accomplishment takes place within this framework. Work is seen as generally suitable for either sex, with more concern for assigning work according to individual abilities and preferences. Decision making is shared between the sexes. Decision-making responsibility depends on ability and preferences rather than gender. Male values of achievement, money, and performance rank equally with female values of nurturing, quality of life, and caring for the less fortunate.

Country Clusters

Examining clusters of countries that share similar values can be a useful approach for international managers. One of the most extensive studies resulting in country clusters was carried out by Ronen and Shenkar (1985). This was a synthesis of previous research and identified eight clusters of countries. Countries that did not fall into one of the clusters were identified as independent. These clusters are illustrated in Exhibit 2.2. This research is more than twenty years old, but it provides helpful insights, in spite of the limited number of countries included (note the earlier discussion on the dearth of information, even today, on a wider array of countries).

The countries included in Exhibit 2.2 reflect the available research. The clusters can be helpful to managers who have to decide on the degree to which cultural adaptation is needed when moving cross-culturally. A manager interacting with colleagues from within the home cluster can expect relatively similar values and easy adaptation—Australians interacting with Canadians will be on somewhat familiar territory. Moving outside the home cluster can be relatively more difficult because of the likely diversity of values and greater need for adaptation—a Mexican going to Saudi Arabia is likely to be faced with more cultural adaptation than the Australian working in Canada.

The countries included on the list are those in which appropriate research has occurred. Sometimes it is possible to make informed judgments regarding the likely position of countries that are not represented, based on information about their cultural antecedents and neighbors. For example, we might surmise that Ecuador would be similar to the other Latin American countries because it shares geographic location and a variety of antecedents (language, religion, history) with these other countries. On the other hand, Brazil shares many of these as well, but because of language differences (Portuguese rather than Spanish) we might be less inclined to include it in this group without more specific information.

Limitations of Country Cluster Information

Country clusters can help international managers, but there are some limitations to consider. For example, geographic regions such as Africa and Eastern Europe are not represented, and within clusters, major countries are missing (e.g., Brazil in Latin America and the People's Republic of China in the Far East), and managers may be particularly interested in one of these countries or regions. The clusters are based on variables studied in the past; thus it is possible that different clusters would emerge if different variables were studied. These clusters do not identify the relative similarity between clusters, and this might be an important consideration for international managers. The clusters might overemphasize similarity within a cluster or dissimilarity among clusters, and countries within a cluster do differ and those in different clusters can exhibit some similarities.

Exhibit 2.2

Country Clusters

Cluster 1—Anglo	Canada, Australia, New Zealand, United Kingdom, United States
Cluster 2—Germanic	Austria, Germany, Switzerland
Cluster 3—Latin European	Belgium, France, Italy, Portugal, Spain
Cluster 4—Nordic	Denmark, Finland, Norway, Sweden
Cluster 5—Latin American	Argentina, Chile, Colombia, Mexico, Peru, Venezuela
Cluster 6—Near Eastern	Greece, Iran, Turkey
Cluster 7—Far Eastern	Hong Kong, Indonesia, Malaysia, Philippines, Singapore, South Vietnam, Taiwan
Cluster 8—Arab	Bahrain, Kuwait, Saudi Arabia, United Arab Emirates
Independent (not closely related to the other countries)	Japan, India, Israel

The Role of Country Clusters in International Decisions

Grouping countries into culturally similar clusters is helpful to international managers in a number of ways. If we consider some typical concerns of international managers, we can see how country clusters might be used. The following examples are by no means inclusive; there are many additional ways in which country cluster information can be used by international managers. These examples should, however, give a sense of how this information can be factored into international management decisions.

- Members of a cluster can be expected to share basic cultural values, and people in all the countries in a cluster are likely to behave in relatively similar ways. Managers with experience in one country (say, Norway) can then move relatively easily to another country in the same cluster (say, Finland). This does not mean that everything in Finland will be the same as in Norway. Rather, it means that the experience gained in Norway is likely to be helpful in adjusting to Finland, although it is important to note that Finnish is quite unlike the other Nordic languages.
- Managers in one country in a cluster can move to others in the same cluster with a minimum of culture shock and with relatively little need for adaptation. Movement from one cultural cluster to another can be expected to be somewhat difficult. Managers in one cluster moving to another cluster need to be particularly aware of the effect of cultural differences. They need to expect culture shock and be prepared to adapt to the new cultural experience.

- Countries in different clusters are likely to exhibit different cultural values and the people to behave in relatively dissimilar ways. Managers moving from a country in one cluster (say, Singapore) to a country in a different cluster (say, Argentina) can expect to encounter substantial differences. They can be prepared for this and can adapt their management style as needed.

- Decisions regarding locations for international subsidiaries can take advantage of information provided by country clusters. A firm seeking to expand internationally might initially want to gain experience in culturally similar locations. For example, a Canadian firm might expand to other countries in the Anglo cluster. An international firm with substantial experience may feel there is benefit in expanding to culturally different countries; for example, a Canadian firm could consider places like Saudi Arabia, Portugal, or Indonesia.

- International staffing decisions can benefit from a consideration of country clusters. Allocating personnel to relatively similar cultures (e.g., moving French personnel to French-speaking Belgium*) minimizes the culture shock they could experience. Such a move can be relatively easy, and extensive cross-cultural training and support are not needed. In contrast, a move to a country in a different cluster (e.g., French personnel to the United States) may present a greater challenge. In this move a greater degree of culture shock is likely and, therefore, appropriate training and support should be provided.

- International managers can consider country clusters in relation to joint ventures and strategic alliances. Many alliances fail because of the differing objectives of the parties involved, and to some extent these objectives may reflect the national culture (e.g., Japanese managers are generally believed to take a longer-term view than U.S. managers). Firms entering alliances within a familiar cluster may be able to agree on objectives more easily than in an unfamiliar cluster. When entering an alliance in an unfamiliar cluster, it is important to allow adequate time to discuss objectives in detail and it may be necessary to consider innovative proposals.

- Managers may find negotiations follow similar procedures within clusters but can change quite dramatically between clusters. Managers who are aware of this are likely to be better negotiators because they will prepare for and use the similarities and differences that exist.

- Managers need to consider whether management practices and approaches can be transferred from one country to another. Management practices are more likely to be generalizable within cultural clusters. Managers who

---

*It is important to recognize that Belgium itself is quite diverse, and the Flemish region may not be at all Latin European.

have successfully worked in one country can have some confidence that they can be effective in other countries in the same cluster.

- International managers often have to make decisions about expanding to new locations. Given a choice of expanding to two locations that are equally attractive in other ways, cultural similarities and differences may be a deciding factor. Expansion to new locations within a familiar cluster is likely to involve fewer unexpected occurrences than expansion to an unfamiliar cluster. In contrast, the differences that are inherent in a new cluster may provide opportunities that do not exist in culturally similar locations.

- Subsidiaries of international firms are often grouped based on similarities of activities, and regional groupings are fairly common. Country clusters provide one basis for deciding on regional groupings. Countries within a cluster can be expected to share some characteristics such as language and religion and to express relatively similar values. These similarities suggest that taking a common approach to countries within a cluster is appropriate.

- Marketing in different countries can be a major challenge for international managers. A major concern for marketers is taking advantage of efficiencies offered by standardized marketing approaches while adapting to cultural differences. Country clusters provide input into decisions regarding marketing standardization and adaptation. The relative similarity of countries within a cluster suggests that greater standardization may be appropriate, while differences between clusters highlight the need for adaptation.

World Values Surveys

The World Values Surveys (Ingelhart 2012) were designed to measure major areas of human concern, from religion to politics to economic and social life. Two dimensions emerge as the most important and explain more than 70 percent of the cross-cultural variance on scores of more specific values.

The two dimensions are:

The Traditional/Secular-rational values, which reflect a contrast between societies in which religion is very important and those in which it is not. Societies near the traditional end emphasize the importance of parent–child ties and deference to authority, instead of standards and traditional family values. They reject divorce, abortion, euthanasia, and suicide. These societies are high on national pride and a nationalistic outlook. Societies with secular-rational values have the opposite preferences.

The second major dimension relates to Survival and Self-expression. The wealth accumulated in developed societies has led to their taking survival for granted, and priorities have shifted to an emphasis on subjective well-being, self-expression, and quality of life. Self-expression values have a priority on environmental protection, tolerance of diversity, and rising demands for participation in decision making in economic and political life. Self-expression values include a shift in child-rearing values, from an emphasis on hard work toward an emphasis on imagination and tolerance and a rising sense of subjective well-being that is conducive to an atmosphere of tolerance, trust, and political moderation. Societies that rank high on self-expression values also tend to rank high on interpersonal trust, which leads to a culture of trust and tolerance, in which people place a relatively high value on individual freedom and self-expression, and have activist political orientations.

The website presents maps that group countries according to cultural values. One map has the following groupings:

Islamic—Algeria, Bangladesh, Egypt, Ethiopia, Indonesia, Iran, Iraq, Jordan, Morocco, Pakistan, Turkey, Zambia, Zimbabwe;

Africa—Ghana, Mali, Nigeria, Rwanda, South Africa, Tanzania, Uganda;

Confucian—Hong Kong, Japan, People's Republic of China, South Korea, Taiwan;

Protestant Europe—Denmark, Finland, Germany, Iceland, Netherlands, Norway, Sweden, Switzerland;

Catholic Europe—Belgium, Croatia, Czech Republic, France, Italy, Luxembourg, Slovakia, Slovenia, Spain;

English Speaking—Australia, Canada, Great Britain, New Zealand, Northern Ireland, United States;

Latin America—Argentina, Brazil, Chile, Colombia, El Salvador, Guatemala, Mexico, Peru, Puerto Rico, Uruguay, Venezuela;

South Asia—Cyprus, India, Malaysia, Thailand, Vietnam, and

Orthodox—Belarus, Bulgaria, Macedonia, Moldova, Romania, Russia, Serbia, Ukraine

Islamic, Latin American, and African countries score relatively high on traditional values; Confucian and Protestant European countries score relatively high on secular-relational values. Confucian, Orthodox, and Islamic countries score relatively high on survival values; Protestant Europe and English-speaking countries score relatively high on self-expression.

This approach to cultural values adds to our understanding of values around the world and how they influence behavior and thus management. One interesting finding related to the World Values Survey is that shared values influence the likelihood that countries will do business together. Countries that share imperial ties trade 188 percent more than those who do not share these ties. Among other findings, 68 percent of foreign direct investment into the People's Republic of China came from places where ethnic Chinese are the biggest group; similarly, the top five sources of Indian investment all have large Indian populations. In terms of Britain's former colonies, trade flows were 13 percent higher than would be expected, capital flows were 24 percent higher, and people flows 93 percent higher. Cultural bonds appear to matter in terms of international business.

Smith and Peterson (1988) Event Management Approach

This approach considers how people make decisions and how culture impacts the sources used in decision making. The original research asked middle-level managers in more than sixty national cultures to rate the extent to which each of eight specified work events were handled on the basis of guidance from eight different categories of norms, rules, and roles. Work events included events like hiring a new subordinate. Sources of guidance included statements like "my own experience and training." The eight sources of guidance were formal rules, unwritten rules, subordinates, specialists, coworkers, superiors, own experience, and wide beliefs. More recently family and friends were added as sources of guidance.

These sources of guidance are largely self-explanatory; however, brief explanations are set out below:

Formal Rules (written, specified policies, procedures, and other systems designed to clearly guide behavior). Some cultures rely heavily on such rules for making decisions and see them as constraining and compelling behavior; others see formal rules only as guiding decisions and behavior, but believe that it is not necessary to follow the formal rules at all times. In the case of hiring a new subordinate, those that feel formal rules are important would follow the procedures set out in the Human Resources manual.

Unwritten Rules (norms and beliefs, or "the way we do things here," that guide behavior). Some cultures rely heavily on unwritten rules to make decisions and guide behavior; others do not. In the case of hiring a new subordinate, those who feel that unwritten rules are important would refer to the norms, such as "when we hire, we try to bring in new blood" or "seniority is very important in our organization."

Subordinates. Some cultures believe strongly in participation and rely substantially on input from subordinates when making decisions; others do not believe that subordinates need or want to be involved in decision making. In the case of hiring a new subordinate, those who feel that input from subordinates is important would discuss the new hire with a variety of lower-level subordinates to get their thoughts on filling the position, and subordinates would participate in the hiring process.

Specialists. Some cultures believe strongly in expertise and rely on the input of specialists in order to make decisions; others feel that specialists can provide only partial input. In the case of hiring a new subordinate, those who rely on specialists would hire a search firm to identify and check appropriate candidates.

Co-workers. Some cultures look to co-workers for advice and input when making decisions; others see co-workers as relatively unimportant. In the case of hiring a new subordinate, those who rely on co-workers would discuss the new hire with a variety of co-workers and have them participate in the hiring process.

Superiors. Some cultures rely largely on superiors for decision making and often will not make a decision until it has been approved by a superior; others believe superiors should be kept informed, but that decisions should be made at the level where they have to be implemented. In the case of hiring a new subordinate, those who rely on superiors would want the superior to be involved in all aspects of the hiring process and to make the final decision on the candidate to be selected.

Own Experience. Some cultures rely on each individual's own experience to make decisions; others believe that your own experience is too subjective. In the case of hiring a new subordinate, those who rely on their own experience would not seek input or advice but would manage the hiring process themselves and would select a candidate based on the type of person who had been successful in the past.

Wide Beliefs. Some cultures base their decisions on the wider beliefs of the society, which go well beyond the individual, group, or organization; others see organizational decisions as much more company-specific. In the case of hiring a new subordinate, those who rely on wide beliefs would base the hiring process and decisions on the general societal norms and beliefs; for example, hiring family members is considered wrong in some societies, but is accepted and even encouraged in others.

Family. Some cultures look to the family and the family values when making decisions; others think it inappropriate for the family to be involved in organizational decisions. In the case of hiring a new subordinate, those who rely on family would get advice from family members regarding the new hire and would discuss potential candidates with these family members.

Friends. Some cultures look to friends and get advice from them when making decisions; others do not see friends as being able to contribute to organizational decisions. In the case of hiring a new subordinate, those who rely on friends would get their advice regarding the new hire and discuss potential candidates with them.

The sources of guidance are related to different types of cultures. Consider some examples:

- Reliance on own experience and training is likely to be most favored in individualistic national cultures, while reliance on coworkers is likely to be favored in collective cultures.
- Reliance on widespread national beliefs about right and wrong is likely to be more favored in traditional national cultures.
- Reliance on a superior is likely to be favored in a hierarchical society high on power distance, while reliance on subordinates is more likely in a society that is low on power distance.
- Reliance on rules and specialists is likely to be favored where certainty is important and uncertainty avoidance is high.

Exhibit 2.3 summarizes the results reported by Smith, Peterson, and Schwartz (2002). Reported levels of reliance on ten sources of guidance averaged across eight events are given for demographically heterogeneous samples from sixty-one national cultures. The scores were standardized across sources within respondents to discount response bias. Positive scores therefore indicate above-average reliance on a given source relative to other sources, while negative scores show below-average reliance. Some sources have positive scores for all nations, indicating they are frequently employed in all contexts; others are almost all negative. We could consider these patterns as representing universal aspects of contemporary management.

This approach provides an interesting and helpful dimension to understanding the influence of culture on international management, because it focuses specifically on decision making and behavior, and identifies easily understandable information on cultural influences on decisions and behavior. As an example of how this approach can be used:

> The author was conducting a cross-cultural seminar for a British organization with an office in Barbados. The managers felt that there were tensions between the personnel from the UK and the local Barbados personnel and thought that a better understanding of cultural differences would be helpful. Participants in the seminar were generally interested and involved throughout the seminar; however, the aspect of the seminar that was greeted with the most enthusiasm, and proved to be the highlight, was a table comparing Barbados and the UK on the sources of guidance. Barbados personnel were heavily rule oriented, while the UK employees relied on their own experience or on subordinates. Essentially the reaction around the seminar room was "now

Exhibit 2.3

National Scores on Sources of Guidance from Event Management Research

Nation	Formal rules	Unwritten rules	Sub-ordinates	Specialists	Co-workers	Superiors	Own experience	Wide beliefs	Family	Friends
Argentina	-08	05	-07	-43	-07	32	61	-44		
Australia	47	07	-23	-53	-36	50	70	-62		
Austria	05	-04	08	-30	-43	29	103	-69		
Barbados	48	-02	-31	-44	-26	47	77	-82	-191	-169
Belarus	-07	-20	-06	-33	-37	65	67	-30		
Brazil	42	04	-27	-35	-23	42	68	-69	-165	-156
Bulgaria	37	-11	-39	-71	-46	44	75	03		
Canada	22	07	-03	-48	-05	42	59	-78	-183	-182
Chile	34	-10	-31	-57	-20	41	65	-21		
China	36	-28	-36	-28	-23	56	27	-04	-129	-120
Colombia	15	-08	05	-30	-17	-06	66	-27		
Czech Republic	10	-32	01	-26	-41	33	122	-69		
Denmark	-10	-08	62	-57	-34	-06	97	-47		
Finland	-59	06	34	-40	-21	26	118	-66		
France	05	18	05	-56	-30	45	80	-77		
Germany	-04	-29	36	-25	-42	25	116	-78		
Greece	44	02	-43	-70	-43	47	111	-48		
Hong Kong	45	22	-21	-83	-41	72	48	-43		
Hungary	-32	-32	26	-05	25	35	119	-137		
Iceland	-27	01	-08	-60	-02	53	104	-68		
India	33	00	-07	-60	-17	30	36	-14	-82	-115
Indonesia	64	06	-48	-55	-53	34	58	-07		

(continued)

Exhibit 2.3 (continued)

Nation	Formal rules	Unwritten rules	Sub-ordinates	Specialists	Co-workers	Superiors	Own experience	Wide beliefs	Family	Friends
Iran	18	10	-64	-48	-20	37	49	08		
Israel	22	23	-07	-71	-30	45	102	-84		
Italy	11	-24	12	-21	-22	20	80	-56		
Jamaica	51	05	-38	-48	-22	84	34	-72	-171	-163
Japan	38	-23	01	-56	-29	42	61	-34		
Kenya	56	-33	-45	-25	-06	64	47	-61		
Lebanon	33	03	01	-31	-23	40	29	-53		
Macao	33	16	-11	-66	-27	49	49	-42		
Malaysia	55	-05	-14	-56	-25	44	21	-20		
Mexico	30	04	-29	-23	-27	45	30	-29		
Netherlands	-05	06	34	-49	-37	-04	94	-40		
New Zealand	26	06	-12	-58	-04	26	69	-53		
Nigeria	55	-13	-12	-35	-16	35	19	-36	-105	-114
Norway	12	-29	16	-60	-09	11	76	-25		
Pakistan	37	07	-24	-45	-29	45	42	-44		
Philippines	37	33	-24	-55	-50	54	31	-20		
Poland	27	-54	-33	-46	-49	71	76	-58		
Portugal	41	22	-24	-45	-50	64	101	-114		
Qatar	61	-13	18	-55	49		40	-98	-168	-172
Romania	24	-42	-32	-38	-43	40	85	03		
Russia	17	-22	-05	-63	-34	48	94	-93	-190	-180
Saudi Arabia	38	17	11	-40	03	-15	31	-50	-144	-142

Singapore	37	22	-15	-57	-42	18	55	-20
Slovakia	01	04	-14	-35	-36	42	88	-53
S. Africa (white)	21	-04	-21	-47	-15	57	68	-61
S. Africa (black)	46	-11	-24	-46	-19	46	46	-38
S. Korea	27	32	-18	-53	-38	36	24	-12
Spain	29	-01	-26	-44	-22	56	50	-48
Sri Lanka	34	09	-04	-48	-28	37	44	-47
Sweden	38	-27	13	-37	-49	11	80	-33
Taiwan	58	-60	-31	-35	-26	47	43	04
Tanzania	39	-32	-09	-17	06	40	21	-48
Thailand	17	-44	37	-52	-16	28	43	-13
Turkey	12	18	-21	-78	-12	84	49	-52
Uganda	60	-21	-43	-31	02	71	34	-72
Ukraine	-04	-21	-06	-39	-15	88	59	-62
UK	18	-07	-06	-54	-30	40	99	-63
USA	26	02	-10	-61	-16	58	54	-56	-168
Zimbabwe	76	-18	-41	-70	-44	69	68	-67	-173

Source: Peterson, M.F., and P.B. Smith, 2008.

Note: Formal rules = "Formal rules and procedures"; Own exp = "My own experience and training"; Wide beliefs = "Beliefs that are widely accepted in my nation as to what is right."

I understand." The Barbados personnel had been complaining that the UK managers wouldn't follow the policies and procedures, and the UK managers had been complaining that the Barbados personnel were inflexible and wouldn't take any initiative. Once the participants understood the reasons for these differences, they felt they would be better able to interact effectively. The Barbados personnel thought they could be more accommodating to UK initiatives, and UK personnel agreed to try harder to follow the rules.

As Exhibit 2.3 illustrates, there are data for a large number of countries using this approach and many of these countries have not been included in other research measuring culture. This research serves to greatly expand understanding of cultural variations around the world.

Alternative Cultural Models

For those who want to explore these concepts in more detail, there are a wide variety of cultural models that may be useful to managers working internationally, in addition to those described in this chapter. For example:

Schwartz (1999) used multidimensional scaling of the country means for the following values to validate seven value types and identify national differences:

1. *Conservatism* or *embeddedness* emphasizes maintaining the status quo, propriety, and restraint of actions or inclinations that might disrupt the solidarity of the group or the traditional order in which people are embedded.
2. *Intellectual autonomy* emphasizes the desirability of individuals' pursuing their own ideas and intellectual directions independently.
3. *Affective autonomy* emphasizes the desirability of individuals' pursuing affectively positive experience.
4. *Hierarchy* emphasizes the legitimacy of an unequal distribution of power, roles, and resources.
5. *Egalitarianism* emphasizes transcendence of selfish interests in favor of voluntary commitment to promoting the welfare of others.
6. *Mastery* emphasizes getting ahead through active self-assertion.
7. *Harmony* emphasizes fitting harmoniously into the environment.

He summarized his seven country-level value types as constituting three dimensions: *embeddedness versus autonomy, hierarchy versus egalitarianism,* and *mastery versus harmony.*

Trompenaars and Hampden-Turner (1998) surveyed the values of more than 11,000 organization employees in forty-six countries. Smith, Peterson, and Wang

(1996) used multidimensional scaling to identify two reliable country-level dimensions within the Trompenaars databank. The first of these was named *egalitarian commitment versus conservatism* following Schwartz's use of these terms. Those favoring egalitarian commitment endorse abstract principles of what is right and just and believe that jobs should be filled on the basis of impersonal criteria such as qualifications. Those favoring conservatism prefer their immediate circle to outsiders. This includes values such as loyalty to one's boss and job appointments based on connections or family relationships. The second dimension was defined as *utilitarian involvement versus loyal involvement.* This contrasts involvement in the organization that is contingent on meeting one's individual goals with involvement based on a long-lasting identification with the organization's goals as one's own. These two dimensions incorporate several that proved closely correlated with one another from among the larger number of dimensions proposed by Trompenaars. Trompenaars himself continues to distinguish seven dimensions of cultural variation, but the remaining dimensions have not yet been reliably measured.

Space does not permit examination of these models in detail here. The models that we have looked at in detail are among the most popular in the international management literature, but international managers might find it helpful to identify additional models and review them to decide which are most relevant in specific circumstances. For example, the individualism/collectivism construct has been examined (Triandis 1972), and some authors have concluded that it is not simply a continuum from individualistic to collectivistic but, rather, that there are different types of individualism and collectivism; specifically, he identified horizontal and vertical dimensions of individualism and collectivism. Some people find this approach particularly insightful and useful internationally.

In addition to developing new concepts and models of culture, the existing ones are also evolving over time. For example, the Hofstede model has recently added new dimensions based on new work. Readers are encouraged to consider the most up-to-date information rather than be limited by what is included here.

Ethnocentrism and Parochialism

Some anthropologists believe that cultural attributes develop as a response to the environment and become a preferred way of behaving for a group of people because they help the people survive. It is not surprising, then, that cultural preferences are associated with right and correct ways of behaving. Consequently, other ways of behaving are seen as bad and incorrect. If "our way" somehow contributed to our survival, it is hard to admit that "their way" can also be acceptable. This view of the world is referred to as an *ethnocen-*

tric view. Ethnocentric means that our view of our own and other cultures is centered on the belief that our culture is superior to other cultures.

Adler (1997) described a similar view of one's own culture as being best in terms of *parochialism.* Parochial people also assume that the home culture is superior, but the assumption arises for different reasons. The assumption of superiority arises not because cultures are compared but because differences are not recognized. Parochialism often arises when someone simply lacks knowledge about other cultures.

Ethnocentrism implies that the belief in the home culture's superiority is conscious, while parochialism implies only that the home culture is believed to be superior because little is known of other cultures. Both ethnocentrism and parochialism are common among managers who have to deal with people in foreign locations. Managers need not feel guilty about ethnocentrism or parochialism, given their frequent occurrence. Managers do need, however, to recognize that they are likely to exhibit either or both of these attitudes and that these attitudes will inhibit their ability to work effectively in other cultures. The first step is to recognize the prevalence of these attitudes. Once they are recognized, one can begin to change them. Changing these attitudes begins with developing a better understanding of one's home culture.

Variation Within Cultures

Models of cultural values are helpful in understanding cultural similarities and differences. In essence, however, they are stereotypes. Any culture is far more complex than such models would suggest, and it is important that this complexity be recognized. One can think of cultural stereotypes as describing the values of a typical member of a particular culture, but must acknowledge that any culture is made up of individuals, many of whom do not share the typical values. In working with people from other cultures, both of these aspects need to be considered. To illustrate both cultural preference and individual variation, consider two cultures, Alpha and Beta. Alpha might be a culture described as valuing personal initiative and Beta as valuing group harmony (the United States and Japan, respectively, would fit these descriptions to some degree). These values are measured on an individualism scale.

If these preferences are considered as describing the average in these two societies, these cultural values can be pictured graphically as normal curves. In Exhibit 2.4, the y axis represents the relative frequency of occurrence of individualism in society and the x axis represents a continuum from low individualism to high individualism. The individualism preferences of the two cultures, Alpha and Beta, are pictured on the graph. As Graph A illustrates, there are some Alphans who are quite concerned with group harmony (contrary to their average) and there are some

Betans who are quite concerned with personal initiative (contrary to their average). It is possible to talk of the Alphans as generally being high on individualism and concerned with personal initiative, and the Betans as generally being low on individualism and concerned with group harmony. At the same time, individuals within both the Alpha and Beta cultures can vary from this general preference. In contrast, it is possible, although unlikely, that there could be virtually no overlap between two cultures, as in Graph B. Two cultures can also be very similar and yet reflect a subtle difference in preferences. This would be the case in Canada and the United States, two countries often seen as holding similar values yet with some differences in their cultural values. This is illustrated in Graph C, where there is a great deal of overlap between the cultures, yet the norm structures for each country are slightly different.

Exhibit 2.4   **Variations in Cultures**

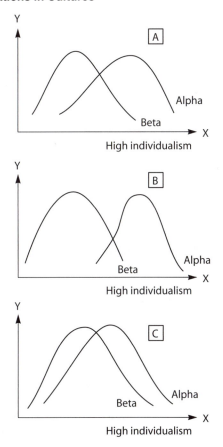

Beyond National Culture

A focus simply on national culture can be somewhat misleading if one limits consideration to this level. There are clear cases where cultures transcend national boundaries (for example, the British culture in many former colonies) and other cases where several cultures are evident in one nation (for example, multiculturalism in Canada). Equally, because cultures change in response to the environment, degrees of similarity and difference change over time. On the whole, as discussed earlier, from the organization's viewpoint, a focus on national cultures is an appropriate beginning. Within this framework, subcultures, overlapping cultures, and forces for convergence and divergence need to be considered.

Understanding Subcultures

Identifying subcultures and their values is vital in some situations and can be particularly useful to international managers; for example:

- A subculture may hold values that are in sharp contrast to those of the broader national culture. If a manager is interacting substantially with members of such a subculture, he or she will need to appreciate and accommodate these differences. Sikh immigrants to Canada still maintain their cultural heritage and believe in the importance of wearing turbans. The Royal Canadian Mounted Police—Canada's famed Mounties—found it was necessary to accommodate this cultural custom in order to attract and retain Sikhs in the force.
- The values of a subculture can be more similar to a foreign manager's own cultural values than those of the broader national culture. A manager might want to seek out members of this subculture in situations where similar values are desired. A manager from a largely Christian country such as the United Kingdom might find some similarity of values with the Christian minority in Japan and might seek out this group at certain times, particularly in times of personal grief.
- Members of a subculture whose values are in conflict with the broader national culture may not be integrated into the workforce easily. Contrasting values may cause personal conflicts among employees from different groups. A manager must be sensitive to these potential conflicts and identify ways of dealing with them. The indigenous Malays and the Chinese in Malaysia have been described as exhibiting sometimes radically different values that can lead to conflicts at work. These are partially due to conflicting religious practices—the Malays, for the most part, are Muslims, while the Chinese are Confucians or Buddhists—and

partially due to attitudes toward work—the Malays are seen as easygoing and working to live, while the Chinese are described as concerned with getting ahead and viewing work as more central to their lives.

- Synergy can develop where employees with different values work together, because they may view the same situation from varying perspectives. Managers who can effectively control interactions among employees with different values can benefit from the development of new and innovative ways of thinking. The Bata Shoe Company has subsidiaries throughout the world and finds that by bringing its diverse marketing managers together in Canada, new ideas for products and marketing approaches can be developed.

- Working with a variety of subcultures within one national location provides many of the same experiences as working in a new national culture. Managers can increase their cross-cultural sensitivity by seeking out members of different cultural minorities and interacting and working with them on an ongoing basis. The United States is made up of many groups that maintain their cultural heritage in spite of being Americans. Some companies have made a virtue of this cultural diversity; for example, Monsanto is reported to have developed specific programs to ensure that all employees are culturally aware.

Understanding Overlapping Cultures

Subcultures are often encountered and cannot in practice be ignored by international managers. The same is true of cultures that overlap national boundaries. There are many situations where groups in different countries share similar values. In fact, the subcultures identified previously (e.g., the Sikhs) can be found in many countries and their values are somewhat similar in each location. The similarities in values are often attributable to shared ethnicity or religion; some examples illustrate this potential overlap:

- Rastafarians (members of a religious sect originating in Jamaica) can be found throughout the Caribbean and in Canada, Japan, the United Kingdom, and the United States. Those values and customs associated with their religious beliefs remain similar even when they have been integrated into societies outside Jamaica.

- The Jewish people often exhibit similar values no matter where in the world they have settled. To some extent this is because of shared religious beliefs, but even nonpracticing Jews feel a kinship with other Jews in different parts of the world, and many Jews see this as a shared cultural heritage, not simply a religious similarity. Similarly, Gypsies, no matter where they live, have some values in common.

- The British left a clear mark on many of their colonies, and the governing class in former British colonies retains many British characteristics.
- Boundaries of many nations have been demarcated in such a way that cultural groups have been divided. These groups often share more culture with their counterparts in other countries than with the nation in which they live. The Kurdish people of Iran, Iraq, and Turkey provide a good example of this division of an ethnic group. Ethnic Russians living in many of the new states formed from the USSR are in a similar situation.

It can also be helpful for international managers to identify overlapping cultural values that may be found in different locations. Familiarity with the cultural values of a group in one location can then be useful in identifying values of a counterpart group elsewhere.

The Importance of Cultural Values for International Managers

Managers in international businesses need to understand and appreciate a variety of differences among nations. Among other differences, nations exhibit varying cultural profiles; thus, understanding the cultural environment is a component of the international manager's task. Managers who have worked in foreign locations acknowledge that understanding the culture in those locations is necessary if one is to manage effectively. Virtually all of the activities undertaken by managers are affected, at least to some degree, by the cultural environment. Consider some examples, which show the importance of culture in the management process:

- International firms need to negotiate with various foreign constituencies. Success in these negotiations rests on understanding the cultural profile of the negotiators.
- Cross-border strategic alliances are becoming more and more common between firms with different strategies and objectives, because of their cultural differences. To succeed, managers may need to understand the cultural factors that influence organizational strategies, objectives, and practices.
- Managers in foreign locations frequently find that employees behave in ways that are quite different from these managers' expectations, which are rooted in their own culture.
- Expatriates (employees working outside their home country) find that culture shock affects their general ability to function well in foreign locations. Cultural understanding and adaptability have been

identified as contributing to better expatriation of managers and their families.

• Foreign guest workers provide services in a variety of locations around the world (for example, Indonesian maids in Dubai, Caribbean farm workers in Canada, Mexican migrants in the United States). These guest workers often have very different values from their employers.

• Various functional aspects of organizations, such as accounting, finance, and marketing, can differ markedly from one location to another. For an organization to be effective overseas, these functional aspects must fit the local culture yet continue to relate to the home culture.

There are a wide variety of websites that provide cross-cultural information for travelers and international managers. One that readers may find particularly relevant is offered by the *Economist*. This is a series of fifteen-minute audio guides called "Doing business in," which promises to give business travelers the knowledge they need to survive in the world's most important business centers. Each installment features candid insights and expert advice from *Economist* correspondents. The *Economist* suggests users of these guides can learn from someone else's mistakes.

Summary and Conclusions

The relationship between national culture and international management is an extremely complex one. The discussion in this chapter is necessarily limited in scope and depth. It should, however, provide the reader with a basic understanding of the issues associated with developing and using cultural understanding to enhance international operations. A particular aim of this chapter has been to provide a structured approach to studying and understanding culture. To this end, several models of cultural values were presented in some detail. There are many other models that may be useful. Individual managers will want to consider these as well, and to select models that seem most relevant to a given situation. For example, in some situations, the individualism/collectivism contrast might seem helpful; in others, a society's view of humans as good/bad or changeable could be most relevant, and so on.

It is important to be aware of the Western biases inherent in these discussions of culture and management. For example, the management process—consisting of planning, organizing, staffing, directing, and controlling—is familiar to most readers because that is how business and management are usually approached in North America and Europe, but consider the following:

1. Is planning a necessary part of management? If events are pre-determined, planning may at best be a waste of time and at worst a questioning of a higher power.
2. Should firms be formally organized? If personal influence is important in day-to-day activities, it may not be appropriate to identify positions within the firm.
3. Can people be allocated to fill positions within the firm? If people prefer to work at tasks as they arise, it may not be helpful to allocate them to specific slots.
4. Does management actively seek to direct and motivate subordinates? If people believe that they should work hard only for personal achievement, it may be counterproductive for management actively to direct and motivate them.

This inherent bias in Western thinking about management illustrates a major challenge for international cross-cultural management. Effective managers should not take anything for granted. Openness to the possibility that the world is not the world you know and accept is constantly necessary. In addition, because culture is complex, the astute manager needs to go beyond "sophisticated stereotyping" to make sense of apparent cultural paradoxes that can occur (Osland and Bird 2000).

References

Adler, N.J. 1997. *International Dimensions of Organizational Behavior.* 3rd ed. Boston: PWS-Kent Publishing.

Chinese Cultural Connection. 1987. "Chinese Values and the Search for Culture Free Dimensions of Culture." *Journal of Cross-Cultural Psychology* 18(2): 143–164.

England, G. 1978. "Managers and Their Value Systems: A Five Country Comparative Study." *Columbia Journal of World Business* 13(2): 35–44.

Heller, F.A. 1988. "Cost Benefits of Multinational Research on Organizations." *International Studies of Management and Organization* 18(3): 5–18.

Hofstede, G. 1980. *Culture's Consequences.* Beverly Hills, CA: Sage.

Inglehart, R. 2012. "National-level Value Scores by Country." World Values Survey. http://www.worldvaluessurvey.org/wvs/articles/folder_published/article_base_111 (accessed March 4, 2012).

Kluckhohn, A., and F. Strodtbeck. 1961. *Variations in Value Orientations.* Westport, CT: Greenwood Press.

Kroeber, A., and C. Kluckhohn. 1952. *Culture: A Critical Review of Concepts and Definitions.* Cambridge, MA: Papers of the Peabody Museum, Harvard University.

Lane, H., and J. DiStefano. 1988. *International Management Behavior: From Policy to Practice.* Scarborough, Ontario: Nelson Canada.

Osland, J.S., and A. Bird. 2000. "Beyond Sophisticated Stereotyping: Cultural Sensemaking in Context." *Academy of Management* 14(1): 77–78.

Punnett, B.J., and S. Withane. 1990. "Hofstede's Value Survey Model: To Embrace or Abandon?" *Advances in International Comparative Management* 5: 69–90.

Rokeach, J. 1973. *The Nature of Human Values.* New York: Free Press.

Ronen, S., and O. Shenkar. 1985. "Clustering Countries on Attitudinal Dimensions: A Review and Synthesis." *Academy of Management Review* 10(3): 435–454.

Schwartz, S.H. 1999. "Cultural value differences: Some implications for work." *Applied Psychology: An International Review* 48: 23–48.

Smith, P.B., and M.F. Peterson. 1988. *Leadership, organizations and culture: An event management model.* London: Sage.

Smith, P.B., M.F. Peterson, and S.H. Schwartz 2002. "Cultural values, sources of guidance and their relevance to managerial behavior: A 47 nation study." *Journal of Cross-Cultural Psychology* 33: 188–208.

Smith, P.B., M.F. Peterson, and Z.M.Wang. 1996. "The manager as mediator of alternative meanings." *Journal of International Business Studies* 27: 115–137.

Terpstra, V., and K. David. 1985. *The Cultural Environment of International Business.* Cincinnati, OH: Southwestern.

Triandis, H.C. 1972. *The Analysis of Subjective Culture.* New York: Wiley.

Trompenaars, F., and C. Hampden-Turner. 1998. *Riding the Waves of Culture: Understanding Diversity in Global Business.* 2nd ed. New York: McGraw-Hill.

3

The Political and Regulatory Environment

Introduction

The global nature of the business environment, discussed in chapter 1, suggests that national economies are much more closely linked now than in the past. The forces for cultural convergence, discussed in chapter 2, suggest that countries are becoming more alike in some ways, one of which is democracy. To some this suggests that national governments are becoming less relevant. At the beginning of the twenty-first century, regional and global organizations such as the World Trade Organization and the United Nations are playing an increasingly important role in determining what national governments can and cannot do in terms of trade and investment. In addition, there has been a proliferation of regional trade agreements over the past fifteen years. These regional agreements require that countries cooperate closely and sometimes subordinate their national interests to regional interests. The Internet can also often transcend national regulations. The question arises as to the degree that national policies have relevance in this global environment. In 2012, the problems faced by some nation-states in the European Union, such as Greece, illustrated the trade-offs between national sovereignty and obligations to the larger group.

The demise of the nation-state has been predicted before, but nation-states, so far, have remained viable entities. Notwithstanding the forces for convergence, the forces for divergence are also strong and suggest strong divisions among countries. The regional and global organizations have, as part of their mandates, the duty of reinforcing national sovereignty. International firms do not, in fact, operate internationally and outside of the regulations imposed by nation-states. Rather, their operations are subject to the preferences of national governments, which are demonstrated in what firms are permitted to do and what they are prohibited from doing. For example:

- A Jamaican firm that wants to export ackees (a Jamaican vegetable, made famous by Harry Belafonte when he sang, "ackee and rice, salt fish is nice, and the rum is fine any time of the year") to the United States must pass U.S. government inspections to ensure that the food meets safety standards, and the goods are subject to search to ensure that they contain only the stated products.

- A U.S.-based firm, such as Hilton Hotels, that invests in the People's Republic of China (PRC) must obtain government permission to invest and to import the supplies that it requires from outside of the PRC.
- A Canadian university that sends professors on a teaching exchange to Croatia needs the Croatian government's approval and work permits for the professors before they can take up their teaching duties.

The *Oxford English Dictionary* definition of a nation-state is a territory with its own government; thus, each nation-state follows a particular political system and has its own government. Each nation-state also has a legislative system that governs the behavior of anyone within its territorial boundaries. Corporations, like people, are subject to the legislative system and thus required to behave in ways that comply with its rules. In most countries, there is a particular body of legislation focusing on corporations that determines how they can be structured, owned, and operated. Further, in many countries there are laws that deal specifically with foreign corporations.

In spite of the globalization of the business world, the political and regulatory environment remains a major area of understanding for international managers. The political and regulatory environment is important "at home" as well, but at home this environment is generally well known and well understood. For example:

- American managers know what political contributions are allowed in the United States; they are familiar with the major parties' beliefs about the role of government in business; they understand the relationships with their local representatives, and so on.
- Canadian managers are conscious of the political tensions between Quebec and the other provinces; they are proud of the government's provision of a social safety net; they expect their government to work closely with the U.S. government, and so on.
- Nigerian managers are at ease with the need to provide small tips, and larger bribes, to government persons; people in Barbados know the difference between the BLP (Barbados Labour Party) and the DLP (Democratic Labour Party); UK managers understand the Conservative government's relationship with unions; Hong Kong managers know when it is best to stay out of politics.

The point of these examples is that managers working in their own countries may not need to do a political assessment, because they will be reasonably familiar with this environment and it is easy to stay current. The same is not true of a manager operating outside the home country. A thorough understanding of the political and regulatory environment is critical for the foreign manager. Such an understanding allows the manager to make decisions that are appropriate, given the host country's political context. This chapter will explore a number of aspects of the political and regulatory environment that need to be understood. First, different types of political systems are described; next, government, business, and societal relationships are considered; and finally the concept of political risk is explored. All of these are discussed from the point of view of a manager's need to consider these issues.

Political Systems

The political system refers to the structure of the government in a nation-state. There are a number of distinct governmental structures, which are described briefly in the following pages. Space constraints allow only a very superficial explanation of these structures. A manager going to a foreign country with a political system that is different from that at home would want to read more about the unfamiliar system.

- *Sovereign systems.* Some countries have a supreme ruler, or sovereign, who selects government personnel. The ruler is usually in the sovereign position based on birthright. Typically, the sovereign is succeeded at death and a designated child in the ruling family, usually the eldest son, commonly succeeds to the sovereign position. Government personnel may change at any time when the sovereign determines there is a need for change. Saudi Arabia is one example of a sovereign system. Countries can also change from a sovereign system, as Nepal did in 2007 when, under pressure from Marxist rebels, the monarchy was deposed.
- *Dictatorships.* Some countries have a supreme ruler whose position is based on personal power. For example, military dictatorships are led by a person who has the support of the military. Typically, the ruler in a dictatorship is replaced when he/she no longer has the support necessary to maintain the needed power base. The leader can be overthrown in a military coup, through a war with another country, assassination, or by a popular uprising. In recent years, the Taliban in Afghanistan were removed in a U.S.-led war (the Taliban were not necessarily led by a single dictator), the Philippine government changed in a popular uprising, and the Pakistani leadership in a military coup. In some situ-

ations, dictators choose to hold democratic elections or establish their family as the ruling family. In Bhutan, a previously largely isolated country, the head of state implemented a limited democracy in 2008, and Bhutan might be called a democratic theocracy—that is, it includes aspects of a sovereign ruler and aspects of a democracy.

- *Multi-party democracies.* Some countries have popular elections to select their leaders. Typically, democratic countries hold elections at specific times, and people over a certain age may vote for their preferred candidates. There are usually two or more political parties vying for power, and the candidates are usually associated with the parties, which have stated views on various aspects of government. In these countries, some government personnel change at election time, depending on the outcome of the vote. The United States, Europe, and much of the British Commonwealth (the United Kingdom and former colonies) are multi-party democracies.
- *Constitutional monarchies.* Some countries have democratically elected governments, as well as a ruling family and a sovereign as the ceremonial head of the government. These countries function as democracies, but the monarch is technically the head of state. The United Kingdom is a constitutional monarchy with a king or queen (Queen Elizabeth II in 2012). Normally, a monarch serves for her/his life, but in the United Kingdom there have been discussions as to whether the queen should resign to give her son Prince Charles an opportunity to serve as monarch while he is still relatively young (*relatively* being a subjective term, as he is nearly seventy).
- *Single-party systems.* Some countries allow only one political party, typically the Communist Party, and government personnel are selected from among party members. The communist system is based on the idea of widespread elections for low-level government personnel, higher-level officials selected from these, and so on. This would seem to suggest that communist government officials change on a regular basis. The reality in communist countries has been that one leader with supreme power emerges and retains dictatorial power. Fidel Castro in Cuba has been supreme ruler of a communist country, however, his brother Raul has taken over because of Fidel's illness and has been undertaking some economic and political reforms since 2008, moving toward freer markets and, perhaps, democracy. It will be very interesting for international managers to watch these developments in Cuba. In such a situation, the government actually changes through an internal party struggle where a new leader emerges, often when the current leader dies, or, in the Cuban case, is unwell. The Soviet Union was a communist state, but most of the countries that were part of the Soviet Union have opted for other forms of government, although those that are now democracies often have a communist party as one of their parties.

- *Colonies.* Some countries are not sovereign, but are ruled by other countries and are called colonies. Often these countries vote for local government officials, but the head of state is dictated by the colonial power. In Britain's colonial empire, the head of the colonial government was a governor appointed by Britain. Most of Britain's former colonies are now independent, but some have chosen to retain their colonial status. In some colonies, leadership changes at specified times. Some territories are similar to colonies but are not considered colonies; this is the case with Puerto Rico and its relationship to the United States, or the French territories in the Caribbean, which are considered departments of France.

Events in 2011 and beyond in the Middle East illustrated the importance of understanding the political situation in any country where one may do business. The countries of the Middle East had in many ways been seen as "stable" and therefore good for doing business. These countries had been governed by long-standing rulers, often in power for thirty, forty, or more years. Underneath this apparent stability however was a bubbling resentment of the repressive nature of the rulers. Egyptians, for example, had been under "emergency law" since 1981 and were ready for change. The demonstrations and changes in the Middle East, called the "Arab Spring" by reporters, resulted in major and ongoing changes in the region. We do not know what the final result of the Arab Spring will be, but these events illustrate the importance for international managers of the political environment.

Managers need to understand the political system of the country where they work, because the type of system determines who makes the rules, how they are enforced, and if they are likely to change. For example, in multi-party democracies, candidates for office are encouraged to explain their policies, thus likely policies are known and discussed; there is both a ruling party and those in opposition, so that the implementation and enforcement of policies is scrutinized closely; elections occur at specified times and can be incorporated into business plans and decisions. In contrast, in dictatorships, policies are often not explained and may be based on maintaining power, enforcement may be on the basis of relationships, and change may come at any time if there are shifts in power.

The political system is also closely linked to the economic system and the degree of government involvement in business, and these relationships are important for managers. To explore these relationships, consider the following contrasts:

• Multi-party democracies are traditionally free-market economies and believe in capitalism. A free-market economy is one where the demand for and the supply of goods and services determine the price for those goods and services. Consumers are free to buy the products and services they want. Producers are free to make the products and services that they believe the market wants. There is a clear distinction between the public sector (government services) and the private sector (business), and most economic activity takes place in the private sector with little government intervention.

• One-party states are traditionally centrally planned economies. A centrally planned economy is one where the government determines the supply of goods and services, and identifies a price for them based on its beliefs and its estimate of the needs and demands of the people of the country. Producers are told what to produce, and the choices available to consumers are limited to what is produced. The private sector essentially does not exist, because the factors of production are controlled by the government.

The above descriptions represent the extremes of a free-market economy compared to a centrally planned one. The United States would be considered to be a traditional free market, while Cuba would be a traditional planned economy. Even in the United States, however, there is some government ownership and intervention, and in Cuba, there is some private industry. The People's Republic of China, the world's largest communist country, is experimenting with a mix of central planning and free markets, and these efforts are likely to increase now that it has become a member of the World Trade Organization. There are many in-between possibilities. Some countries have mixed economies, where the vital factors of production are government owned and centrally planned, but private industry is allowed. These are often called socialist countries. A country like Canada has essentially a free-market economy, but the government is more involved in providing social services than is the government in the United States.

During the 1990s, following the collapse of the Soviet Union and accompanying the growth in globalization, there was a substantial move toward freer markets. Central planning was seen to have failed in the countries where it had been tried. Government ownership and intervention were believed to be the cause of inefficiencies in many industries and locations. Many countries deregulated industries and privatized those that had previously been government owned and operated. The result has not been uniformly successful, and at the beginning of the twenty-first century there are questions being raised regarding the wisdom of relying too heavily on the private sector. The "Occupy" movement (originally "Occupy Wall Street") that spread around the world in 2011 and beyond essentially felt that capitalism had gone too far, and that 1 percent of the world's population controlled the vast proportion of the world's wealth. This movement appealed to many of the 99 percent, even if they did not actively participate in demonstrations, and raised many questions about the results of capitalism if it is left unfettered.

Managers can expect that there will be more government intervention and regulation in the coming decade. This is likely for a number of quite disparate reasons. Consider the following events since the turn of the century:

- The terrorist attacks of September 2001 in the United States have resulted in tighter security around the world. This means that the activities of firms and their managers are being scrutinized more closely now. For example, airport security in the United States has been taken over by the government. In 2008, in many airports around the world a new regulation had been put into place that limited liquids and gels in hand luggage to three ounces, or about 100 milliliters.
- In late 2001, the collapse of a large company in the United States, Enron, and subsequent revelations about Arthur Andersen's accounting and audit methods, had made the public suspicious of corporate reports.
- There is a substantial push for greater transparency in corporate reporting, and managers will have to comply. Self-regulation by the auditing/ accounting profession has been questioned, and greater scrutiny by governmental or quasi-governmental bodies, such as the U.S. Securities and Exchange Commission, is now required.
- The subprime lending crisis in the United States came to light in late 2007 and led to the near collapse or failure of banks in various countries.
- In 2008, in response to concerns about governance in Chinese companies, China's securities provider launched a new index that rates corporate governance in China-listed companies with the hope of improving governance practices.
- Financial institutions were bailed out by various governments in the years following the 2008 recession, and then they paid substantial bonuses to their executives, raising questions about both the bailout and the bonus system.
- Continuing disparity between rich and poor countries has encouraged many to question the worldwide benefits of globalization. Managers will face greater pressure to demonstrate that their decisions, and their firms' activities, are beneficial to the countries where they do business.
- The World Bank and other international institutions have questioned their traditional thinking about economic development, debt, and debt relief, and the amount and role of aid to poor countries.

- Poorer countries are pushing for a greater say in world trade decisions, and countries generally are questioning the power relationships in global organizations, such as the role of the Security Council at the United Nations.
- The "Occupy" movement brought disparity between the 1 percent richest people in the world and the 99 percent "rest" to the attention of the world.
- The European Union suffered a severe crisis, with some countries continuing to grow economically and others remaining in severe recessions; this brought into question the viability of the common currency, the euro.
- Some countries did well economically, through the "global" recession, particularly the BRICS countries (Brazil, Russia, India, China, and South Africa).

Free markets have not been a panacea for the world, but central planning certainly was not successful. Nation-states will continue to experiment with different forms of government and different approaches to their economies. China's experiments both on the mainland and in Hong Kong have been interesting because they have resulted in a phenomenal reported economic growth rate. For most of the developed world, managers can expect that free markets will continue, but that there is likely to be closer government scrutiny and more regulation. For the developing world, managers can expect continued welcoming of foreign investors, but with more host government concern for clear host country benefits to be associated with incoming investment. Global warming and the state of the environment are likely to play an important role in how markets evolve in the coming decades. One is reading more and more about so-called "green" developments in business, and these may well be the growth areas of the future.

Government, Business, and Society

The previous discussion has shown that there are close links between government, business, and society at large. Governments, at least nominally, are in place for the benefit of society at large. Private enterprise, or business, provides both benefits and costs to society. Businesses provide employment and security, they produce needed and desired goods and services, they pay taxes and dividends, and they develop new systems and technology. Businesses are not naturally ethical, however, and managers' primary objective of making profits is not always consistent with society's general welfare. Businesses, thus, are often seen as contributing to the gap between the rich and the poor, damaging the environment, profiting from exploiting the disadvantaged, and generally being a cost to society. News coverage of the subprime lending situation in the United States, the earlier Enron collapse, and the multi-million-dollar executive salaries, suggest a few people have profited enormously while others have suffered, and these events clearly encourage this view.

The reality is somewhere between the extremes. Businesses provide both benefits and costs for society. It is the government's role to maximize the benefits while minimizing and controlling the costs. How a government accomplishes this depends on its view of the role of business. For the international manager, it is not only important to understand this view, but also vital to know how a host government views business generally and foreign businesses in particular.

Government View of Business

Governments may view private sector businesses on a continuum from very positive to very negative. At the positive extreme, businesses have been described as the engine of growth. At the negative extreme, businesses have been described as exploiters of the poor. During the 1990s, along with privatization, free markets, and free trade, private enterprise enjoyed a generally positive image. By the early 2000s, this image was changing.

Managers at home and abroad in the 1990s were welcomed as knowledgeable and capable of producing both extraordinary profits and social benefits. There was a lot of talk of a new economy that would go on growing, essentially forever. The new economy did not continue, unfortunately. Growth stopped, and countries experienced recessions. Fear of terrorism replaced optimism, at least temporarily, in the United States. Conflicts around the world continued. The effects of global warming seemed ever more dramatic. By 2003, business was no longer seen as saving the world, but rather as contributing to its economic, environmental, and social degradation. By 2012, the "Occupy" movement exemplified a negative view of business as contributing to the gap between the rich and poor, within countries as well as between countries.

The situation is more complex, with some businesses addressing the world's challenges (for example, charities such as the Gates Foundation, companies developing better technologies, new ideas such as the Grameen Bank founder's concept of an ethical corporation that reinvests for the good of society), while others are seen as taking advantage of the world and the poor (for example, petroleum companies reaping excessive profits because of high oil prices, Chinese companies selling fake drugs). The key for a manager is to understand how her/his company is seen in a particular location.

Where the prevailing view of business is positive, managers face a relatively benign political and regulatory environment. They can expect private investment to be welcomed, government personnel to be helpful, incentives to be provided, and regulations to be minimal. This was the environment that managers grew accustomed to at the end of the twentieth century.

The current environment has not changed to a negative extreme, but it has become more cautious. Investment is still welcome, but government personnel are raising more questions; incentives are there, but some countries are reviewing them, and more regulations are being considered. Terrorism, unrest, and global warming concerns have all resulted in attempts to make regulations much tighter in terms of trade and investment. In this environment, international managers can expect that their firms will receive more attention than in the previous decades. At the same time, there are ongoing efforts to make trade and investment freer, and technological innovations are making it easier for companies to carry out activities across borders that are difficult to trace. Managers in today's complex business environment face an uncertain world.

View of Foreign Business

Within the general context of whether businesses are seen as positive or negative, foreign businesses may have a different image from domestic ones. In some locations, foreign businesses are seen as providing more opportunities, better management, increased access to technology, and generally as being superior to local firms. In other locations, the reverse is the case, and foreign businesses are seen as a form of neocolonialism—imposing foreign cultural values, ignoring local conditions, exploiting host country resources, and generally a negative to be endured for the sake of some job creation and provision of foreign capital. In yet other locations, the two views are combined in a love–hate relationship where foreign companies are both admired and distrusted.

Where the prevailing view of foreign businesses is positive, managers can look forward to a pleasant, nonthreatening environment. Well-qualified locals will seek out foreign firms for employment; government personnel will make themselves readily available to foreign managers; managers in local firms will want to learn from their foreign counterparts. Where the view is that foreign business is negative, it will be hard to attract good employees, government personnel will be difficult to access, and local managers will avoid foreigners. In the first case, foreignness is an asset, and managers should want to be seen as foreign. In the second case, foreignness is a drawback, and managers will want the firm to blend in as much as possible and themselves to be seen as adapting to local conditions.

Often the view of foreign firms and managers is a mix of admiration and distrust. In Canada, American managers may be held up as examples of excellence but disliked as arrogant. In the 1980s, many Americans admired Japanese management but thought the Japanese unfair in business practices. Indian managers may pride themselves as being more British than the British, but may not want to work with the British. In these situations, the foreign manager has to evaluate the pros and cons of foreignness, with the objective of portraying the positive side and countering the negative. For example, in the previous Canadian example, the American manager wants to be sure he or she does not display arrogance by being overly pro-American.

In the following section, the typical love–hate relationship between host government and foreign business is summarized. First, the positives of foreign direct investment (FDI) are outlined, then the negatives, followed by the incentives and restrictions that often accompany FDI.

Positives of Foreign Direct Investment

FDI can provide many benefits, particularly for developing countries. These all mean that countries seek investment and provide incentives to encourage investment. For example, investors can provide:

- capital and technology for host country growth, development, and modernization where capital and technology cannot be generated internally;
- expertise and skills that do not exist locally;
- training to develop domestic expertise and skills;
- access to markets, distribution, and resources available to, or controlled by, foreign firms;
- employment for locals who would otherwise be unemployed;
- positive contributions to the balance of trade through import substitutes or exports;
- foreign exchange through investment or export earnings; and
- revenues from personal and corporate taxes and tariffs.

The positive side of FDI provides foreign managers the opportunity to ensure that the host government sees how a firm's investment will benefit the host country. The positives also underlie the incentives that governments offer to foreign investors. When investors take advantage of incentives, it is to their benefit if they can identify the positive outcomes for the host country. These positive aspects of FDI cannot be considered in isolation. There is a negative side as well, as the following illustrates.

Negatives of Foreign Direct Investment

The host government may see foreign investment as potentially providing the benefits outlined previously, but it may also see a downside to this investment, and this downside may be magnified if the host is a developing country. For example, investment can result in:

- increased dependence as countries rely on investors for capital, expertise, and technology instead of developing it themselves;
- decreased sovereignty as countries depend on foreign investors and make decisions to suit investors rather than their own people;
- exploitation through the use of nonrenewable resources and low-skilled jobs;
- provision of inappropriate technology that is either so advanced it is not transferable, old and outdated, or otherwise inefficient;
- outflows of capital in the form of dividends, profit repatriation, and intra-firm transactions; and
- displacement of local firms because they cannot compete with foreign investors.

The negative view of FDI has to be understood and considered by foreign managers. If the view of foreign investors is generally negative, then the foreign managers will need to be able to counter the potential accusations from the local government, media, unions, and so on by clearly illustrating that the benefits of the investment to the host country outweigh the costs and by finding meaningful ways to contribute to the host country.

Incentives and Restrictions

The result of the love–hate relationship is a combination of incentives for investment and regulations imposed on investment (see Exhibit 3.1). The incentives are intended to promote the positives and the regulations to limit the negatives. Incentives and regulations are generally applied across the board to all investors; however, there is often also room to negotiate the terms of any agreement with the host government. If managers understand the reasons for incentives and restrictions, they are in a better position to negotiate arrangements that are beneficial for their firm. Managers need to identify the benefits of their investment and ensure that appropriate incentives are associated with these benefits. For example, in a country with high unemployment, if an investor can guarantee certain employment and training levels, the host government may be willing to provide low-rent facilities. At the same time,

Exhibit 3.1

Some Typical Incentives and Restrictions for Foreign Direct Investment

Typical *incentives* for investment have been:
    Tax holidays
    Exemptions from tariffs
    Accelerated depreciation allowances
    Provision of land and factory shells
    Low-interest loans
    Low utility rates
    Duty-free zones
Typical *restrictions* on investment have been:
    Local ownership participation
    Local content
    Specified employment levels
    Reinvestment
    Location limitations
    Export promotion or import substitution
    Restricted access to local markets

managers should openly examine the potential costs and be able identify how these can be minimized. For example, if the company plans to repatriate most of its profits, managers should recognize this as a cost to the host country. In this situation, identifying some opportunities, even if relatively small, for reinvestment in the host country allows the company to mitigate the cost somewhat. The restrictions listed in Exhibit 3.1 are clearly intended to limit the costs identified as associated with foreign investments. The incentives are meant as enticements to encourage investors to choose a particular location for their investment. Investors should weigh these incentives and restrictions in different locations and factor them into investment decisions.

View of the Home Country

An additional issue for the foreign manager is how her/his home country is perceived in the host country. Even where business is seen as a positive force and foreign businesses are favored, firms from particular countries may be seen negatively. Vice versa, foreign business can be thought of negatively, but firms from a particular country might be favored. The view of the home country is usually a function of overall relationships between home and host countries, as well as specific past experiences with firms from a specific country. Where the home and host country have a generally good relationship, firms can expect a positive reception. Canada and the United States work closely together as countries, and each is the other's largest trading partner—U.S. firms in Canada and Canadian firms in the United States usually find doing business in the other country relatively easy. In contrast, U.S. relations with Arab countries are quite mixed, and U.S. firms doing business in the Arab world face mixed reactions from governments as well as the population at large.

It would likely surprise many Americans to learn that a poll in Arab countries in early 2002 that asked for words to describe America identified "terrorist" as the most common. At the same time, American politicians were saying that if they could describe their position logically to the Arabs, surely they would understand. Many people in the Middle East, Africa, and elsewhere around the world do not understand the U.S. position on the Israel–Palestine conflict; they do not understand why the United States considered Iran, Iraq, and North Korea to be part of an "axis of evil"; they believe the war in Iraq was misguided and unjust; they do not understand how the Guantánamo prisoner situation has been allowed to continue. . . . In other words, they do not understand the Americans. Many Americans, in turn, are bewildered by these attitudes and do not understand why the rest of the world no longer seems to be their friend.

Managers working in foreign locations are often faced with similar conflicting views. This makes their work difficult and complex. They are in the position of wanting to support the home viewpoint but needing to live with the host viewpoint. The need for cultural awareness and sensitivity, discussed in chapter 2, is evident in dealing with the political environment.

The potential for host countries seeing foreign investors as negative, or investors from particular countries as undesirable, leads to the concept of political risk in international firms. The following sections discuss political risk and its assessment and management.

Types of Political Risk

The risk associated with the political environment is essentially the likelihood that a government will take actions that have an unexpected, negative impact on a firm. These actions can include:

- government confiscation of a firm's property with no compensation to the firm;
- government expropriation of a firm's property for compensation to be determined by the government;
- government acquisition of a firm's property for a sum determined by an objective third party;
- government imposition of taxes on foreign firms;
- government passage of regulations that make it difficult for foreign firms to operate efficiently and effectively;

- government encouragement of negative attitudes toward a particular firm or foreign firms in general; and
- government spearheading and supporting a buy-local campaign that discriminates against foreign firms.

Political risk is generally defined to include three major categories: forced divestment, unwelcome regulations, and interference in operations.

Forced Divestment

Forced divestment means that a government requires that a company give up its assets against its will. The government may acquire the company's assets itself, or it may force the company to give up the assets to other parties. At worst, a government may confiscate the assets of a company with no compensation. This is unusual except where there is clear evidence of wrongdoing on the company's part. The Cuban takeover of foreign companies in 1960 is often considered a confiscation, because the companies received no compensation for their assets; however, the Cuban government maintains that it offered compensation that was not accepted by the companies. More often the government forces a sale of assets, either to the government itself or to other local interests. Forced divestment may focus on one company when a government expropriates the assets, or it may entail the nationalization of an entire industry. In these cases, payment is made for assets, but in this situation, many companies believe their assets are substantially undervalued and that they are unfairly compensated. Sometimes payment is made in the local currency, which may not be readily convertible, or in government bonds, which are not negotiable and subject to foreign exchange risk. Again, companies consider this to be unfair treatment.

The impact of forced divestment can be substantial for a company or industry, and the risks must therefore be assessed carefully. The likelihood of forced divestment is, however, relatively low. The period from 1970 to 1977 was a period when a substantial number of forced divestments took place around the world; a reported high of nearly seventy such acts took place in 1975 (Minor 1990), still a relatively small number. From 1980 to the present there have been few forced divestments. In contrast, privatization has been more common in this period. Governments have returned assets to former owners or sought private sector buyers (often foreign) for government-owned companies.

Forced divestment or nationalization is most often undertaken by a host government against a foreign company, either because the company is seen as having a negative impact on the host, or because the host believes it can run the company for its own benefit. Interestingly, in 2008, the UK government announced that it would nationalize the Northern Rock Bank, a UK bank, because of the problems the bank had suffered due to bad loans associated with the U.S. subprime loans. The UK government had provided substantial financing to stop a run on the bank in late 2007. The government claimed that nationalization was necessary to save the bank, but shareholders did not agree.

While the impact of forced divestment is substantial, it is a one-time event. Unwelcome regulations can be of more ongoing concern for many companies, as discussed in the following section.

Unwelcome Regulations

Governments can impose new restrictions that affect a firm's ability to operate effectively and profitably in a particular location. Unwelcome regulations include new taxes, local ownership or management requirements, reinvestment provisions, limits on size or location, and foreign exchange restrictions. If these regulations are expected, then managers can make decisions to deal with them. The risk occurs because they are often unexpected. Decisions made without taking the restrictions into account may no longer be appropriate when the restrictions are imposed. In contrast to forced divestment, governments do not usually reimburse firms for losses in profits resulting from the imposition of regulations, so it is particularly important for managers to assess and manage these events.

Generally, new and unwelcome regulations are imposed either to raise revenues for the government (e.g., new taxes) or to encourage particular aspects of development (e.g., local ownership). If managers invest in understanding a government's priorities, they are more likely to be able to predict government regulations. For example, if the government is concerned with unemployment, it may impose local employment requirements; if it wants to establish a broadly based industrial complex, it may require local sourcing and technology development; if improving local management skills is important, it will likely want training for local managers. If managers can predict likely regulations, they can plan for them. Managers can also choose to be proactive and implement plans to help achieve development objectives, thus building an image as a good corporate citizen.

Unwelcome regulations were prevalent in the 1970s but have become less common in the 1990s. Many countries around the world have recently sought to promote themselves as good places to do business, and thus to attract foreign investors. Along with this has been a decrease in regulations. There are still many regulations, however, and, as noted previously, firms are likely to be examined more closely in the coming years. Terrorism, conflicts, poverty, and apparently unethical corporate activities are all likely to result in increased attempts to control business activities.

In addition to unwelcome regulations, governments can interfere in company activities in a variety of more subtle ways as outlined in the following section.

Interference in Operations

Interference in operations refers to a government action that makes it difficult for a firm to operate effectively. This includes government support and encouragement of unionization, negative comments about foreigners and foreign businesses, and discriminatory support of local businesses. Governments may engage in such activities for a variety of reasons. They may believe that a foreign firm is detrimental to local development and thus that opposing the foreign firm will increase the government's popularity. In some circumstances, anti-foreign sentiment might allow the government to remain in power. In other situations, anti-foreign sentiments are based on historical events. The Japanese occupation of Korea before and during World War II means that Japanese firms are not always welcomed in Korea. American firms may find the South Korean environment friendlier.

This type of political risk is particularly difficult to assess and manage because it is often motivated by current political sentiment and can occur in different and subtle forms. Forced divestment and unwelcome regulations have an immediate and identifiable impact on operations. The activities described as interference with operations may be less obvious and the related effects unclear. Yet while not immediately obvious, the effects can nevertheless have a major impact over time (through lost sales, increased costs, difficult labor relations, and so forth). Managers should therefore consider this aspect of political risk to be as important as the other two.

Understanding the reasons for various types of political activity enables managers to assess the likelihood of a particular activity occurring and to devise ways to manage such occurrences.

Assessment and Management of Political Risk

Assessment of political risk is a relatively informal activity in many companies, although some companies have detailed systems of political risk assessment and management in place. For example, the following systems have been described (Punnett and Ricks 1997):

- At Xerox, each managing director of a major foreign affiliate prepared a quarterly report listing the ten most salient political issues in the local environment. These issues were analyzed in terms of their implications for Xerox, and alternative action plans for dealing with them were prepared. These reports went to the operating vice president and the director of international relations at the company headquarters, who considered the combined implications of all the reports. Decisions about responses to political events were made by the operating vice president and director of international relations, incorporating the managing directors' recommendations. These decisions were incorporated into the company's annual plans.

- At Chemical Bank, political spreadsheets were completed for each location. Significant political issues and actors were identified for each location, and the actors were evaluated in terms of their stands on issues, their power to enforce a stand, and their degree of concern about it. Overall, this was used to provide a rating for a given location and details regarding political issues of concern. The spreadsheets were completed by local managers and reviewed at headquarters.

- The Royal Bank of Canada used a ranking method to gauge the relative risk in different countries (according to Bertrand 1990). The ranking was based on economic, business, and political issues. Economic issues included the economic structure and resources (including natural resources), recent economic trends and policies, foreign debt and liquidity, and short- and long-term economic outlook. Business issues included the quality and skills of the labor pool and business leaders, the legislative environment (including rules for ownership and taxation), and the financial strength and competitiveness of the country's top companies. Political issues included the quality and stability of the government, as well as social factors such as the impact of special interest groups, civil unrest, and relationships with its neighbors, major powers, and Canada. Once the bank had all the data, it ranked countries from 0 (worst) to 100 (best). At least once a year the bank's Country Review Committee reviewed all countries in which the bank did business.

Sophisticated political risk analysis systems are computer based and incorporate a wide variety of country and company data. Concerns about terrorism and Internet security are likely to lead to a greater emphasis on political risk analysis in many companies. The following discussion considers sources of information on political risk, factors that suggest risk, and approaches for managing risk.

Sources of Information

Information for political risk assessment comes from external and/or internal sources. External sources include banks, accounting firms, consultants, trade officials, and country risk services. A variety of these organizations publish books on individual countries that include a political analysis. The CIA (Central Intelligence Agency) Factbooks and The *Economist* Intelligence Units are two well-known sources of country information. In addition, organizations such as Business International and Business Environmental Risk Intelligence specialize in assessing and rating country risk. Each source provides a somewhat different viewpoint, and managers will want to utilize several. These external sources of information are a good starting point, but they focus on the country only.

In order to assess political risk validly, managers need to consider their company and the country in question. This means that internal sources of information are as important as external. Managers with substantial company history and international experience, employees who have lived or worked in a particular country, as well as regional and local managers can all provide somewhat different perspectives. Combining these provides a rounded look at any situation. Larger companies have staff departments that specialize in political risk assessment and management, but smaller companies generally rely on a more informal process.

Factors Affecting Political Risk

The degree of political risk that a company faces is a function of both the country where business takes place and the particular company and its type of business. For example, for most companies, political risk would increase in times of civil unrest. For a company that provides negotiations services, which are valued by both sides in the civil unrest, the situation is the reverse. This is clearly the case of companies providing security in Iraq during the war. This is an extreme example, but serves to illustrate the point that what is risky for one company may be neutral or safe for another. There are certain characteristics of countries and companies that generally suggest increased political risk, and these are discussed in the following sections. It is the job of the international manager to apply these generic concepts to the specifics of the company's situation.

Country Characteristics

Generally, instability is associated with increased risk. Instability implies uncertainty, which implies risk. Instability and uncertainty imply political risk from a business perspective because the government may behave in unexpected ways. Characteristics such as type of government, level of economic development, and stability of social and political systems make a country more or less risky. For most companies, frequent government changes, an unstable economy, and social upheavals increase the business risk associated with a particular location. War, revolution, and terrorism increase personal and property risks, as well as business risk. When a gap exists (as is the case in many less-developed countries) between what people expect (particularly in terms of material goods) and what they have access to, the population may be hostile toward foreigners, who seem to be better off than locals; this also increases the degree of political risk, as the governments will be conscious of this hostility.

Although instability, war, and terrorism imply increased risk for many companies, it is also true that some companies benefit from them and a fair number are not affected. At the extreme, a company whose business is selling guns or training executives to counter terrorism benefits from situations that most companies would seek to avoid. A company that provides material goods at a low cost might be attracted to a location where the expectations/reality gap is high. Other companies are involved in businesses that are not particularly affected by changes in government, the economy, or society—for example, a company that manufactures cardboard boxes might fall into this category—and therefore they can to some extent ignore these instabilities.

Industry and Company Characteristics

Certain industries appear to be more subject to government activity than others. This is usually because these industries are seen as being important to a country's welfare and development, and the government therefore wants to maintain control over them. An interesting ongoing issue is the attempt to control Internet access by a variety of countries, such as the People's Republic of China, Myanmar, North Korea, and various Arab countries experiencing civil unrest. In addition, industries that are highly visible to the local population are important to governments in maintaining political control. Extractive industries (e.g., petroleum, mining), those that use natural resources (e.g., agriculture, tourism), as well as infrastructure (e.g., banking, insurance, railroads, airlines, communication) and defense are all seen as important and are highly visible. Historically, these have been most subject to government intervention, sometimes to the point of nationalization.

The makeup of a company also affects the degree of risk that it faces—factors such as ownership, management, technology, and size may mean that a company faces more or less risk in a particular country. It is quite possible that there could be two companies operating in the same foreign country and the same industry with one facing substantial political risk and the other very little.

If a company is seen as a good corporate citizen by the government and the host county population, then it is less likely to face political intervention. Local ownership, local management, good employee relations, use of local suppliers, contribution to development goals, and provision of appropriate technology are all characteristics of good corporate citizenship and tend to lower the likelihood of government intervention.

In contrast, a foreign company can also make government intervention difficult by controlling critical aspects of the local business outside the host country. Control of technology, needed resources, distribution systems, markets, and so on makes the subsidiary dependent on the parent and means that it is hard for the government to intervene effectively.

These two sides of the vulnerability to political risk picture lead to two distinct risk management strategies, which have been described as defensive and integrative (Gregory 1989). Although based on research some twenty years ago, these approaches are still applicable in general terms; however, their specific application will be influenced by technological developments. Essentially, defensive strategies focus on maintaining control and power with the parent company, while integrative strategies aim to develop a positive local image for the company. The investor needs to examine the political situation in the host country to select the appropriate strategy.

Defensive Political Risk Management

These defensive strategies make it difficult and costly for the host government to intervene in a company's operations:

Finances

- Borrow locally so that negative host government actions affect local creditors.
- Raise capital from a variety of sources so that many parties will be affected by unwelcome government action.
- Joint-venture with multiple parties, each of whom may be able to influence the host government.
- Obtain host government guarantees for loans and investment.
- Maximize profit repatriation and minimize retained earnings and reinvestment so that there is little net investment at risk.

Management and Logistics

- Minimize the use of host nationals in strategic positions and limit locals to junior and symbolic positions, keeping parent nationals in control.
- Train and educate necessary host nationals at headquarters, ensuring understanding of the home culture, objectives, and approaches.

- Locate a critical segment of processing outside the host country so that the local enterprise cannot operate on its own.
- Spread production among several countries to avoid dependence on any one country.
- Concentrate research and development in the parent country to increase local dependence on the parent.

Marketing

- Control transportation so that the subsidiary cannot operate effectively without the parent.
- Maintain a strong global trademark, corporate image, and so on, so that they cannot be used without the parent.
- Control the markets through intra-firm buying, or through long-term agreements with customers (including agents, distributors, and end users) so that the subsidiary has no market without the parent.

These strategies do not necessarily enhance the investing company's image locally, but they keep the company quite independent and can be seen as increasing its power relative to the host country. During the 1960s, when nationalizations were more common, a number of countries found that they took over the assets of foreign companies but could make little use of them because the investing companies controlled the markets, distribution, technology, and so on.

Integrative Political Risk Management

Often, companies that are strongly integrative are perceived as local companies. The following integrative strategies aim to make the foreign subsidiary an integral part of the host society so that any adverse government action has an impact on many local entities as well:

Financial

- Establish joint ventures with local partners so that local interests will be concerned with the local company's success.
- Sell shares on the local stock exchange ensuring broad-based interest in the company's profitability.
- Establish open and transparent reporting systems and ensure that internal transfer pricing systems are fair in order to dispel any fears of exploitation or unethical behavior.

Management and Operations

- Employ a high percentage of locals at all levels in the organization to give the company a positive local image and to show trust in local personnel.
- Ensure that expatriates understand the local environment and behave in culturally sensitive ways.
- Establish commitment among local employees so that the workforce is loyal to the company.
- Maximize local sourcing and research and development to increase benefits to the local economy.
- Use local subcontractors and professionals so that the local economy would be hurt by any negative government action.

Government Relations

- Develop and maintain channels of communication with the government so that the company is aware of the political climate and understands political events.
- Negotiate fairly and be willing to renegotiate when the situation changes so that the government can see the benefits of the foreign investment.
- Provide expert advice if asked by the government, but be wary of becoming too closely linked with a particular government or political group.
- Provide public service, such as sponsorships for the arts and culture, sporting events, and educational events, which add to the company's positive public image.

These strategies enhance the company's corporate image and mean that the government is unlikely to interfere in company operations. The local image of the company, as well as its interdependence with local entities, means that any negative government action has widespread local implications.

Managerial Choices

Managers have many options in terms of structuring the operations in a particular country. As indicated earlier, choices about ownership, management, finances, logistics, marketing, and so on can affect the degree of political risk that a company faces. The strategies were described as defensive or integrative, but this is by no means an either/or choice for managers. These strategies are usually mixed. For example, the Bata Shoe Company employs largely integrative strategies in its operations around the world. The company is often thought of as a local company—it uses local managers, buys inputs locally, and sells in the local market. The company also maintains 100 percent ownership in its subsidiaries and will close a subsidiary as soon as it believes it is no longer safe or worthwhile to operate in a particular country. Another company might be integrative in terms of ownership, having local partners, but the parent company controls critical aspects of technology. The combinations of defensive and integrative tactics are numerous. Managers have to exercise judgment and weigh the pros and cons of the available tactics (in terms of the local subsidiary, its relationships with other subsidiaries and the parent, and in terms of the parent) and try to identify the best mix in a particular location.

It is important for the manager making this choice to evaluate the company's operations in the context of the country in question. Neither country nor company can be looked at in isolation. It is the interaction between the company's chosen policy and activities, and the government's view of these activities, that is important. This interplay determines the degree of political risk that the company faces.

Summary and Conclusions

This chapter has discussed the political and regulatory environment in which companies operate. This environment, and the nation-state's power, remains a critical aspect of doing business today, in spite of globalization. It is important for managers to understand the political environment wherever they operate; in foreign locations this environment is unfamiliar, thus understanding it can be difficult. The manager in a foreign location needs to know how the government operates and changes, what its policies are, and how it views business, particularly foreign businesses from particular countries. The relationship between host governments and foreign investors can be uncertain and this leads to the concept of political risk. Managers in foreign locations need to be able to assess the degree of political risk that their company faces. They also need to evaluate and choose among the various options available in terms of managing the risk they face.

In spite of globalization, the nation-state remains the unit whose laws and regulations govern the activities of the firm. International companies need to be aware of the impact of their activities on those nations where they operate. This impact will determine, to some extent, the relations that the company has within a particular country, and this, in turn, will affect the company's success and profitability.

References

Bertrand, K. 1990. "Politics Pushes the Marketing Foreground." *Business Marketing* (March): 51–55.
Gregory, A. 1989. "Political Risk Management." In *International Business in Canada,* ed. A. Rugman, 310–329. Scarborough, Ontario: Prentice-Hall Canada.
Minor, M. 1990. "Changes in Developing Country Regimes for Foreign Direct Investment." Monograph. Columbia: University of South Carolina Press.
Punnett, B.J., and D. Ricks. 1997. *International Business*. Cambridge, MA: Blackwell.

4

The Role of History and Geography in International Management

Introduction

Both history and geography play an important role in the development of culture. They therefore also play a significant role in determining how people behave. The model of culture and behavior that was introduced in chapter 2 identified history and geography as basic antecedents that influence the development of cultural values. While it is intuitively clear that history and geography are important to international managers, surprisingly little has been written identifying the specific need for these managers to understand the history and geography of the countries where they do business. This chapter will provide an overview of historical and geographical issues, looking at their relationship to each other, their contribution to the development of culture, and the role they play in international management decisions. Throughout the chapter, many examples are used to illustrate these points. We begin with three examples that show the role of both history and geography in three separate locations.

A good example of the twin roles of history and geography is the Inca civilization of South America. The Incas flourished in a large area of South America for a period from about 1200 to 1500 c.e. before being conquered by the Spanish (although it is important to recognize that the descendants of the Incas still make up a major portion of several Latin American populations, including Peru, Bolivia, and Ecuador). The Incas flourished largely because they were able to supply the people of the region with food. The Peruvian archaeologist Federico Kauffman-Doig explained how the development of the Inca civilization was clearly linked to the geography of the region.[1] The region was unduly affected by weather patterns created by El Niño and La Niña, which caused the extremes of drought and floods. This meant that access to food was a critical aspect of life in the region. The Inca rulers' ability to provide the needed food through an extended and sophisticated system of agriculture, storage, and distribution made them all-powerful as well as revered. Kauffman-Doig identified the role of geography in culture by saying that the same culture would not have been likely to develop if food had been plentiful (as it was in other parts of South America); thus, the Inca civilization and culture was based on a need to provide food in a location where food was often scarce. The Inca people consequently accepted the directives of their rulers, the Incas, willingly, and were accustomed to waiting for these directives. One unfortunate effect may have been that when the Spanish captured the Inca ruler and finally killed him, the Inca people were leaderless and easier to conquer.

The modern state of Turkey also illustrates the twin effects of geography and history on cultural values. Geographically, Turkey sits between Western Europe and the Arab states of the Middle East. This location has meant that the people of Turkey are pulled in two opposing directions—toward "modern" Western values and attitudes and toward "traditional" Islamic values and attitudes. Before Ataturk came to power in the 1920s, there were essentially two ways of behaving: two sets of schools, two languages spoken, and so on. Ataturk reformed the country into a secular one, emphasizing the Western, "modern" approaches. It is not so easy to remove tradition, however, and in Turkey today there are families who dress traditionally, go to religious schools, and want to establish an Islamic, rather than secular, state. Turkey's geographic location makes it strategically important as well. For example, following the September 11, 2001, terrorist attacks on the United States, the U.S. government and its allies saw Turkey as a pivotal supporter in the fight against terrorism and a location from which an attack on Iraq could be launched. This did not win approval with the more traditional people of Turkey or some of its neighbors.

Turkey will undoubtedly continue to be pulled in different directions because of its location and historical developments. It continues to seek membership in the European Union, but the European Union continues to require changes in Turkey's regulations, indicating the contradictory forces in Turkey. Turkey has long banned the headscarf in public spaces, including schools and universities (public and private), courts of law, government offices, and other official institutions, suggesting Turkey's secular nature. However, more recently, Turkey reversed its position banning the headscarf in universities. Some people see this as extending rights to all women, including those who wear the headscarf; others see it as a move away from secularism.

The United States and Canada have a rather similar geographic and historical basis. Canada is farther north, and the United States includes more warm territory, but there are similar climates in both for the most part. Both countries were settled by Europeans at much the same time, and both remained colonies for a substantial period. One would expect the people of these two countries to express very similar values, and for the most part they do—both are individualistic and self-reliant. An interesting difference is seen, however, if we look at the language used in their respective constitutions. The Canadian constitution talks of seeking "peace, order and good government" while the U.S. constitution talks of "life, liberty, and the pursuit of happiness." These are clearly very different views of life. The American statement reflects the breakaway from the British, who were at the time of the American Revolution seen as oppressors who took lives and stifled liberty and the pursuit of happiness. The Canadian statement reflects a gradual maturing from colony to independence, as part of the British Empire, which was seen as providing peace, order, and good government, which Canadians wished to continue.

Some additional examples illustrate the relationships between history and culture, geography and culture, and their relationship to behavior.

History and Culture

Jamaicans describe themselves as high on masculinity (using the masculinity/femininity cultural dimension described by Hofstede 1980)—and Jamaicans say that they like tangible rewards, such as "flashy" cars, for performance.[2] This cultural value is attributed to the historical fact of slavery and the prohibition of slaves' owning property. Jamaicans believe that when the slaves were freed, owning property became of especial importance and has since become an integral part of the culture. In the 1600s, Jamaica was known as the "pirate capital of the world" for many years, and as pirates are certainly known for their distinctive dress and behavior, one can hypothesize that this is reflected in the Jamaican preference for dress and music that can often be described as dramatic or extreme. Foreigners sometimes interpret Jamaican behavior as threatening, when it is simply normal Jamaican behavior.

Geography and Culture

People in the tropics are often described as "laid back," with relatively little concern for time compared to their counterparts from colder climates. In Latin America this is often referred to as the "*mañana*" syndrome, that is, people may seem to prefer to put off for tomorrow (*mañana* in Spanish) anything that does not have to be done today. In Jamaica the equivalent expression is "soon come," and in other parts of the Caribbean "jus' now"—both implying action at some indeterminate time in the future. This cultural attitude has been attributed to the geographical reality of the tropics, where days remain essentially the same length throughout the year and temperatures change little, so the passage of time is of relatively little interest. In cold parts of the world, the passing of each year is marked by the lengthening and shortening of the days and the changing temperature, and a consequent concern with time because survival depends on using the period of warm weather to be prepared for the cold. Consequently, people in the tropics are less concerned with time than their counterparts in temperate countries. First-time foreign managers in tropical countries often express frustration at people's apparent willingness to put off tasks and ignore punctuality.

History and Behavior

South Koreans can be somewhat hostile toward their Japanese neighbors. This is not because the Koreans are culturally a hostile people, but because the history of Japanese occupation of Korea, although half a century old, is still fresh in the minds of many Koreans. The event that is now part of history directly influences the behavior of some South Koreans. This can be challenging for Japanese managers operating in South Korea.

Geography and Behavior

The Greeks close their businesses in the early afternoon, reopening in late afternoon and well into the evening. This is attributed to the extreme heat that Greece experiences in the summer, which makes it difficult to work during the afternoon hours. This geographic reality influences business hours for the Greeks and also means that the Greeks eat dinner late (10 P.M. or later) and socialize and do business long into the night and early morning. Many North Americans, accustomed to dining early (as early as 5 or 6 P.M.), find it difficult to adjust to these Greek patterns.

This chapter explores some of the ways in which history and geography influence both cultural values and behaviors. We begin by looking at history and geography as they relate to values and behavior; then we consider their relationship to other cultural antecedents, specifically language and religion. We finish the first section by examining different maps of the world and how they influence our thinking about the world. The subsequent section looks at how history and geography affect doing business internationally—trade and investment decisions, international strategy, and dealing with current events. Throughout, we illustrate the points with examples drawn from around the world and consider the importance of understanding a country's history and geography from a managerial perspective.

Understanding History and Geography

The first discussions in this chapter focus on understanding history and geography and seeing how they relate to each other, to cultural values, and to behaviors.

History, Values, and Behavior

History is defined by the *Oxford Dictionary of Current English* as "a continuous record of events." As such, a country's history encapsulates all that has happened in the country, and between it and other countries. A country, at a particular point in time, is thus the result of its history. Understanding a country's history is fundamental to understanding the country and its people.

The people of the United States are often described as individualistic, self-reliant, and creative. The Europeans who settled the United States were rebels and pioneers. When they reached the New World (as they thought of it), Americans, as we now call them, were seeking a new land where they could build what they considered a better life than they had in Europe. Some of these new Americans were religious rebels and others were seeking their fortune. Both groups were willing, usually eager, to make their own way in their new world. If they were to succeed, they needed to be individualistic, self-reliant, and creative. These cultural values have thus become an integral part of the "American way." In turn, these values have attracted others with similar values from many parts of the world. The "American way" is today reflected in U.S. public policy and the educational system and social structure of the United States; it encourages values like those mentioned above and provides support for people with these values. History has thus played a clear role in the development of American cultural values.

In addition to shaping cultural values, history also shapes more spontaneous behavior. The terrorist attacks on New York and Washington, D.C., in 2001 brought Muslim fundamentalists to the fore as potential enemies of the United States. The people of the United States value diversity; nevertheless, some reacted negatively toward people of the Islamic faith or even those who appeared to them to be Muslim. This reaction toward Muslims did not reflect a fundamental American value; rather, it represented an immediate reaction to current events. These events could, however, influence fundamental American views in the future. This should not suggest that all people of the United States value diversity. There also exists an "us versus them" mentality in the United States, where WASPs (white Anglo-Saxon Protestants) are seen as the rightful "Americans" and everyone else as intruders. The continuing challenges faced by African Americans, the descendants largely of African slaves, even today speak to U.S. ambivalence to diversity. Of course, the 2008

Democratic primaries—where a black candidate and a woman fought hard for the nomination—auger well for a more encompassing view emerging in the United States, with women and African Americans having equal status to white males. Many people are still surprised that there is a black family in the U.S. White House in 2012, and see this development as indicating that African Americans are finally being accepted as equal in the United States.

International managers are well advised to understand the history of any country where they do business. This understanding should encompass events in the distant past, as well as more recent ones. It should include the local perspective, as well as the perspective from outside the country. Understanding a country's history allows a manager to place local values and behaviors in context. Often this means understanding the stresses and conflicts that exist within a country; for example, if one is doing business in Ireland, it is important to understand the situation in Northern Ireland and to be aware of the religious, secular, and historical bases for the conflict there. Similarly, if one is doing business in Sri Lanka, it is important to understand the ethnic tensions related to the Tamil population, whose historical roots in southern India create tensions with the native Sinhalese. Understanding the basis for conflict does not imply sympathy with dissidents, such as the Irish Republican Army or the Tamil Tigers, only an understanding of the bases for the conflicts, and public and societal actions in response. Both the IRA and the Tamil Tigers reached cease-fire agreements with the governments of their respective countries in 2002, and many international business analysts believed that these agreements should result in increased international trade and investment for both Northern Ireland and Sri Lanka. As a direct outcome of the peace agreement with the Tigers, the Sri Lankan head of state visited a number of potential investing countries in the summer of 2002 to encourage them to consider Sri Lanka as a place to do business (reported on the BBC News, July 20, 2002). Peace appears to have become a reality in Northern Ireland, with attendant economic benefits; unfortunately, the same was not true of Sri Lanka, where the peace agreement expired and hostilities reemerged. The Tigers were defeated by the Sri Lankan army in 2009, but accusations of crimes against Tiger supporters remain in the news.

Geography, Values, and Behavior

Geography is defined by the *Oxford Dictionary of Current English* as "form, physical features, climate, population, etc." By definition, then, the geography of a country is essentially coterminous with national culture. Understanding a country's geography is therefore also fundamental to understanding the country and its people.

As discussed previously, the people of the United States are described as individualistic, self-reliant, and creative. These characteristics are clearly linked to the history of the United States as discussed previously. The characteristics are also linked to the country's geography. The European settlers of what would be the United States faced a vast, mostly uninhabited land. In order to survive and prosper, many had to fend for themselves, find their way through the wilderness and across mountain ranges, and hunt, fish, and farm. These early settlers needed to innovate in times of need. Those who were individualistic, self-reliant, and creative survived and set the cultural standard. The great mountain ranges that had to be crossed to reach new lands provided the Americans with natural challenges to overcome and supported a sense of dominance over the environment. Americans continue to have a strong sense of self-reliance and a willingness to face difficult obstacles. The individualism and self-reliance that are valued in the United States are not always seen as positively elsewhere, however. Americans are sometimes described by others as arrogant, pushy, loud, and overbearing. American individualism makes people from some cultures quite uncomfortable. Native Americans, in contrast to the European settlers, had developed a harmony with the same wilderness. One can speculate that those born into such an environment learn that it is best to live with it, while those who come to it from elsewhere, with a sense of adventure and conquest, seek to dominate this environment.

Geography also shapes more immediate behavior. Dress codes in the tropics are often different from those in colder climates. A Program Chair for the Academy of International Business, when it took place in Puerto Rico, advised participants to take note of the tropical locale for the conference and dress accordingly. In many tropical locations, suits and ties are simply uncomfortable, and businesspeople wear alternatives that are considered more acceptable. In such circumstances, the person in a suit and tie looks out of place and is instantly marked as a foreigner. It may be clear in other ways that a manager is a foreigner, but dressing to emphasize one's foreignness is not usually helpful.

One does not often see geography discussed in the context of international business, but an exception was the 2002 Academy of International Business (AIB) Meeting, which had as its theme "Geographies and International Business," attesting to the importance of geography in doing business internationally. A wide variety of papers on the topic were presented, indicating the diversity of geography's impacts on international managers (see Exhibit 4.1 for abstracts of selected papers from the meeting).

In addition to the direct influence of history and geography on cultural values and behavior, there is an indirect link through other cultural antecedents, such as language and religion. These links are explored in the following discussion.

Exhibit 4.1

**Abstracts of Selected Academy of
International Business Papers**

These abstracts from the Academy of International Business (AIB) conference are intended to illustrate briefly some of the ways in which geography can influence international management decisions and to suggest that managers need to consider the role of geography carefully in their decisions and to ensure that decisions are consistent with the geographical reality of their operations.

Kobrin, S., "Safe Harbors Are Hard to Find: The Trans-Atlantic Privacy Dispute, Democratic Legitimacy and Global Governance."

Kobrin discusses the problems faced by managers in a world where markets are global, while social and political institutions are local or national. Economic space no longer coincides with national boundaries, leading to conflicting choices, depending on whether the manager takes an economic, market-based view, or a social and political view. Kobrin addresses protection of data privacy to illustrate the difficulties faced by managers in this context.

Enright, M., "Geographies and International Business: A Three Dimensional Approach."

Enright examines the way in which firm location decisions across countries vary by activity and depend on the availability of resources and knowledge. He considers the advantages associated with the firm's specific know-how and competitive strategy as well as those associated with operating regionally. Enright concludes that the critical element in today's business world is linking the firm-based and region-based perspectives.

Phene, A., and S. Tallman, "The Effects of Regional Clusters on Knowledge Stocks and Flows: Evidence from the Biotechnology Industry."

Phene and Tallman look at knowledge flows across geographic borders in the biotechnology industry. Knowledge flows are investigated in three geographic contexts—intraregionally, interregionally, and between countries. Their results suggest that the factors that are important in between-country knowledge flows are different from those that influence flows within a region or between regions. While the specific focus is the biotechnology industry, the results have implications for any manager concerned with knowledge flows among subsidiaries in different countries.

Wint, A., "The Competitive Advantage of Small Economies."

Wint examines size of economies and its relationship to economic performance. He concludes that small economies that are integrated into world markets are more economically successful, but that this integration implies risks. The international manager needs to be able to evaluate both the opportunities and the risks associated with small economies.

Abo, T., "An Approach for Management Geography: The Case of Japanese Hybrid Factories in the Three Major Regions."

Abo introduces the concept of "management geography." The paper argues that cultural differences are closely linked to the historical contexts of the geography of a country. In turn, the comparative and competitive advantage of nations is shaped by these forces.

Doh, J., Chair, Panel on "Economic and Geographic Integration in the Americas."

A variety of panel papers considered the role of geographic proximity and regional groupings on investment decisions—both in terms of where investment takes place, as well as the form the investment takes.

Source: All papers were presented at the AIB Annual Meeting, San Juan, Puerto Rico, June/July 2002.

Influences on Language, Religion, and Economics

Upcoming chapters will look in more depth at the role of language, religion, and economics in the development of cultural values. Those chapters will give detailed information on languages, religions, and economies around the world. The discussion here highlights the importance of history and geography in the development of language nuances and religious practices.

Discussions of language often identify the way thinking is shaped by the words available to describe particular phenomena:

- "Privacy" in Chinese is described as referring to the group, and the concept of individual privacy is not part of the culture.
- The Arabs are reported to have many words for *camel,* while non-Arab countries basically have only one.

- The Inuit of the far north are reported to describe snow using a range of words that do not exist in other languages.

These language differences can be traced in part to historical and/or geographical realities. The Chinese have had a relatively large population compared to their arable land area, and this would lead to individual privacy being an unusual situation—consequently, privacy would tend to be a group concept. Camels are a means of livelihood and transport in some Arab countries—consequently, describing different characteristics of camels requires a variety of words not required where camels are simply curious animals. Similarly, for the Inuit different kinds of snow are critical to life and death—thus, describing minute details of snow quality is important to them. These are all historical and geographical realities that have influenced language.

The English language can provide interesting snapshots of historical events. Some English words have French origins while others do not. Often there are different words for the same object, and the French version is usually longer. For example, the words "serviette" (French in origin) and "napkin" are synonymous in Canada and the UK, both referring to the same thing. This came about during the Norman rule of England and was further supported in the glory days of France under Louis IV, when the aristocracy and upper classes in England chose to speak French. Interestingly, the French words still have an air of the upper class, so even today when we talk of using serviettes, the word retains its upper-class image and we picture fine dining, and when we talk of using napkins, we think of something much more ordinary. English also incorporates German and Dutch roots for many words, as well as building on a Latin and Greek foundation. These have all been incorporated into the language because of the different groups that have traded with and conquered parts of Britain at different periods in history. American English tends to downplay the French words as somewhat pretentious and favors simpler, plain words, whereas Canadian English has retained many of them. Similarly, American spelling has opted for simplicity—*favor*—where Canadian English retains the British spelling—*favour*.

Religion is similarly influenced by history and geography. Religious taboos can, in some cases, be traced to geography; for example, a number of religions forbid the consumption of pork products, and it may be that this prohibition was originally in response to diseases associated with pork in warm countries and the inability to cook it thoroughly enough to kill the harmful parasite it contained. Religious holidays are often associated with earlier historical periods of rejoicing. Christians celebrate the birth of Christ in December, but some argue that this is because there was a traditional mid-winter celebration that was adopted by the Christians, rather than it being the actual birth date of the Christ child.

Economics is also somewhat a function of history and geography. Singapore's geographic location, combined with a particular set of political policies, has allowed its economy to grow dramatically. Singapore is a small island country that is strategically located in the heart of Southeast Asia with easy access to many larger countries. Hong Kong has had a similar geographic advantage as the gateway to the People's Republic of China. This location, combined with the historical events that made Hong Kong a British colony until 1999, resulted in a unique set of circumstances that made this small island economically very successful.

The brief discussion of the Inca civilization at the beginning of this chapter mentioned the importance of food production, storage, and distribution throughout the Inca Empire. An interesting economic system developed alongside the food system. The Inca population has been estimated at 15 million or more, yet the economy functioned without money, markets, or trade. Provision of food was the glue that bound the empire together and provided the rulers with power and loyalty. The economy was founded on a regime of total reciprocity, and different social strata had clearly defined rights and responsibilities. This system worked so well that the first Spanish arrivals marveled at the infrastructure of roads, bridges, communal granaries, inns and lodges, as well as relay stations making up a postal system, and houses with running water (*Cuzco, Land of the Incas, Guide* 2000).

Language, religion, and economy were identified in chapter 2 as some antecedents to culture and cultural values. History and geography influence culture and values directly, but also through relationships with other antecedents. These previous examples illustrate the potential impact of history and geography on other cultural antecedents. History and geography are always a good place to start in understanding a new country. The following discussion focuses on how people see the world. We examine a number of maps to show that the world can look very different from varied perspectives.

Ways of Seeing the World

Buckley (2002) suggested that there was a need for a closer relationship between cartographers (mapmakers) and international business specialists. Maps are clearly a critical analytic tool and aid to international understanding for managers. A typical map of the world prepared in North America is based on lines of longitude from top to bottom and lines of latitude from side to side, and portrays the world physically, with the Atlantic Ocean in the middle and North at the top. Exhibit 4.2 is such a map.

This is not the only way to see the world. Consider some alternatives. If we put the South Pole at the top of the map, things look quite different. The next map (Exhibit 4.3) is often referred to as the "upside down" map,

Exhibit 4.2   **Map of the World: Conventional**

Exhibit 4.3   **Map of the World: Southern Perspective**

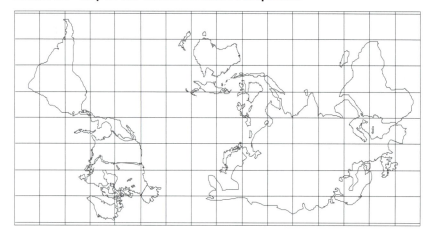

but there is no inherently correct top or bottom of the world. Many of the countries of the Southern Hemisphere prefer this map because it puts them at the top.

If we imagine a map with East at the top, and the lines of "latitude" becoming the vertical lines, things again look quite different. Maps oriented to the East, that is, with East at the top, were used by navigators in the 1500s when typically they were seeking routes to the East. Indeed, the word "orient," meaning to turn toward or point toward, derives from this navigational focus on the East (see Exhibit 4.4).

Exhibit 4.4   **Map of the World: Eastern Perspective**

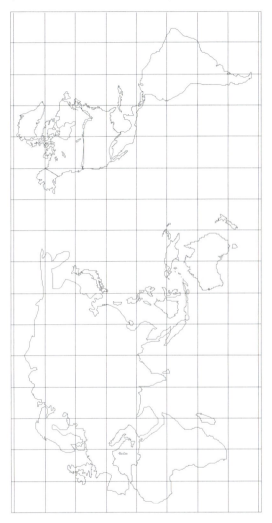

If we take the Pacific Ocean as the central focus of a map, our view changes again. In Exhibit 4.5, the size of the oceans is more evident than in the more typical Western map, which portrays the Atlantic centrally. The *Canadian Geographic World Atlas* (1998) uses this perspective to illustrate the world's oceans. This view of the world is often used in the Far East and features the Asian countries far more prominently than the Americas.

Exhibit 4.5   **Map of the World: Pacific Perspective**

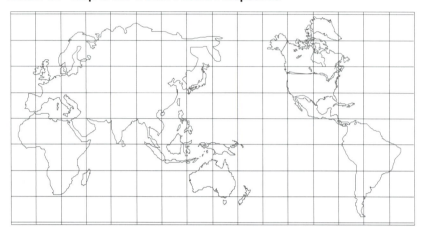

Each of these maps portrays a different world perspective. One or another may be more familiar, depending on where you are from, but each perspective is equally valid. Looking at the world from different geographic perspectives can be a helpful way to understand the world. These alternative perspectives help us to recognize that we normally see the world from our own particular location, and this can assist in identifying our ethnocentrism. When we understand that we are ethnocentric, we can begin to be sensitive to alternative ways of looking at the world. Throughout this book, the focus is on understanding the unfamiliar, dealing with the unexpected, and being flexible in the face of differences. Some of these maps are unfamiliar, unexpected, and different, and they portray concretely this aspect of international management.

There are also many nonphysical map possibilities as well. For example, maps can be based on population, language, economics, and religion, to mention a few. Each of these different ways of examining the world provides understanding for the international manager.

Maps are valuable tools for managers. Numerous studies have shown that many people today are relatively uninformed geographically (the National Geographic Society has made efforts to educate Americans on geography, but with little real impact). This means it is up to the international manager to ensure that her/his knowledge is accurate and up to date.

Managing Internationally: The Role of History and Geography

This section of the chapter relates aspects of history and geography to management issues. We begin by looking at trade and investment, then we look at regional economic linkages and international strategy choices, and finish by considering current patterns and events.

International Trade and Investment

Openness to international trade and investment is often dictated by the size and geographic location of a country. Japan and the United Kingdom are often described as relatively small and thus unable to provide an array of goods and services internally. These countries cannot be self-sufficient and thus have always been trading nations. At the same time, an island state like Japan can be protectionist because it can relatively easily restrict access to its markets.

The United States advocates and promotes free trade but can be largely self-sufficient—the diversity and size of the United States allows it to produce most of the goods and services it needs internally. This has meant that the United States has sometimes introduced protectionist policies with little apparent regard for its trading partners. The United States does import a substantial amount of goods and services from around the world, ranging from oil from Africa and the Middle East through financial services from the Caribbean to toys from China. Nevertheless, because of its diversity and size, it is in a better position to do without these imports than most other nations. U.S. policies regarding wood products from Canada, steel products from Europe, toys from China, and its agricultural subsidies have all caused trade concerns with its trading partners over the past several years.

Protectionist policies are often seen positively in the home country when they are implemented to protect domestic interests. International managers need to recognize that they may be seen in a very different light in countries that are negatively affected by such policies. Managers can find themselves, as the proverb goes, "between the devil and the deep blue sea"—damned if they support their home government's policies and equally damned if they don't.

Trade and investment flows are influenced by government and international policies, as well as by both historical and geographical factors. In recent decades, the majority of the world's trade and investment has been among the "triad" countries—Japan, North America, and Western Europe. Countries in the triad became wealthy in the latter half of the twentieth century. The United States and Canada suffered little physical damage from World War II and developed strong economies built on pent-up postwar demand through the 1950s. At the same time, substantial sums of money were provided for the reconstruction of Western Europe and Japan following the war, allowing industries in those countries to recover and retool. These areas constitute what is now usually called the developed world. Trade within the triad countries has typically been over half of world trade, and they have accounted for over

70 percent of the world's gross domestic product and most of its innovation. Emerging economies are, however, becoming increasingly important in today's business world. China is on track to become the biggest economy in the world, and other countries, including Brazil, India, and Russia, are having a substantial impact on world economies and global business. Nevertheless, the recession that started in the United States in 2008 and the continuing economic problems around the world have shown how interrelated countries are. As the old saying goes, "when the U.S. sneezes, the world catches cold."

This current pattern of trade and investment suggests that businesspeople from the developed world are usually doing business with others also from the developed world. There are substantial differences in business practices and management approaches among these countries, however: managers from the United States can find Japanese managers to be quite different, Canadians are not just like Americans, and the British and French approach decisions from distinct points of view. Interestingly, much of the management literature from the 1970s onward, focused on the triad countries (North America, Europe, and Japan), and a substantial amount is known about the similarities and differences in business practices and management approaches. Managers interacting with other managers in this context face challenges, but they have a body of literature to help them deal with the challenges. In addition, because of the high degree of interaction among the triad countries in the past decades, businesspeople have learned about those differences in style.

The same is not true when one considers the non-triad countries. These countries are less economically developed than the triad countries, and much less is known about their business practices and management approaches. In the first years of the twenty-first century, there has been a substantial call for greater investment in the developing world and more trade between the developed and developing countries. It is not clear whether this will become a reality.

It is also evident that improvements in incomes in the developing world can fuel world economic growth substantially. These countries have fared better during the recession that affected the world for several years after 2008, and they have been participating in world trade and investment to a larger degree than previously. The population of the developing world makes up approximately 80 percent of the world's people. Because many of these people are quite poor, with relatively few in the middle class, they do not have access to many of the goods and services that are considered normal in the developed world (e.g., electrical appliances, cars, computers, radios, and the like). In fact, basic necessities such as running water are uncommon in many places. Increases in per capita income and development of a substantial middle class in these countries would result in a significant increase in demand, which would far outstrip the pent-up demand described as following World War II. This could lead in turn to an extended period of global economic growth.

There are also opportunities among the poor. For example, the use of cell phones in developing countries has opened up a variety of avenues for doing business in these countries—ranging from fishing people being able to access information on prices for their fish in different markets, to banks providing access to accounts by cell phone. There are now well-established businesses supplying solar lighting for poor rural parts of Africa, recharging batteries for battery-powered phones and the like, and even one entrepreneur who travels across Africa showing movies and selling ice cream, all using solar power.

We can expect, therefore, that interactions between managers from a developed background and those from a developing background will increase in the coming years. This will pose a significant challenge for both sets of managers because they have had relatively few interactions in the past and because their behavior norms are likely to differ for economic development reasons, as well as due to the political, cultural, linguistic, religious, historic, geographic, and other social factors discussed in this book. Punnett (2012), in her book *Management: A Developing Country Perspective,* explores these issues and how they are likely to influence management in these countries.

Patterns of trade and investment around the world suggest that countries with a history of trade continue to trade with each other, and countries that are geographically close are likely to be trading partners. The same is true of investment. This means that current trade and investment patterns reflect the history and geography of the countries and companies involved in international business agreements. There are, of course, important exceptions to this, and both trade and investment patterns change over time to reflect changing needs and current events.

Access to needed resources is a major reason for trade and investment in specific countries, which may be far afield and unfamiliar. The limited availability of certain resources means that they must be obtained where they are found. The petroleum industry is a prime example of this. Americans and Europeans consume more oil than they can produce. The oil reserves of the Middle East have meant that the United States and European countries do business in the Middle East, regardless of unfamiliarity, the situation, or the risks associated with these operations. The same is true of access to precious metals, gems, rubber, and a whole array of other natural resources.

The two Koreas, North and South, share what was once one country. As such, one might expect them to be close trading partners, and one might hypothesize, based on geography alone, that North Koreans would do business in the South, and vice versa. This is not the reality. The historic events since the 1950s have left the two Koreas technically still at war, with little interaction between the people or the governments. North Korea remains isolated from most of the world, while South Korea has developed an industrialized economic base and trades with a wide variety of other countries.

Regional Economic Linkages

Regional economic linkages have increased in recent decades. The European Union (EU), which had progressed over more than forty years, represented a substantial integration of twenty-seven European countries in 2012, with five other candidates to join. The North American Free Trade Agreement (NAFTA) has closely linked the economies of Canada, Mexico, and the United States. The Association of Southeast Asian Nations (ASEAN) incorporated Brunei Darussalam, Cambodia, Indonesia, Laos, Malaysia, Myanmar, the Philippines, Singapore, Thailand, and Vietnam in 2003. There are a variety of other regional trade organizations such as Mercosur and Caricom, and still more are in the process of being developed. Countries proposing a regional trade agreement have to notify the World Trade Organization, and there have been more than 400 such notifications.

Most economic linkages incorporate countries that are geographically close together, and this often means that the people who form the links are somewhat similar. In the EU, the countries were originally, and have become by policy, economically alike in terms of inflation, monetary policy, currency values, unemployment, and so on. In Caricom, which encompasses portions of the Caribbean, most members are English speaking, and all share a similar European colonial past. Similarity was also strong in the trade agreement between Canada and the United States, but the addition of Mexico to the NAFTA group added more heterogeneity. Where countries of a regional grouping share history and geography, or language, religion, political and social systems, management regionally will often be somewhat consistent. Although Canada and the United States are not identical, management approaches are similar, and throughout the European countries of the EU, many values remain similar and business practices are relatively consistent.

To some extent this consistency of values and behaviors among a group of linked countries makes it relatively easy to do business within the region and to transfer management from one location to another. This is true for managers from within the region, as well as those coming in from outside. Europeans move fairly easily from one country in the EU to another, and an American firm that develops expertise in a particular EU country can often use this expertise in other EU countries.

Similarities can also be misleading, of course. As mentioned earlier, Canadians are not "just like" Americans. The Canadian constitution, built on "peace, order and good government," and the American on "life, liberty, and the pursuit of happiness" are expressions of fundamental values that may go some way to explaining why Canadians are often seen as more moderate than Americans and have sometimes been described as "polite Americans." It is always necessary, even in the face of apparent similarity, to be conscious of, and sensitive to, differences across national and cultural boundaries.

NAFTA includes Mexico with Canada and the United States and thus adds more diversity to this regional group. Mexico is different from the other two in terms of politics, language, religion, and economic development. Mexican cultural values contrast with those of the other two countries, and Mexican business practices and management approaches are sometimes unlike those found in Canada and the United States. The establishment of the NAFTA regional group was intended to make trade and investment easier among the three countries, and the result has been an increase in intra-regional business arrangements. Consequently, there are more Canadian and U.S. managers doing business in Mexico, and vice versa. This has posed challenges for the managers. The establishment of the regional trade arrangement meant that managers had to understand a new and different environment if they were to take advantage of the opportunities offered by the agreement. The Free Trade of the Americas Agreement (FTAA) intended to encompass all the countries of North, South, and Central America as well as the Caribbean island states, other than Cuba, has been talked of, but little progress made.

The EU is somewhat unusual in that it incorporates a single currency—the euro—that many member countries use. This was intended to facilitate doing business across the member countries and to mitigate the foreign exchange risk, thus encouraging trade and investment throughout the EU. In 2012 the wisdom of a single currency was questioned because of the variation in the economies that made up the European Union. Some countries, notably Ireland and Greece, had very weak economies (and others such as Italy and Portugal also had high debt levels and low economic growth rates). Other countries, such as Germany, had relatively strong economies. A currency devaluation would be appropriate for the countries with weak economies but not for those with strong economies. Some economists felt that this situation would lead to the breakdown of the currency union, and Ireland was planning a referendum on whether the country should continue to use the euro. These events high-lighted the differences among the European countries and the challenges of maintaining consistent economic policies among a diverse group of countries, even when they are considered relatively similar. The problems in Europe also went beyond economics, with some people describing the Germans, for example, as hardworking and productive, while the Greeks, for example, were seen as less so.

International Strategy

Firms' decisions about where to operate (next door, within the region, or around the world), how to operate (export, license, franchise, joint venture), what kind of investment to make (greenfield, brownfield, staggered acquisitions), and what kind of strategic alliance to undertake, are all influenced by a wide variety of factors. On the surface these decisions are economic and business decisions that involve looking at the benefits and costs and making choices that are optimal for shareholders. This simplicity is not reflected in reality, as these decisions are influenced by an array of factors. History and geography appear to be two important ones.

A history of investment appears to beget future investment; for example, UK firms have a history of investing in the United States, and therefore the United States is one of the first places that UK firms consider for investment. Similarly, geography appears to play an important role. More trade and investment tend to take place among countries that are physically close than among those that are geographically distant. There may be economic reasons for this, such as transport costs, but it also seems that managers are more likely to consider close-by countries than those farther afield. Canadian managers first consider the United States, Japanese managers South Korea, Taiwanese managers the PRC, Trinidad managers Barbados or Jamaica, and so on. To some extent, this can be seen as a natural bias toward more familiar territory.

International managers should consciously recognize this bias. Managers need to ask if similarity is an advantage, and if it is, they should capitalize on this. If similarity is an advantage, then it should lead to marketing effectiveness, cost savings from standardization, better management from using like practices, and so on. The UK manager may be able to standardize and transfer practice to the United States. Equally, the reverse needs to be considered: the UK company that invests in the United States because of history may overlook a better opportunity in Chile; the Canadian manager who focuses on the United States may ignore possibilities in India; the Taiwanese businessperson may not consider Africa; and the Trinidad manager who favors Barbados and Jamaica may not realize the potential of China. These geographic biases are both constraints and opportunities; the overlooked often become opportunities once they are recognized.

A Canadian apple farmer in British Columbia (BC) provides a good example of how geographic differences can provide opportunities. The farmer had, like most BC farmers, traditionally sold his apples wholesale, by the bushel, into the familiar Canadian market. He received about CAN$8 per bushel. After seeing a documentary on Japan, he decided to explore the Japanese market for apples. The farmer discovered that if he carefully selected his best apples, made sure they were identical, and packaged them in appropriate small numbers, carefully wrapped, he could sell each apple for about $10 in Japan. The difference was more than enough to cover the additional costs associated with shipping, customs, distribution, and the like, and the apple farmer's margins were substantially higher than in the traditional markets. By looking beyond his traditional, familiar market, the farmer was able to identify and exploit an opportunity.

History and geography also influence choices about how to enter foreign markets. These decisions have major implications for organizational behavior and human resource management. If a firm chooses to export, it limits its personal interactions in its foreign markets, but it must ensure that marketing (pricing, promotion, place, and so on) is handled appropriately for the market. If a firm chooses to invest in a brownfield operation, it is investing in an existing organization that may be facing problems domestically, and thus a completely different set of issues arises—for example, how to motivate alienated workers and revitalize markets. If a firm chooses 100 percent ownership in a greenfield investment, it is undertaking a start-up operation that requires substantial management input and negotiating skill. Each of these strategic and operational choices raises different challenges for international managers.

In the chapters dealing with selection, training, and support of international personnel, these issues are dealt with from a generic perspective. Beyond the generic, the specifics of a particular location's geography and history need to be taken into consideration. A manager dealing with exports requires a certain set of abilities and skills, a manager setting up a joint venture requires a different set, and one managing a wholly owned subsidiary still another. Selection, training, and support need to be tailored to fit the investment in a particular location, given its history and geography.

The Caribbean island states provide a setting for examining the combined influences of geography and history (Punnett 2000) using some of the factors identified previously. Caribbean states are small, and this means they are necessarily open to trade and investment because they cannot survive on their internal resources. The islands have always had open economies, but they have often served protected markets established by the former colonial powers—for example, bananas grown in the Caribbean and sold to European countries have benefited from special support prices. This has meant that many businesses in the region have not been required to be competitive. Management in these island states has been influenced by their history of slavery and plantation economics, as well as their colonial heritage. Typically, management style in these countries has been top-down, with little real participation from lower levels. Many companies are run by owner/managers, with family members as managers and a clear distinction between managers and workers.

The situation has changed for these countries in the twenty-first century, however, and they are under pressure to change their business strategies. Globalization has meant that businesses need to be globally competitive and cannot rely on protection from former colonial masters. The history of slavery, plantation economies, and colonial heritage does not encourage embracing change; rather, this history reinforces acceptance of the status quo. The management status quo, as described above, incorporates hierarchical management, acceptance of orders, and limited communication or trust. These management characteristics are seen as inimical to dealing with the new competitive environment. Caribbean managers are considering how to integrate traditional values with new management needs. Non-Caribbean managers in the region are faced with the question of whether to adopt the Caribbean management style, which is still typical, or to introduce new approaches.

Managers, whether from the Caribbean or from outside, need to recognize these realities and be ready to manage in this context. The individual manager will decide whether to operate in traditional ways or innovate; either choice has consequences, given the context, and these consequences must be thought through. Operating in traditional ways is often comfortable because both managers and employees are familiar with this style of operation. Typically, however, this style does not encourage initiative and creativity, and can stifle growth. Innovation means change and therefore can be difficult for both managers and employees, but it may result in new and improved ways of thinking and acting. The manager has to weigh the pros and cons of each approach and find the right mix of both.

Current Events

Current events are always an important consideration in international management decisions. What happens each day around the world affects managers' decisions about where to do business, what kind of business to undertake, when to do business, with whom, and whom to send to do business. A host of long-term and short-term decisions and actions revolve around what is happening in a particular country or region. For example, when there were major disturbances in Indonesia, Americans were warned by their government not to go there; when tensions increased between India and Pakistan, Europeans were advised by their officials to leave the region. Individual companies and managers also monitor these situations and base their decisions on unfolding events.

Many conflicts that we consider relatively current have roots that are in fact centuries old. The Israel–Palestine conflict has its immediate, or modern, beginnings in the creation of the State of Israel in the late 1940s and the consequent alienation of the Palestinians. In turn, this resulted in the alignment of Arabs with the Palestinian cause, while the Jewish State of Israel was supported by Europe and North America—particularly the United Kingdom and the United States, because of their close ties to the creation of that new state. The creation of the State of Israel is now a part of history that influences many decisions of businesses in the twenty-first century. Yet if one traces Middle Eastern history back over the centuries, it becomes clear that the roots for the conflict date back much further, perhaps four thousand years. We cannot manage around such conflicts unless we understand their origins.

Christopher Columbus's famous journey of 1492, which led to the "discovery" of the New World, has had a profound impact on our world today. The aboriginal inhabitants of the New World felt it was theirs and thus not discovered, and there is evidence that the Scandinavians, the Chinese, and the Africans had visited the New World prior to Columbus's voyage. Columbus came, however, at a time when Western Europe was prepared to invest in exploration of the New World and was actively seeking new routes to the Far East. The coincidence of Columbus's voyage with a willingness of European powers to invest provided the base for current trade and investment patterns. For the next several centuries following 1492, England, France, the Netherlands, Portugal, and Spain saw themselves as explorers, bringing their ways to the rest of the world. They were not always welcomed, but the results of their arrival can be seen around the world in architecture, language, religion, and so on. Instability throughout Latin America can be attributed, at least partially, to the history of conquest and shifting power among European countries, followed by independence movements, combined with continuing differences between native peoples and the descendants of European settlers.

Current events influence a variety of international decisions; for example, many businesspeople are more hesitant about investing in the Middle East because of the current level of conflict, and they are concerned with the apparent instability in Venezuela. These circumstances make a particular country or region seem more risky and mean that managers expect greater returns to compensate for the increased risk. They also can imply risks to individual security, and managers may be unwilling to risk kidnapping, hostage taking, and so on for any returns. International managers need to be historians and geographers as well as expert evaluators of risk, and they need to be constantly up to date on what is happening around the world.

Summary and Conclusions

This chapter has explored the influence of history and geography on doing business internationally. History and geography are closely linked, and both separately and together they have a significant impact on how business is done and how managers manage. International managers are faced with the challenge of doing business in many different environments, and finding ways to manage effectively in these environments is not an easy task. To be effective, managers need a thorough understanding of the varied environments in which they do business, and both the similarities and the differences between these settings need to be examined. A starting point for this understanding is the history and geography of a particular location. A management consultant with experience in a wide variety of countries around the world advises managers to get a good atlas and always to read an in-depth history of the country and region before going to a new location.

Notes

1. Speech at the 2002 International Western Academy of Management Meeting, Peru.
2. Based on in-class discussions with MBA students in international business classes.

References

Buckley, P. 2002. "Geographies and International Businesses." Paper presented at AIB Annual Meeting, San Juan, Puerto Rico, June/July.
Canadian Geographic World Atlas. 1998. Willowdale, Ontario: Firefly Books.
Cuzco, Land of the Incas, Guide. 2000. Cuzco: Centro de Estudios Regionales.
Hofstede, C. 1980. *Cultural Consequences.* Beverly Hills, CA: Sage.
Kauffman-Doig, F. 2002. "Where Ancient Meets Modern." Paper presented at International Western Academy of Management, Lima, Peru, July.
Punnett, B.J. 2000. "Management in the Caribbean." In *Management in the Americas,* ed. M. Warner, 333–341. London: Thompson Learning.
———. 2012. *Management: A Developing Country Perspective.* London: Routledge.

5

Language and Religion in International Management

Introduction

Both language and religion play a critical role in effective management. Language and religion are integral to human action and affect many aspects of people's behavior. The manager who deals with people from different countries needs to be aware of the role of language and religion, and be able to relate easily to people who speak different languages and follow different religious practices.

Many people believe that language influences the way we think, and that the structure of language is rooted in one's culture. For example, it has been demonstrated that where language contains many words for a color, people who speak that language actually see more variations in color than those who speak a language that has only a few words for that color. The English language capitalizes the word "I" no matter where it occurs in a sentence, and this may reflect the high level of individualism found in Anglo countries.

Religious beliefs are often the basis for deciding what is right and wrong, what is encouraged, permitted, or forbidden. Some religions prohibit the eating of certain foods (e.g., beef, pork, shellfish), some religions require certain consumption (e.g., wine and wafers to represent the blood and body of the Messiah in Christian churches). Some religions permit multiple marriage partners; others forbid this. In addition, religion is closely related to cultural values. The Christian Bible states that God has given dominion over the earth to man, and this is reflected in a cultural belief in mastery over nature in Christian countries.

In this chapter we will investigate a variety of aspects of language and religion and their relationship to management.

Language

Let us begin by considering what we mean by language. Language consists of symbols (usually audible, although the deaf use nonaudible sign language) that allow people to communicate among themselves about a wide range of issues and convey a wide range of information from one person to another. Language is perhaps the main feature that differentiates humans from other animals. Other animals communicate, but about simple issues, and they convey a limited range of information. Consider a dog's barking, for example. Different barks convey different emotions (excitement, anger, fear), but the dog cannot explain why it is excited or angry, and it cannot say that it was afraid, but it is no longer afraid, and so on.

Human language allows us to communicate in complex ways. It also defines our life in many ways. Our language allows us to think about our lives, about ourselves, and about our environment. Different languages reflect the primary emphasis and technology of the speakers of that language.

According to Whorf (1956), the language that you normally use influences the way you understand your environment; thus the picture of the world shifts from language to language. To illustrate this point, recall that it was noted previously:

In Arabic there are many words relating to camels, their parts, and equipment. Most of these do not exist in English. The Inuit of northern Canada have words that differentiate among forms of snow. Only a few of these exist in other languages. The many words for camel in Arabic and snow in Inuit languages presumably developed because of the importance of camels and snow in the respective communities. Understanding snow, for example, was essential to Inuit survival, so they developed many ways of describing it.

Deutscher (2010) argues that language does not prohibit its speakers from thinking about anything—for example, if a language does not have a word for privacy, it does not mean that the people who speak the language cannot understand the concept. In contrast, he identifies ways in which language obliges us to think in certain ways. For example: In English, we can say we dined with a neighbor, without saying whether the neighbor is male or female. In many other languages the grammar obliges us to use the masculine or feminine form of the word for neighbor (in French, *voisin* or *voisine*). Genders are assigned to inanimate objects as well. English is apparently unusual among European languages in not assigning genders. The genders assigned to different objects varies from language to language; for example, bridge is feminine in German but masculine in Spanish, apple is masculine in German and feminine in Spanish, and so on. When speakers were asked to grade a variety of objects on a range of characteristics, they described masculine ones with more manly properties and the reverse. Spanish speakers thought of bridges as strong, whereas German speakers thought they were slender and elegant. In another study, French and Spanish speakers were asked to assign human voices to various objects in a cartoon. The French wanted a fork (*la forchette*, female) to speak in a woman's voice, but the Spanish wanted the fork (*el tenedor*, masculine) to speak in a gravelly male voice.

These examples clearly illustrate the interaction between the language we speak and how we see the world. People often say that they cannot speak a language fluently until they can think in the foreign language. These examples suggest that there are good reasons why this is so.

English has become the traditional language of business because many other languages do not contain words for business concepts such as management, operations, finance, and so on. At the same time, there is substantial interest in learning Mandarin because this language is spoken by a large proportion of the people in the People's Republic of China, a major supplier of the world's goods. Mandarin and Cantonese are also spoken in Hong Kong and Taiwan and by a large number of overseas Chinese. There is some evidence that Mandarin may be overtaking English as the most popular second language, but English remains the most spoken language (including native speakers and those who speak it as a second or third language).

These examples illustrate how a language develops from a particular culture and how it reinforces cultural knowledge. Camels have been and continue to be important in the Middle East, thus there are many words to define and describe them. Similarly, snow in the north, business in English-speaking countries— each is important to its society, thus language develops accordingly.

Terpstra and David (1985) illustrated the identification of language with religion and ethnicity with the situation in Sri Lanka. The Sinhalese people of Sri Lanka are predominantly Buddhist and of Aryan ethnicity, while the Tamil are predominantly Hindu, of Dravidian ethnicity. Conflicts between the two groups intensified when the Sinhalese majority wanted to implement Sinhalese as the national language of Sri Lanka. Both Sinhalese and Tamil newspapers referred to the conflict as a "language conflict," yet to outsiders it might have seemed based on religious or ethnic differences.

The importance of language can be seen in many other situations. For example:

- The French Canadians of Quebec have had a strong movement to sepa-rate the Province of Quebec from the rest of Canada. Both French and English are official languages of Canada, but the French believe their minority language status puts them in a negative position.
- In France, the French have grave concerns about the purity of the lan-guage being corrupted by the importation of English words and have a formal group to monitor changes in the language.
- In many of the island countries of the Caribbean, "the Queen's Eng-lish" (i.e., English based on United Kingdom standards) is the official

language, but many people speak a Creole that is heavily influenced by African languages, and different status is often associated with speaking one or the other.

- Mandarin and Cantonese speakers can communicate in writing because they share a written symbolic language. Spoken communication does not work, however, because the verbal forms are quite different.
- The Irish under British rule and the Africans taken to the United States as slaves were forced to speak English and intentionally spoke a form of English, based on their own languages, that was largely unintelligible to their "masters."
- According to Deutscher (2010), some languages do not use concepts such as "left," "right," "behind," and "in front," but instead use the compass—"north," "south," "west," and "east"—and speakers of these languages always, apparently automatically, know where north is.

These examples illustrate that language is important to all of us. We are often proud of the language we speak and relate more positively to those who speak like us than to those who speak differently. This is even true of those who, on the surface, share a language. The author can spot a "fellow West Indian" outside of her home region by their accent and will usually speak to a total stranger because she has identified them as West Indian, whereas she would not consider doing so under other circumstances. Canadians recognize other Canadians outside of Canada by the way they speak, and so do the Irish, Australians, Singaporeans, and so on; in each case, language creates a bond.

Given the importance of language, it can be helpful to international managers to speak the language of those with whom they will work and those they will manage. It is not always possible to learn to speak a language fluently, but managers moving cross-culturally will want to learn some basic aspects of the language of the foreign location, and if their stay will be at all extended, they will want to take language lessons and develop at least a degree of fluency. The fact that English has become the accepted language of business provides a certain advantage for English-speaking managers, but this also has disadvantages. Non–English speakers often learn English, as well as other languages, and this can give them a communication advantage because they can communicate relatively easily with a variety of others. English speakers, in contrast, may be limited to the English that their foreign counterparts speak and thus may need to rely substantially on translators and interpreters. English speakers may also feel that they can get by with English and thus have less incentive to work hard to learn other languages.

Let us now consider some information on languages and language diversity around the world, as well as how managers can deal with this diversity.

Linguistic Diversity

There are many different languages around the world. According to Terpstra and David (1985), estimates range from 3,000 different languages to as many as 10,000, if one includes dialects. Some countries are essentially linguistically homogeneous (e.g., Sweden and Japan), with one main language that virtually all nationals speak and few speakers of minority languages. Other countries, such as India and Switzerland, are linguistically diverse. India probably represents the extreme of diversity with a multitude of languages and an estimated 3,000 dialects.

The Impact of Homogeneity

Countries with little linguistic diversity, that is, those where most of the people speak one language, are described as homogeneous with regard to language. The close link between language and culture means that these countries are usually also homogeneous in terms of culture. The national culture is strong, and subcultures are relatively unimportant. Japan is often used as an example of a linguistically homogeneous country with a strong national culture and relatively unimportant subcultures. This does not mean that there are no subcultures—managers still need to be aware of these—but they are less important than the broader, shared, national culture.

For a manager, going to a linguistically homogeneous country is, in some ways, relatively easy. There is one language to understand and learn, and cultural characteristics are likely to be relatively uniform throughout the country. The challenge is that linguistically homogeneous countries are sometimes particularly parochial and ethnocentric because of their limited exposure to language and culture differences. This means that fitting in with the cultural norms is especially important, and being able to speak some of the language reasonably well may be well worth the effort.

The Impact of Heterogeneity

Countries with substantial linguistic diversity, that is, those where many languages are spoken, are described as heterogeneous with regard to language. The close link between language and culture means that these countries are usually also heterogeneous in terms of culture. In these countries, subcultures are important, and the shared national culture may be relatively weak. India is often used as an example of a linguistically heterogeneous country with many important subcultures and a relatively weak national culture. This does not mean that there is no national culture (Indians as a whole still feel that they share certain cultural characteristics), but the importance of the subcultures cannot be overlooked in a country such as India.

For a manager, going to a linguistically heterogeneous country is, in some ways, rather difficult. There are many languages to understand and learn, and cultural characteristics are likely to differ around the country. On the positive side, linguistically heterogeneous countries are aware, sometimes painfully so, of linguistic and culture differences. This may mean that they are more accepting of differences, and outsiders may be able to fit in relatively easily. Unfortunately, in some locations, such as Sri Lanka, diversity has meant major conflicts between language/cultural groups. Understanding and fitting in with the cultural norms of the subgroups can be critical in such situations.

National Languages

Many countries have an official national language used for official communications. In linguistically homogeneous countries, it is clear that the main language will also be the national language. In heterogeneous countries, the national language can serve as a unifying force. It can also serve as a divisive force, with minority groups arguing over the appropriate national language.

Some countries have opted for more than one official national language. In Canada, for example, both French and English are official national languages, and all formal governmental communication is issued in both languages. In addition, documents from most institutions are available in two languages, and product labels are required to be written in both. Other countries have multiple official languages (Singapore and Switzerland each have four).

Some languages serve as the official language for many countries. Arabic is used in an array of Middle Eastern countries; English is common throughout the British Commonwealth; French is used in many former colonies; Spanish is used in much of Latin America, as well as in the Far East, and the Philippines. The use of a common national language—for example, Spanish—implies a certain similarity in culture. The Spanish-speaking countries of Latin America share certain cultural characteristics with other former Spanish colonies and with Spain. Yet they are also culturally quite different because of variations in history, geography, education, and so on. Sharing a common language implies some cultural similarities, but should not be interpreted as sharing a culture.

Linguistic Hierarchies

In many places the use of a particular language, or the way language is spoken, has clear hierarchical implications; that is, certain languages/

dialects/accents are used by certain people and for certain purposes, and the language/dialect/accent one uses implies a certain social status. In the United Kingdom, for example, the "cockney" accent is often associated with working people while the "etonian" accent is associated with the upper classes. This class differentiation was well illustrated in Shaw's play *Pygmalion,* which was later adapted as the musical/movie *My Fair Lady,* which portrayed a young woman's transformation from a cockney-speaking flower seller to an upper-class socialite entirely based on changing the way she spoke.

English has incorporated words from many other languages—for example, Anglo-Saxon, Dutch, French, and German. The way in which words are used in English is an interesting reflection of history. For example, at one time, the upper class spoke French while the common people used Anglo-Saxon words, and many words currently in use reflect this. In the United States, the dialect of African Americans, as exemplified by rap and hip-hop, is quite distinct from the speech of white Americans. More basically, many people in the United States believe that you can identify an African American on the telephone by the way he/she speaks.

In linguistically diverse countries, a lingua franca or common language often develops to enable people from different language groups to communicate. This common language sometimes becomes the high-status language because it allows greater inter–language group communication. In other cases it becomes the low-status language because it is a hybrid, often simplified, and not seen as a true language. In the United States, one often hears young second-generation immigrants from Spanish-speaking countries using a language that mixes English and Spanish and is sometimes called Spanglish. Similarly, in Singapore, people often speak a mixture that is called Singlish. In some former colonies, the colonial language is the high-status language; this is the case in Kenya, where English is the official language. In others, the colonial language is shunned and local languages have been embraced: in Tanzania, Swahili is the official language.

Managers going to foreign countries need to be aware of these nuances regarding languages and need to be able to pick up on local preferences. In the English-speaking Caribbean, as noted earlier, English is generally high-status. At the same time, speaking Creole is considered a mark of a "true West Indian," so each plays a different role. Many visitors meet the prime minister of one of these states and are struck by the exceptional upper-class English that he or she speaks (the prime minister may well have been educated at Oxford), then hears the same prime minister giving a speech in the market in Creole and cannot understand what he or she is saying.

Linguistic Change

Language is constantly changing. Because language allows us to define and classify our inner and outer environment, we find new words for new developments in these environments. Some of these words are temporary, but many enter the language permanently. Words come and go all the time. The Beatniks of the 1950s coined the word "groovy" to depict a particular inner state that they believed represented a new emotion. Groovy is still used today, but its meaning changes from time to time, possibly because each generation wants its own word for a similar emotion—in time it may become a permanent expression in English, but only time will tell. The development of the Internet in the latter half of the twentieth century led to a variety of new English words and expressions (Internet, World Wide Web, e-mail, search engine, Facebook, Twitter and tweet, and so on) that seem to be constantly changing. Some of these may become permanent, but as the technology changes, other new words will develop. The very way we communicate also changes in response to these changes in technology. A young person in 2012 is probably thoroughly familiar with texting and social networks, but may never have received a written letter in the mail. The ubiquitous nature of electronic communication means that people are in constant contact with their friends and that they feel somewhat lost when this communication is not available.

The demonstrations and uprisings in the Arab world in 2011 and 2012 were partly enabled by the ability of demonstrators to communicate easily with other demonstrators and potential demonstrators. Information was freely available to participants and plans could be exchanged and changed at will. Further, information on events within countries could be shared with the outside world. Governments sought to limit the information that was shared and to shut down or limit in other ways access to the Internet and other communication media, but this had only limited success, due to the wide array of options available to people today.

An interesting exercise is to look at a dictionary of the late 1800s. Many words that are common today—such as airplane, automobile, telephone, television—did not exist. Similarly, many words that are included in such a dictionary are unfamiliar to us today and relate to an essentially rural society. Only thirty years ago, collaboration with people from other cultures and countries meant traveling long distances to meet in person. Today we have virtual collaborations and can work with people essentially anywhere in the world. Today, because of the speed of communication, we also expect decisions to be made quickly and the turnaround time to be more or less instant, and we attempt to multitask so that we do not seem to ignore any communication that we should respond to (as I write these words, I am also monitoring my e-mail and listening to the radio online). The pace of communication today has become faster, and this appears likely to continue.

Managing Language Differences

International managers are faced with language differences as they move around the world, and they have to manage within these differences. Broadly speaking, these managers can learn new languages, or they can use translators and interpreters. The following briefly discusses these options.

Learning New Languages

As an international manager, it is ideal if you can master new languages easily and speak the language of your business counterparts, colleagues, employees, and other stakeholders. People are generally pleased when a foreign manager has taken the time to learn the local language, and your ability to speak "their" language can give you an advantage in doing business.

For managers who are expecting to spend a substantial time doing business with a particular country, or to live in a particular country for several years, it is usually a good idea to learn the local language. This makes communication much easier and more effective, and the effort is well worthwhile. Many people find that once they learn one new language, learning other languages becomes easier. Some international managers who work in many different countries end up speaking, at least passably, a variety of languages.

While speaking the local language is often an advantage, it is not always possible. For example:

- Managers who have to go to a foreign location on short notice do not have time to learn the language.
- Managers who go to many different countries for short periods may find it difficult to learn many new languages.
- Some managers find it difficult to learn new languages.

For these and other reasons, some managers will choose to use translators and interpreters rather than seek to master foreign languages themselves.

Translation and Interpretation

Differences in language around the world mean that international managers have to deal with translations and interpretations. Learning a new language is desirable, but often it is not possible to learn all the languages of all the people or countries where a company does business. Consequently managers rely on translators and interpreters.

An organization's communications often have to be translated into other languages. Communications may be legal documents, instructions for product use, corporate policies and procedures, or public relations releases, that is, a wide array of messages. Organizations usually rely on professional translators (either in-house or external) to do translations from the original language to other languages. Good translation is much more than the translation of words; it is the translation of meaning. Legal documents present a particular challenge if differences in the meaning are found in documents that have been translated. American companies usually include a clause in such documents stipulating that the American English version is the default if discrepancies occur.

We have probably all experienced reading a set of instructions for the use of a product that made little or no sense. This usually occurs because a company has employed a poor translator. In some situations, the poor translation is simply amusing. In others, it can be devastating for the company.

If a message is important for a company, it makes sense to invest the time and effort to ensure that translations are accurate and meaningful. This means, first, using a translator who is thoroughly bilingual and can think in both languages. For further verification, a process of back-translation is often recommended. This is a process whereby the message is translated from Language A to Language B by one bilingual translator, and then the Language B version is translated to Language A by a second bilingual translator. The two versions in Language A are compared for important discrepancies. This is a somewhat complex and costly process, but it ensures that translations are accurate and thus is well worthwhile for important communications.

Translations are now available on the Internet, and these services are likely to become more common. These translations are subject to the same errors as other translations. If a message is important, Internet translations should be used cautiously—several might be used and the results compared. In addition, a back translation process can be used; have the translated version translated back to the original language and compare the two versions.

Where communication is important, it is advisable to have a native speaker comment on the translated version prior to making it public. This can avoid mistakes by innuendo, as well as ensuring that the translated version sounds natural. A translator will be concerned with accuracy and may provide an accurate translation that does not sound natural. A final examination by a native speaker will identify this.

Many managers in foreign locations rely on interpreters to communicate with their foreign counterparts. Even where the manager speaks the foreign language to some degree, an interpreter can be a valuable asset. The interpreter provides assistance with unfamiliar words or phrases, as well as nuances of the language. For example, the Japanese often use interpreters when negotiating with Americans even though they speak English reasonably well. This is believed to give the Japanese an advantage because they have more time to consider the positions put forward by the other side—often they can hear and understand what the Americans say in English, and they consider it while the interpreter repeats in Japanese.

Good interpreters need to be completely bilingual, that is, fluent in both languages, so that they can move easily from one language to another. Working with an interpreter is not easy, however, as you speak to your foreign counterpart in your language, then wait while the interpreter speaks in the foreign language. Your foreign counterpart speaks in the foreign language, and you listen although you may not understand, and then you listen while the interpreter speaks in your language. Clearly the process takes much longer than direct communication. You also need to place complete trust in the interpreter that the interpretation is accurate. For this reason, it is advisable to have your own interpreter rather than relying on one provided by your foreign counterparts.

There are many stories of people involved in negotiations who listen to a speech of a couple of minutes by their foreign counterpart only to have the interpreter say, "he said, 'no.'" When this happens, you inevitably wonder if that was all that was said. There is a great story of an American dignitary in China telling a joke about American football during a speech. The interpreter knew that the audience could not possibly understand the joke, so instead of repeating the inappropriate joke, he said to the audience, "The dignitary has made a joke, please laugh." Everyone laughed, and the dignitary's dignity was saved.

Interpreters provide invaluable assistance in allowing people to communicate when they do not speak a common language. Working well with an interpreter takes some skill, and it is a good idea to have practice before attempting an important set of interactions.

Both translation and interpretation rely on the skills of the professional linguist. Even the best translators and interpreters might not be familiar with certain colloquial or technical expressions. For example, a colleague tells of using the English expression "out of sight, out of mind" in a Middle Eastern country. This expression was translated/interpreted as "blind and crazy"—not exactly what the speaker had meant. It is always important to choose your words and phrases carefully in such situations, to speak simply and clearly, to avoid expressions that may be misunderstood, and to recognize that verbal humor often does not translate.

Religion

Pick up any newsmagazine or newspaper, turn on the news on television or radio, check out your favorite blog or Twitterfeed, and you will very likely find stories that relate to religion. Wars have been and are fought because of religion, and people commit crimes for religious reasons. Religion also encourages people to be good, generous, and caring. Religion is fundamental to people's behavior. Even those who claim to follow no religion find that their behavior is in effect based on their non-belief—that is, they are careful to focus on reason and empirical reality, rather than accepting the unprovable beliefs postulated by various religions. In effect, each religion provides explanations for what humans do not and cannot know—for example, explanations of death and what happens after death.

For most people of the world, religion is extremely important. To live a good life and hope for something after death in this world, one needs to follow the tenets of one's religion. This essential nature of religion means that international managers must be prepared to accept the many different religious beliefs that they encounter as valid for the people who hold them. People hold their religious beliefs dearly and may be willing to die for them; few would do so for other beliefs.

Interestingly, even in countries where religion is not considered very important, and the society is essentially secular, the evidence of religious traditions is often still important. For example, Canadians would generally say that Canada is a secular society and that religion is relatively unimportant in everyday life. Nevertheless, when the mayor of Toronto recently called the traditional Christmas tree a "holiday tree," Torontonians were outraged. While many Canadians are not Christians, Christmas time remains a major holiday season, and little business other than retail gets done during the latter part of December.

In Nepal it is normal to see holy shrines along the street, in the windows of houses, and hanging in trees. A visitor to Canada from Nepal remarked that she was surprised to find that the people of Canada were very religious and had similar religious traditions to those in Nepal. Her hosts were mystified until she pointed out the ghosts hanging from trees, the lighted carved pumpkins in windows, and the skeletons in front of shops. Of course, it was Halloween in Canada—a celebration for children that is now thought of as nonreligious, but which is, in fact, based on religious tradition.

Many historical events have occurred under the banner of religion; for example, there are the Islamic conquests, the Crusades, and the emigration of European religious dissenters to the New World, to mention only a few. The terrorist attacks by supporters of al-Qaeda in the United States, Bali, and elsewhere were apparently driven by religious beliefs, and many conflicts around the world are driven by religious animosities. Even those belonging to different sects of the same faith are often at variance with each other, an example being the Roman Catholics and Protestants, both Christian, in Northern Ireland.

Religion has been defined as "a socially shared set of beliefs, ideas and actions which relate to a reality that cannot be verified empirically" (Terpstra and David 1985, 79). Religious ideas provide answers to such unanswerable problems as ignorance, suffering, and injustice. The very fact that religious beliefs cannot be verified empirically is what makes them such strongly held convictions. People do not seek to prove their religious beliefs, they simply accept them on faith; thus, it is usually not possible to change those beliefs. International managers, therefore, generally acknowledge the beliefs of those they work with and accommodate these beliefs.

The Expression of Religion

When we seek to understand religion and its impact on behavior, we need to look both at the macro and micro levels. At the macro level, religion drives many collectively held, deep-seated beliefs about what is right and what is wrong, what is moral and what is immoral. In 2003, when preparations were being made by the United States and its allies to enter into a war with Iraq, much discussion revolved around religious teachings on what constituted a just war. Some people believed the war with Iraq to be a just war religiously; others argued that it was not. At the micro level, religion influences many individual behaviors, such as what we eat and wear, whom we talk to and work with, when we rest and pray, how we marry, and so on.

Consider some examples and their impact on doing business:

- The Jewish population, although representing a relatively small proportion of the population in the United States and elsewhere, are a major force in the business world. It is important for non-Jewish businesspeople to be aware of their Jewish counterparts' beliefs. For example, the Sabbath in Judaism is from sundown Friday to sundown Saturday, and it is preferable not to schedule business meetings during this period.
- Muslims do not eat pork and are offended by others eating pork. Non-Muslim Malay Chinese eat pork regularly. Firms in Malaysia have had problems between Muslims and non-Muslims because of their differing food practices.
- Indian Hindu women often wear traditional saris, which leave their upper stomach exposed. At a factory in Barbados, which employed Indian women as well as Barbadians, the locals complained about this, and the

Indian women in turn complained about the locals wearing skirts that were too short.

- In most Islamic countries, local women dress very conservatively and cover their heads. Western visitors have found that it is best to follow this tradition and have adapted their normal Western dress to be more in keeping with Islamic norms. Most female reporters covering news in Islamic countries now wear headscarves.
- The Sikhs wear a turban for religious reasons. In Canada, the Royal Canadian Mounted Police (Mounties) sought to attract people from many minority groups, including the Sikh religion, but found this caused problems because the Sikhs refused to wear the traditional Mountie's hat. Eventually the policies were changed to allow the Sikh Mounties to wear turbans at work.
- Australian companies that employ Muslims typically allow these employees to pray at various times during the workday and provide appropriate facilities for prayer.

There are many other examples that could be given to illustrate how religious beliefs affect doing business. The former illustrate the importance of taking these beliefs into account. Each religion has its own set of special holidays and traditional days of rest. These are important to adherents of the religion, and managers have to take these into account in scheduling operations. Similarly, each religion has its taboos and requirements, and if these can be factored into the business structure, managers are more likely to succeed.

Major Religions of the World

To give the reader a basic idea of how religions differ, the following discussion considers the major religions of the world and very briefly outlines some of the tenets of these religions.[1] The religions discussed (Buddhism, Christianity, Hinduism, and Islam) are practiced by about 70 percent of the world's population. Another approximately 20 percent are nonreligious, 5 percent are adherents of various folk religions, and the balance belong to other faiths, such as Judaism, Sikhism, Jainism, Confucianism, and so on. All of these faiths are important, and managers should have some understanding of each, but due to space limitations, only the major religions are mentioned here and only a very brief summary of each of these is possible.

Buddhism

Buddhism is an ancient religion that originated in India in the sixth century B.C.E. and spread east throughout Asia. There are two major Buddhist branches, Theravada and Mahayana. Theravada means "the teaching of the elders" and is based on the original teachings of the Buddha. This branch is older and more conservative. Mahayana means "the greater vehicle" and is based on the belief that the Buddha did not mean to stop with the original teachings, but to develop a greater vehicle that would encompass all peoples. Adherents of this branch are often adherents of another religion as well as Buddhism.

"Buddha" is a title that means "Enlightened One." The title is associated with Siddhartha Gautama, a prince in the north of India whose early life was free of unpleasant experiences. It is said that one day he walked out of his palace and saw an old man, a dead man, and a begging monk. He was so disturbed by the reality of human suffering that he left his home and family to wander as a hermit in search of answers to the problems of human suffering. After years of wandering, instruction, and meditation, he meditated for forty days under a sacred tree and reached enlightenment. Enlightenment for Gautama was "the middle way"—neither the self-indulgence that he had known as a prince, nor the asceticism of Hinduism (which he had tried), but moderation in all things.

Buddhism is based on the following beliefs (taken from Terpstra and David 1985, 93):

The Four Noble Truths

> All existence is suffering.
> Suffering is caused by desire, and all desires (material, sensual, and so on) are never fulfilled forever.
> Suffering ceases when desire ceases.
> The Noble Eightfold Path leads to the cessation of suffering.

The Noble Eightfold Path consists of:

> Right view is understanding and accepting the Four Noble Truths.
> Right thought is freedom from lust, ill will, cruelty, and untruthfulness.
> Right speech is abstaining from lying, talebearing, harsh language, and vain talk.
> Right conduct is abstaining from killing, stealing, and sexual misconduct.
> Right livelihood is the avoidance of violence to any living thing and freedom from luxury.
> Right effort is avoiding and overcoming what is evil and promoting and maintaining what is good.

Right awareness is contemplating the fact that the body is transitory and loathsome, contemplating the feelings of oneself and of others, and contemplating the mind and other phenomena.

Right meditation is complete concentration on a single object to achieve purity of thought, thought free from all desires, hindrances, and distractions, and, eventually, free from all sensation.

Traditional Buddhist monks are organized in monastic orders and typically live in seclusion from the world. They are easily recognized by their shaven heads and saffron-colored robes. These monks follow very strict and extensive rules and do not work. Modern Buddhism is, however, characterized by its diversity.

Christianity

With its roots in Judaism, the Christian religion is based on the teachings of Jesus Christ, whom Christians consider to be the son of God. Although Jesus was born to a Jewish family, Christians believe that his mother (Mary) was a virgin and that he was conceived by the Holy Spirit. The Western, Christian calendar is based on the approximate time of his birth about 2,000 years ago. Jesus disagreed with some of the traditional religious beliefs of his society, and as an adult, he developed a following—including twelve men known as the Apostles, who worked closely with him and later recorded his teachings in the New Testament of the Bible. As Jesus became more and more popular and his disciples grew in number, he was viewed as a threat to those in political power. His punishment was death by crucifixion. Christians believe that following his death, Jesus rose from the dead and, by the power of the Holy Spirit, ascended into heaven. Thus, the cross and the dove, which represent his death and resurrection, are major symbols of Christianity.

Christians believe that Jesus died to save humans from their sins, and that if you believe in him, you will have eternal life. Simply, his teachings are based on the Ten Commandments that God gave to the prophet Moses, and especially the ideals that you should love your neighbor as yourself, be concerned for the less fortunate, and live peaceably among others. Christianity also encompasses the belief that God gives us gifts and talents that we should use to glorify him.

There are two main branches of Christianity: Roman Catholicism and Protestantism. The Roman Catholic Church has a global structure, with the Pope at its head—the Pope is believed to be God's representative on earth and to speak for God. Priests in the Catholic church are men, and they must take oaths of celibacy and poverty. The Protestant branch is made up of a variety of subsets (e.g., Anglicans, Episcopalians, the United Church), and these subsets have differing structures. Many Protestant denominations ordain women as well as men, and ministers are allowed to marry and have families. Protestantism has also been credited with "the Protestant work ethic," which encompasses the idea that hard work is good and that success based on hard work is positive.

There are a wide variety of minor Christian sects, whose beliefs are based on alternative interpretations of the teachings of Jesus. In some parts of the world, these sects actually predominate. For example, in the English-speaking Caribbean, there are a large number of adherents to sects known as "Spiritual Baptists," "Jehova's Witnesses," and "Seventh Day Adventists." Seventh Day Adventists are prohibited from working on the Sabbath, which is celebrated, as in the Jewish faith, from sundown Friday to sundown Saturday.

Hinduism

The Indian subcontinent is the home of Hinduism, and the majority of Indians are Hindus. The practice of Hinduism varies widely from place to place and depends on the location as well as social status; thus, to describe this religion is difficult. Most Hindus venerate cows. Cows are considered sacred (this is the origin of the English expressions "sacred cow," and "holy cow"), and beef is not eaten by most Hindus. Hinduism also revolves around hierarchies of inequality (gods and people are ranked according to purity).

There are many gods to whom the Hindus pray; some are more important, some less so. People are ranked in a caste system, and caste was the basis for the division of labor and social status (people are, literally, born to rule, born to farm, and so on). The caste system resulted in a well-defined and highly stratified society. While this has changed somewhat in India, where the caste system is technically not legal, the idea of caste is still important to practicing Hindus. The system is based on the concept of rebirth; if a person lives a good life, according to the dictates of their particular caste, in the next incarnation they will have improved their purity and thus their status. One way to improve one's purity is to perform rituals at various stages of the life cycle (birth, puberty, marriage, and death). Many Hindus spend substantial sums of money on these rituals because they see them as an investment that will eventually lead to nirvana, where one escapes the cycle of rebirth and attains endless serenity.

In many ways, Hinduism is more than a religion, it is a way of life, with its beliefs woven into everyday activities. Hindus around the world continue to live by traditional beliefs even though, in other ways, they seem to Western colleagues to be thoroughly Western. Many North Americans are surprised, for example, to learn that Hindu friends are arranging marriages for their sons and daughters, even though these sons and daughters are highly educated, and, further, that marriages are generally arranged between families of the same caste.

Islam

Islam is the infinitive of the Arabic verb meaning to submit and is exemplified by the willingness of the Prophet Abraham to submit to the Lord's will by sacrificing his son Isaac. The word Muslim is the present participle of the same verb and denotes one who is accepting and submitting to God's will. The expression "inshallah," which is translated to English as "God willing," is used to describe the belief that everything, good and evil, proceeds directly from divine will.

The beliefs of the Islamic faith are based on the Koran, its holy text. There is no formal clergy in Islam, but scholars versed in the Koran play an important role as interpreters, preachers, and teachers. In Islamic countries there is no separation between church and state. Sharia, the law of Islam, details how an individual should behave and the punishments for misbehavior. In some Islamic countries where Sharia is practiced, the punishment for stealing is amputation of the offending hand; the punishment for women who commit adultery is death by stoning. Many of these practices are difficult for Westerners to understand and accept, but to some Muslims they are the law as provided by God. Muslims are expected to observe five duties (Terpstra and David 1985, 98):

The Five Pillars

Reciting the creed: "There is no god but God, and Mohammed is the Prophet of God."

Practicing prayer: There are five required prayer periods during the day, with ritual prayers in Arabic, and congregational prayer at noon on Fridays is incumbent on all adult males.

Fasting: During the month of Ramadan, the ninth month of the Muslim calendar, Muslims abstain from food, drink, smoking, and sexual intercourse from dawn to sunset.

Giving alms: Mohammed was especially concerned with the fate of the poor and destitute, and every Muslim is expected to give to help the poor.

Pilgrimage to Mecca: Adult Muslims who can afford it are expected to undertake a pilgrimage to Mecca during the twelfth month of the Muslim calendar.

There are two major Islamic sects, the Shiites and the Sunnis. The Sunnis are the majority overall, but in some countries Shiites dominate. The Shiites have a more formal hierarchy, religious leaders have more prominence, and they are less accepting of non-Muslim, especially Western, behavior. The sects share similar beliefs, but early disagreements over Mohammed's successors have resulted in a continuing separation of the two.

Other Religious Beliefs

There are a wide variety of other beliefs that the international manager may encounter. For example:

- There are people who believe that all objects in nature (trees, stones, and so on) have their individual spirits and that one can appeal to these spirits to help or hurt.
- There are people who worship their ancestors and appeal to them to intervene in ordinary, daily events.
- There are people who believe in magic and witchcraft and that certain people are endowed with special powers, which they can wield for good or evil.
- Spiritual practices, such as obiah and voodoo in the Caribbean and candomblé in Brazil, are based on African traditions, and are still observed, and certain practitioners are believed to have special powers.

We cannot begin to explore in any depth the major religions of the world or the many alternative beliefs that international managers may encounter; in addition, some religions, such as Judaism, play a particularly important business role in certain countries. The aim of this chapter is simply to alert managers to the key role that religion plays in behavior and to briefly explore some of the religious similarities and differences that may be found around the world. Some countries are essentially homogeneous in terms of religion; others contain a wide array of religions. Some religions are very tolerant of other beliefs; others are closed to and unaccepting of others. The international manager needs to be aware of all these variations. The importance and nature of religion, particularly the reliance on faith, means that managers doing business or working in a foreign location should identify the religious parameters of the foreign country in order to be sure that their own behavior conforms reasonably to those parameters.

Summary and Conclusions

This chapter has explored linguistic and religious characteristics from an international management perspective. Both language and religion are closely connected to culture and cultural values. Each influences the culture of a group of people, and each is an expression of that culture. Language and religion have a substantive impact on people's behavior; thus, international managers need to spend the time to understand each of these in the different countries where they operate. This chapter has given a brief overview of linguistic and religious variations around the world and suggested how these variations can influence the international manager, as well as how the manager can prepare for, and work with, the variations encountered.

Note

1. Much of the information in this section is drawn from Terpstra and David (1985).

References

Deutscher, G. 2010. *Through the Language Glass: Why the World Looks Different in Other Languages.* London: Metropolitan Books.
Terpstra, V., and K. David. 1985. *The Cultural Environment of International Business.* Cincinnati, OH: Southwestern.
Whorf, B.L. 1956. *Language, Thought and Religion.* New York: John Wiley.

6

Economic Development and the Management of Organizational Behavior and Human Resources

Introduction

In an article entitled "Steel the Prize" (2006, 64), the *Economist* discussed the takeover battle between Tata, an Indian conglomerate, and CSN, a Brazilian steelmaker, for Corus. Corus is the Anglo-Dutch company that absorbed British Steel. This may be the face of the future—two giant companies from developing countries fighting over a developed-country asset. Tata has become a global power in the business world with Tata Motors, Tata Consultancy, and Tata Steel identified as its major areas of worldwide focus (Official Board 2012). China's carmakers continued to copy cars from traditional automakers ("Carmaking in India" 2006, 64), but China also had a goal to become the number one producer of electric cars, a Shenzhen-based company was expected to become the world's largest DNA sequencing laboratory ("Banyan" 2010), and Chinese-owned businesses are investing around the world. Dubai has established itself as a global financial and tourism center, including a man-made ski hill in the desert ("Dubai's Financial Center" 2006; "The New Titans" 2006). Companies small and large from developing countries around the world are now investing in the developed world. The existing literature on management interactions between developing and developed countries implicitly assumes that managers from developed countries will be adapting to the environment in developing countries, yet the reverse may be more and more the reality of the management challenges of the twenty-first century.

In many ways this is contrary to traditional thinking about developing countries, which have until quite recently been seen only as the recipients of aid and investment from the developed world. And while this may be changing, the developing countries are still the poorer countries of the world. It remains true that the rich countries account for most of the world's gross domestic product (GDP) even though they represent only about 20 percent of the world's population (the richest 20 percent of the world earn about 85 percent of the world's GDP, and the poorest 20 percent only 1 percent). Much of this chapter will discuss the implications of wealth, or its lack, on management in developing countries; however, throughout, readers should keep in mind the changing world in which we live, because it is this changing world that will determine what constitutes effective management.

Approximately 80 percent of the world's population lives and works in countries characterized as "developing," but most of our know-how about organizational behavior and human resource management revolves around the developed world. Developing countries have received little attention from management writers, yet understanding management in these countries is particularly relevant in today's global business environment. Fifteen years ago, a writer noted that the evolution of a global marketplace is redefining the arena for international business, and managers should be aware that "prior examinations have focused primarily on locations in the industrialized regions of North America and Western Europe, [and] our theories, models, and practices exhibit a significant 'Western' influence" (Thomas 1996). This is even more so today as globalization has continued. This means that traditional organizational behavior/human resource theories may not be applicable in the "rest of the world." Similarly, an evaluation of publications in the cross-cultural management field commented that "there is a risk of creating two distinct branches of management literature: global and North American" (Baruch 2001, 116). This chapter focuses on differences between richer and poorer countries, and on levels of economic development. The differences are important factors that affect management, particularly in terms of people's behavior and, in turn, human resource choices.

The developing world provides an array of products and services to the developed world and is a very large market for the developed world as well; thus, the two worlds are inextricably intertwined. As incomes increase in poorer countries, average people will be able to afford many of the goods and services that are currently available only to the rich; this increased consumption can stimulate economic growth in the developing as well as the developed world. The workforce in the developing world is young (whereas that in the developed world is aging) and has the potential to provide an enthusiastic and hardworking group of employees for many years. There are many opportunities on which managers from both sets of countries can capitalize, but they need to understand each other to be able to do so. Managers from the developed world are often attracted to the developing world by its numbers: large potential markets, a substantial potential workforce, and available resources. Managers are unsure, however, of the reality of doing business in developing countries because they experience a business environment very different from what they know at home. Managers from the developing world also see the advantages of their own large markets, workforce, and potential to supply the developed world with new and unique products and services, but these managers are also unsure of the reality of doing business in an environment different from the one they know. This chapter examines some of the differences between developed and developing countries in the context of their impact on effective management practices.

We begin with an examination of development issues and consider what is meant by level of economic development and what economic development means to international managers. The chapter explores a variety of factors that characterize development and how these are likely to impact on behaviors in organizations and human resource choices.

Understanding Development Issues

Many people think first of poverty when developing countries are mentioned. According to a report on the BBC in April 2002, a poll of Europeans showed a negative view of developing countries, predominantly focused on poverty and illness. There is another side to developing countries that managers should recognize. Developing countries have substantial potential (Punnett 2008, 2012):

- Developing countries account for about 80 percent of the world's population, representing a substantial potential market and workforce. China and India together have a population of over 2 billion people.
- Per capita incomes have been growing in developing counties, albeit not as quickly as in the developed world, and there is a growing middle class in many countries.
- A substantial number of developing countries achieve high scores on the United Nations Development Index, a composite index that indicates the presence of good education, health care, and quality of life. These countries are recognized as good places to live and do business. Countries as diverse as Barbados, Singapore, and the United Arab Emirates are among these.
- Some developing countries, such as India, have large numbers of highly trained and qualified people. Others, such as Zimbabwe, have had good infrastructures. Still others, such as Barbados, have stable governments and high literacy rates. Cuba is an example of a developing country with excellent medical facilities. These characteristics of developing countries mean that they can be attractive to foreign businesses; these

characteristics should also mean that businesspeople from developing countries can be successful themselves in foreign ventures.

- Many development organizations are emphasizing support of developing countries in their efforts to make the most of their resources in a global business environment. Such support provides opportunities for both indigenous and foreign companies. Many development agencies from Europe, Japan, and North America provide resources in the form of loans, grants, and insurance aimed at initiatives in developing countries.

- A number of developing countries—for example, Argentina, Brazil, China, India, and Nigeria—are physically large and may offer access to substantial reserves of natural resources. This is reflected in the emergence of BRICS (Brazil, Russia, India, China, South Africa) as a bloc of countries developing rapidly and playing a major role in international affairs.

- Developing countries are increasingly realizing that there is power in numbers and that they do not have to accept the economic dictates of the more developed countries. The formation of the G20 in 2003 is one example of this new realization. The G20 is a group of developing countries whose objective is to champion the interests of developing countries in global forums.

- Many developing countries have had substantial periods of economic growth. The miracle of the Asian Tigers may be tarnished in view of financial and political events since the late 1990s; nevertheless, the economic growth in these countries was often referred to as an "economic miracle." Singapore's per capita GDP in 2010 was US$41,122, compared to US$47,200 for the United States, illustrating the levels that some developing countries have reached (World Bank 2012). These growth rates suggest the economic potential of the developing countries as a whole.

- Many developing countries have relatively warm climates that are attractive to the growing aging population of the developed world. "Baby boomers" from the developed countries have substantial wealth and may see the countries with warm climates as a place to enjoy retirement.

Definitions of Development

Defining where, or what, the developing world is, is problematic (Punnett 2012). According to the United Nations (2000), "The term 'developing countries' includes low- and middle-income economies and thus may include economies in transition from central planning, as a matter of convenience. The term 'advanced countries' may be used as a matter of convenience to denote the high-income countries."

Definitions of "development" are sensitive because the concept of development is value-laden, and managers need to be aware of these sensitivities. Different groups interpret the word "development" differently at different times. Being classified as "developing" can be advantageous for a country when, for example, it wants to receive development aid or other donor assistance. At other times a country may want to think of itself as developed, for example, when it wants to attract foreign investment and high-technology firms. The United States Council for International Business (1985) used the following definitions, which remain helpful in understanding the most commonly accepted distinctions between developed and developing countries:

Developed Countries

Industrialized countries are distinguished from developing countries or less developed countries (LDCs). Generally, the term "developed" is understood to refer to the members of the Organisation for Economic Co-operation and Development (OECD). As of 2012, country members include Australia, Austria, Belgium, Canada, Chile, Czech Republic, Denmark, Estonia, Finland, France, Germany, Greece, Hungary, Iceland, Ireland, Israel, Italy, Japan, Korea, Luxembourg, Mexico, the Netherlands, New Zealand, Norway, Poland, Portugal, Slovak Republic, Slovenia, Spain, Sweden, Switzerland, Turkey, the United Kingdom, and the United States. This shows substantial enlargement over the past decade (OECD 2012).

Developing Countries

This term is used most commonly at the United Nations to describe a broad range of countries including those with both high and low per capita national incomes and those that depend heavily on the sale of primary commodities. These countries usually lack an advanced industrial infrastructure as well as advanced educational, health, communications, and transportation facilities.

The lack of precise definition is further complicated by the myriad of additional terms used in conjunction with or as substitutes for the term "development." Some examples:

Underdeveloped Countries and LDCs

Poorer, developing countries were often called "underdeveloped" some fifty years ago. This terminology has been described as a carryover of colonial condescension and was changed to "less developed countries" (LDCs) in order to be less demeaning. This term has also been considered negative and now is seldom used for the developing countries as a group. The term LDC now describes the "least developed countries," the poorest nations in the world, which receive particular development attention from the United Nations. In 2012 the least developed countries represented 12 percent of the world's population but accounted for only 2 percent of the world's GDP and 1 percent of world trade. There were forty-eight LDCs, using this second definition. The United Nations Office of the High Representative for the Least Developed Countries, Landlocked Developing Countries and the Small Island Developing States (UN-OHRLLS) identified thirty-three of these countries in Africa, fourteen in Asia, and only Haiti outside of these regions (United Nations 2012).

Third World

The Third World designation for developing countries was used in contrast to the First World, OECD countries, and the Second World, communist countries. The Third World encompassed the countries that were not aligned with either the First or Second Worlds. Since the collapse of the Soviet Union, this terminology is less frequently used, but Third World is still in relatively common usage, when referring to the poorer countries of the world.

North/South

The majority of the richer countries are north of the majority of the poorer countries. The North/South distinction began through an attempt to be neutral, and North/South terms are used by many development organizations in the context of a North/South divide. People in the North are seen as the "haves," and those in the South seen as the "have-nots." The north–south division is, of course, not an entirely "correct" depiction of the development country situation, with countries such as Australia and New Zealand clearly richer but situated in the Southern Hemisphere.

Transitional, Industrializing, Emerging Countries

As some countries have embraced new economic forms, they have recently been considered as becoming developed or industrialized. The countries of the former Soviet bloc have been described as "transitional economies," and countries with substantial industrial bases, such as South Korea, Taiwan, and Brazil, have been described as "industrializing" or "newly industrialized countries" (NICs). These countries are also increasingly described as "emerging countries" or "emerging markets" to indicate the substantial potential markets that they represent. Recently, the so-called BRICS countries have been the focus of attention, and all are having a substantial impact on the world economy and world trade and investment.

The varying terminology of development stems from attempts to wrestle with several concerns. There are clear differences among countries in terms of their economic resources and level of industrialization. The United Nations and various development organizations, as well as the general population, want to recognize these differences. Much as with the term "development" itself, words used to recognize differences in development levels are inevitably value-laden. Newly devised terms carry with them the promise of value neutrality; as this neutrality fades and embedded connotations take over, new terms arise (as noted, LDC used in the 1950s was later thought to be demeaning, so "developing countries" became its more acceptable replacement). "Developing" versus "developed," however, suggests that one set of countries has reached a desired level of economic achievement to which the other set should aspire. The North/South terminology sought to differentiate without judging, but this approach did not succeed either. In effect, the rich and powerful North was usually depicted in a negative light as exploiting the poor and powerless South, both with mutual antagonisms.

The terrorist attacks of September 11, 2001, have made people everywhere more conscious of the way words can have different meanings to different people. Hence, sensitivity in the use of language is often important when people relate to others of different backgrounds. As recent events have made clear, "jihad" does not mean the same thing to all Muslims, and it is often interpreted differently by non-Muslims. "Crusade" is used commonly in English to mean any concerted and continuing effort, but to Middle Easterners it clearly refers to the Christian holy wars against the Arab world. Development terminology is no exception. Managers should be aware of the diverse terminology used to describe countries that fall into different economic classifications and be conscious of the various implications these terms may carry.

The issue of describing differences without making judgments is likely to continue. The term "developed world" will be used here to refer to the OECD countries and the rest of Western Europe, and the term "developing world" will refer to the rest of the world. The major distinctions between "developed" and "developing," in this context, are that developed world countries, on average, have a higher per capita income than do the developing world countries, and they rank higher on the United Nations Development Index. What these distinctions mean for managers is that the business environment can be substantially different in the two regions. The next sections provide an overview of some of the main characteristics that differentiate the developing countries from the more developed ones.

Characteristics of Developing Countries

The developing world encompasses a large and diverse group of countries. It includes the very small island states of the Caribbean and Pacific and the extremely large subcontinents of China and India. It includes a variety of political forms—communist states, kingdoms of various kinds, and democracies. It includes all ethnic groups, all races, and all religions. The discussion of shared characteristics in such a heterogeneous group should not be interpreted as suggesting that the countries will be alike. Each country or region has its own unique mix of characteristics that makes it special; nevertheless, an understanding of shared characteristics can assist in building an understanding of management in the group of countries we call the developing world.

There are two important measures that underlie the characteristics of development—real per capita GDP and the World Bank Development Index. The real GDP is the total domestic economic production, adjusted for local purchasing power, and per capita GDP is total production divided by the total population. The World Bank Development Index is a measure that incorporates factors other than economic production, such as health and education, to assess the broader quality of life in a country. There is a high correlation between per capita GDP and the development index. All of the countries that have high per capita GDP rank high on the development index. In fact, the top fifteen countries consist of OECD countries plus Iceland.

The lists in Exhibits 6.1 and 6.2, from the United Nations *Human Development Report,* show the thirty "most livable" countries in 2007 and the thirty "least livable."

A substantial number of countries rank high on the development index but are not high in terms of per capita GDP. In 2007 (United Nations 2007), the following countries were considered high in terms of the development index and are in the top fifty countries: Argentina, the Bahamas, Bahrain, Barbados, Brunei, the Czech Republic, Chile, Costa Rica, Croatia, Cyprus, Estonia, Greece, Hong Kong, Israel, Latvia, Lithuania, South Korea, Kuwait, Malta, Poland, Qatar, Seychelles, Singapore, Slovakia, Slovenia, the United Arab Emirates, and Uruguay. (This list changes somewhat from time to time, but it has remained much the same for the past decade.) The fact that many countries with lower per capita GDP rank high on the development index indicates significant development that is not measurable purely in terms of income. These countries have done well in providing a high quality of life for citizens, an achievement that underscores the need to understand both the similarities and differences among developing countries.

Exhibit 6.1

"Most Livable" Countries, 2007

1.	Iceland	16.	United Kingdom
2.	Norway	17.	Belgium
3.	Australia	18.	Luxembourg
4.	Canada	19.	New Zealand
5.	Ireland	20.	Italy
6.	Sweden	21.	Germany
7.	Switzerland	22.	Israel
8.	Japan	23.	Greece
9.	Netherlands	24.	Singapore
10.	France	25.	Korea, Rep. of
11.	Finland	26.	Slovenia
12.	United States	27.	Cyprus
13.	Spain	28.	Portugal
14.	Denmark	29.	Brunei Darussalam
15.	Austria	30.	Barbados

Source: United Nations Development Programme, *Human Development Report 2007/2008.* Available at hdr.undp.org.

Exhibit 6.2

"Least Livable" Countries, 2007

1.	Sierra Leone	16.	Angola
2.	Burkina Faso	17.	Rwanda
3.	Guinea-Bissau	18.	Guinea
4.	Niger	19.	Tanzania
5.	Mali	20.	Nigeria
6.	Mozambique	21.	Eritrea
7.	Central African Republic	22.	Senegal
8.	Chad	23.	Gambia
9.	Ethiopia	24.	Uganda
10.	Congo, Dem. Rep. of the	25.	Yemen
11.	Burundi	26.	Togo
12.	Côte d'Ivoire	27.	Zimbabwe
13.	Zambia	28.	Timor-Leste
14.	Malawi	29.	Djibouti
15.	Benin	30.	Kenya

Source: United Nations Development Programme, *Human Development Report 2007/2008.* Available at hdr.undp.org.

The Impact of Level of Development

The developing world is characterized by fewer economic resources than the developed world. More simply, developing countries are poorer than developed ones. From a management perspective, the consequences of poverty are clear:

- People are concerned with basic needs or, in the "better-off" of these countries, with achieving economic stability.
- Infrastructure is limited. Roads, railways, ports, and other physical facilities are nonexistent in some locations and only adequate in the "better-off" developing countries.
- Social services are limited. Education, health, and other social services are nonexistent in some locations and only adequate in the "better-off" developing countries.
- Resources are scarce, and projects need to be clearly justified to warrant governmental or nongovernmental support.

In spite of the relatively high rating for some countries on the United Nations Development Index, the economic disparity between the developed and developing countries is startling in many ways. Some statistics illustrate the level of disparity that exists:

- In 2007, the richest 20 percent of the world earned 85 percent of the world's GDP, the middle 60 percent earn 13 percent, and the poorest 20 percent earned only 1 percent.
- In 2007, the highest reported GDP per capita (adjusted for purchasing power) was in Luxembourg with $80,800 and the lowest was the Congo with $300.

Of even greater concern is the growing disparity between the rich and poor countries. Comparisons of per capita gross national product (GNP) for the top and bottom 20 percent of all countries over the past almost two centuries show a dramatic increase in wealth disparities. In 1820, the ratio was 3:1; in 1870, 7:1; 1913, 11:1; 1960, 30:1; 1990, 60:1; and in 1997, 74:1. There is no question that the rich have been growing richer, and the poor have not been catching up. The disparity within richer countries was a growing concern as exemplified by the "Occupy" movement (which started as "Occupy Wall Street" in 2011 and spread essentially around the world). This disparity is important from a management perspective, and managers in the developing countries feel disadvantaged by it. The lack of economic resources in the developing countries means that there are few resources for government expenditure on infrastructure.

The following examples illustrate some of the differentials in selected resources between the developed and developing countries:

- High-income countries consume 5,783 kilowatt hours of electricity per capita per year; middle-income countries consume 1,585; and low-income countries consume 188.
- High-income countries have 92 percent of their roads paved; middle-income countries have 51 percent paved; and low-income countries have 19 percent paved.
- High-income countries have 286 newspapers per 1,000 people; middle-income countries have 75; and low-income countries have 13.
- High-income countries have 1,300 radios per 1,000 people; middle-income countries have 383; and low-income countries have 147.
- High-income countries have 269 personal computers per 1,000 people; middle-income countries have 32; and low-income countries have 4.
- Developed countries have 253 doctors per 100,000 people; developing countries have 76.
- Tuberculosis rates are 15 percent in developed countries, 79 percent in developing countries.
- Low–birth weight babies have incidence rates of 6 percent in developed countries, 18 percent in developing countries.
- Enrollment in primary school is close to 100 percent in developed countries and about 86 percent in developing countries. Enrollment in secondary school is 96 percent in developed countries and 60 percent in developing countries.

These comparisons illustrate the dimensions of the gap between the rich and poor countries. Richer countries have more to spend on infrastructure, both physical and intellectual. Developing countries have less to spend on infrastructure; thus they often lack roads, railways, and ports; their people have limited training; and medical care can be limited, as is access to information.

Access to information through the Internet is often identified as contributing positively to development and providing a means to overcome economic constraints. The Internet can potentially provide everything from basic schooling to contact with the best medical authorities and research scientists. There is little question that the Internet can provide substantial benefits for the poorer countries, but, as Bill Gates, founder of Microsoft, has noted, Internet access is not helpful when you have no water or electricity. The richest 20 percent of the world accounted for about 90 percent of Internet users. As long as that imbalance continues, one cannot think of the Internet as a tool for development. Yet the development of wireless communication technology may provide increased opportunities for the developing world, and some developing countries are doing well in terms of technology. This suggests potential for the developing world. Interestingly, low-technology products also provide opportunities. Wind-up radios have given low-cost easy access to information and news media in parts of Africa that had no such access previously.

The preceding discussion focuses on differences between the two sets of countries. An additional area of interest is the economic or income equality/inequality that exists within a country—that is, the disparity between the rich and the poor. This is measured by the Gini index. Scores on the Gini index range from zero (perfect equality) to 100 (perfect inequality), therefore the lower a country's score the less income disparity there is. In the most recent Gini index published, the "better" countries included Bosnia-Herzgovina (26), Canada (32.6), Croatia (29), Czech Republic (25.4), Finland (26.9), Hungary (26.9), Japan (24.9), Norway (25.8), Romania (31), Slovakia (25.8), Sweden (25), Uzbekistan (26.8)—essentially Eastern European and Scandinavian countries plus Canada and Japan. The "worse" countries were Argentina (52.8), Bolivia (60.1), Botswana (63), Brazil (58), Colombia (58.6), Costa Rica (49.9), El Salvador (52.4), Gambia (50.2), Haiti (59.2), Honduras (53.8), Lesotho (63.2), Malawi (50.3), Mali (50.5), Namibia (74.3), Niger (50.5), Panama (56.4), Papua New Guinea (50.9), Paraguay (57.8), Peru (54.6), Swaziland (60.9), Zimbabwe (61)—essentially Central and South American and African countries plus Haiti and Papua New Guinea. The United States had a score of 40.8, higher than the "better" countries but lower than the "worse" ones, probably reflecting a large, relatively well-off middle class combined with very high executive salaries and a growing number of billionaires.

In addition to purely economic differences, there are demographic differences between the rich and poor countries. The following section summarizes some of the most important of these.

Demography and Development

There are several important demographic differences between developed and developing countries. These include population growth, population dispersion, age distribution, literacy and numeracy levels, and gender roles.

Population Growth

According to the United Nations Population Fund (2012), the world population is expected to hit 10.1 billion by 2100, reaching 9.3 billion by the middle of this century. Essentially all of the growth is expected to take place in less developed countries and will be predominately among the poorest populations in urban areas. Population growth rates were substantially higher in the developing world, at 2 percent, than in the developed, which grew at a rate of 0.6 percent for the period 1975 to 1997 (see Exhibit 6.3). This is also

Exhibit 6.3 **World Population Estimates**

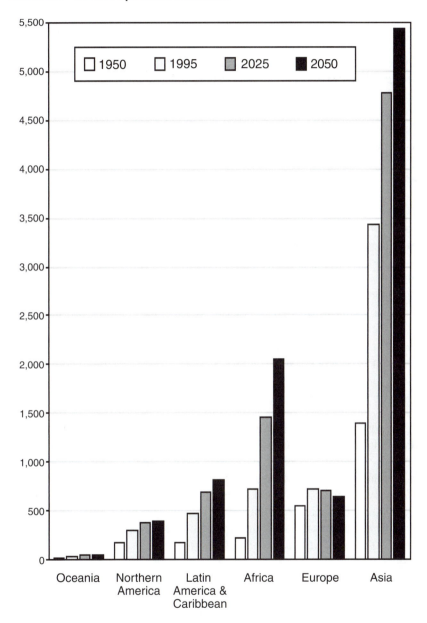

Source: Adapted from United Nations, *World Population Prospects* (New York: United Nations, 1998).

evident in fertility rates in the developing world, which are at 5 conceptions per woman as compared to 1.9 in the developed world. These differences are expected to continue. Combined with the increasing income disparity previously outlined, this means a growing proportion of the world will be poor and a smaller percentage of the world population will control an increasingly greater share of the resources and wealth. This situation does not sound like one that is sustainable, and managers need to be aware of the tensions that are created by such a situation. At the same time, the developing world's positive attributes of a large potential market and workforce are increasing as its populations grow.

Population Dispersion

The world as a whole is becoming more urban. About 50 percent of the world's population lives in cities, but the developing world is still substantially more rural than the developed world. In 1997, 78 percent of the developed world lived in cities compared to only 38 percent of the developing world. Sub-Saharan Africa, East Asia, and southern Africa were still relatively rural, but the rates of urbanization were highest in these regions. In developing countries, the cities are seen as the places where opportunities exist, and major movements of people from the rural areas to the urban often result in cities that are overcrowded and underserviced, with a substantial number of people living in very poor circumstances.

Age Distribution

The average age of populations in developed countries is increasing while that in developing countries is declining. In 1995, the over-65 population in developed countries was about 15 percent compared to 5 percent in developing countries. This gap was predicted to widen by 2015 to 18 percent over 65 in developed countries and a constant 5 percent in developing countries. Developing countries thus have an increasing abundance of younger, less experienced workers. If education and training are available for these workers, they could provide the base for a productive workforce.

Literacy and Numeracy

Literacy and numeracy rates are higher in the developed countries. Yet there are developing countries with good educational systems, and there is concern about the deterioration of education in North America and Europe. Nevertheless, on average, people in developed countries have access to better education, which results in functional literacy and numeracy as the norm. This is not the case in the developing world. The lower literacy and numeracy rates in the workforce of the developing world have major implications for the type of work that can be done, the use of technology, the testing and training that is needed, the need for supervision, and the opportunities for advancement. For example, a U.S. company with a subsidiary in a small island state hired a local manager to run the subsidiary. The local manager came well recommended by local contacts, was intelligent, articulate, and related well to the local workers. She was interviewed by a representative from headquarters and seemed to be an ideal choice for the position. Initially, operations went well, but it soon became clear that there was a problem as major discrepancies surfaced in terms of inventory levels and accuracy counts of parts shipped. The underlying problem was finally uncovered: The manager could not do the basic arithmetic of adding and subtracting, and operating the subsidiary relied on these skills. No one had thought to ask about these skills because they were simply assumed.

Gender Roles

Gender role distinctions are more pronounced in developing countries. In some places, laws discriminate against women in terms of land ownership, family inheritance, education, and a variety of other factors. Women often do much of the work within the family household and receive little, if any, compensation for their labor. Where there are minimum-wage regulations, these may favor men. The United Nations computes a gender-related development index that incorporates male/female differences in life expectancy, education, literacy, and GDP per capita. Countries that score high on the overall development index also score high on the gender development index. The richer and more developed countries thus appear to provide more equal opportunities for women than do the poorer, developing countries. These differences in how women are viewed and treated can cause problems and obstacles to success. For example:

- Where women are in a subordinate position, it is often impossible to make full use of their expertise and experience. Managers from developed countries working in less developed ones may have problems implementing the equal opportunity policies that they feel are appropriate because people in these countries may be offended by such policies.
- Male managers from developing countries may have difficulty interacting with women counterparts from developed countries and may feel compromised, both religiously and socially, by such interactions.

- Women from developed countries working in countries where women are treated differentially may face barriers to effective performance.
- When women's role is defined as homemaker, it is difficult for women to work outside the home.

Although there is still substantial discrimination in favor of men, particularly in the business and professional world, the role of women is changing in many developing countries. Women are playing an increasingly active role in business. These women are often especially committed, hardworking, and innovative. They can be seen to provide an additional benefit for those who do business in these countries. An example of successful women in developing countries is offered by the Grameen Bank of Bangladesh, which has made a series of small loans to women to support their developing businesses. The Grameen Bank has found that their small-business female clients are successful and meticulous about repaying their loans. Interestingly, in the English-speaking Caribbean, there is substantial concern over the marginalization of young men, with the vast majority of university graduates being women. A recent book entitled *Successful Professional Women of the Americas: From Polar Winds to Tropical Breezes* (Punnett et al. 2006) illustrates the potential of women in spite of the challenges they often face. According to Secretary of State Hillary Clinton, women are drivers of economic growth and the United States has launched efforts to spur economic growth by strengthening women's entrepreneurship and creating opportunities for women to participate fully in the global economy (e-mail correspondence from U.S. Embassy, Barbados).

Culture and Development

Hofstede's work on culture was discussed in chapter 2. Interestingly, some of Hofstede's dimensions of culture seem to differ, depending on level of development. The developing countries, for the most part, are low on individualism and high on power distance. This means:

- Individualism: The richer, more developed countries view the individual as the more appropriate focus of attention, while the poorer, less developed countries view the group as the appropriate focus.
- Power distance: The richer, more developed countries see equality as a desirable goal and minimize power differentials, while the poorer, less developed countries accept differences in power as appropriate.

These cultural variations between the two sets of countries are certain to affect management practices and to result in difficulties when managers from one set interact with personnel from the other. Hofstede discusses development assistance. With individualism, "donors will want to serve certain categories, like the urban poor or the small farmers," while "leaders in the receiving countries may, for example, want to repay their own village or tribe for its sacrifices in providing them with an education and enabling them to get into their present power position." With power distance, "donors' representatives try to promote equality and democratic processes at the receiving end" and "tend to be disturbed that they cannot avoid powerful local leaders who want to use at least part of the aid to maintain or increase existing inequalities" (Hofstede 1991, 6).

Similar reactions are likely in the approaches to management in the two sets of countries. Hofstede notes that there is no clear distinction between the sets of countries in terms of his uncertainty avoidance and masculinity indices. In general, however, the developing countries tend to be somewhat higher on uncertainty avoidance and the developed countries somewhat higher on masculinity. Higher uncertainty avoidance indicates a preference for situations that are well defined and clear, with risk aversion and possibly with relatively low entrepreneurial capacity. Higher masculinity indicates a competitive approach with a preference for tangible rewards. The following graphs illustrate the cultural profiles of developed and developing countries (see Exhibit 6.4). Using data from Hofstede's (1991) study, countries were classified as high, moderately high, moderately low, or low on the four cultural value dimensions of individualism, power distance, masculinity, and uncertainty avoidance. The developed and developing countries were compared on each of these value dimensions.

Other cultural characteristics that have sometimes been identified as distinguishing developed countries from the developing are need for achievement and beliefs about locus of control. Some developing countries have been described as having a relatively low need for achievement. This characteristic is perhaps attributable to the limited economic base in these countries, which means that other needs are paramount. A low need for achievement, like high uncertainty avoidance, has been associated with limited entrepreneurial activity (McClelland and Winter 1969).

Some developing countries have also been described as more likely to believe in an external locus of control than an internal one (Punnett 1999). This means that in those countries people are more likely to attribute events in life to external forces, perhaps the gods, luck, or their ancestors, rather than to their own actions. For example, in the Caribbean dialect, if someone is late for the bus, they say, "de bus lef me" (where in North America one might say, "I missed the bus"); if they drop a glass, they say, "de glass mash" (where in North America one might say, "I dropped the glass"); when a Caribbean employee reported on a woman

Exhitit 6.4   **Comparison of Cultural Value Profiles:
Developed/Developing Countries**

a) Region comparison: Individualism

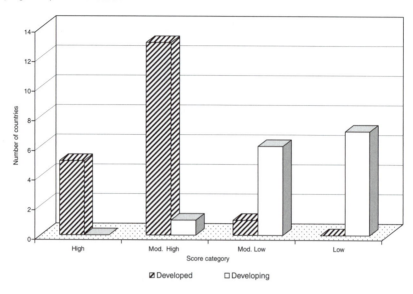

b) Region comparison: Power distance

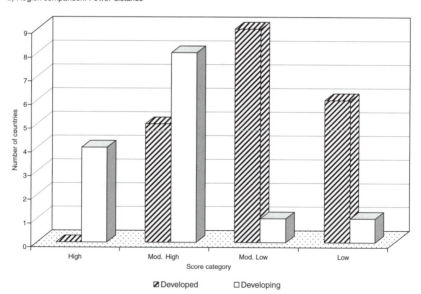

c) Region comparison: Masculinity

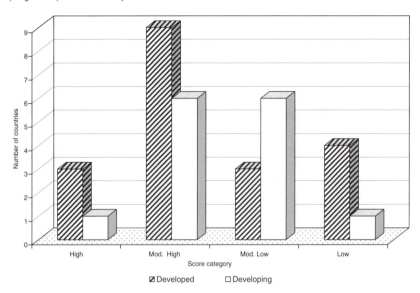

d) Region comparison: Uncertainty avoidance

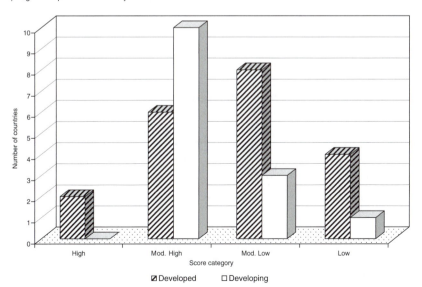

falling at work she said, "de groun slip from under she" rather than "she slipped and fell." These examples indicate a high degree of external attribution.

North American organizational behavior literature describes a fundamental attribution error as the inclination to attribute personal positive outcomes to internal factors in ourselves such as intelligence and hard work and negative personal outcomes to external factors in the environment such as a lousy teacher, the economy, and government rules. Conversely, when others do well, we attribute the positive outcome to external factors, and when they do poorly, we attribute the negative outcome to internal factors in them (Segall et al. 1990). Note that in the example of the woman slipping, the reverse is the case; that is, the negative outcome for another is attributed to external factors. Managers will want to remember that such attributions are culturally conditioned and will want to avoid attribution errors.

Not surprisingly, the World Values Survey classifies many developed countries as "social-rational" and "self-expressive" and developing countries as "traditional" and "survival oriented." This seems to be concordant with the richer/poorer distinctions that have previously been discussed. It is not surprising that generally poor countries will be concerned with survival and traditions, and generally richer countries will be more concerned with individual self-expression and social and rational issues.

People in different developing countries will not necessarily all behave in similar ways. Cultural values may be expressed quite differently in various locations. Moving from a developing country to a developed one, or vice versa, will, however, inevitably involve substantial cultural adjustment. Managers should be prepared for these variations when working with counterparts from the other region.

Politics and Development

The developed countries generally have well-developed democratic processes, while the developing countries are more likely to be ruled by a powerful individual or an elite group. Those developing countries that are democracies are relatively new democracies. The United Nations reported that the percentage of "some form" of democracy in country-level governance increased worldwide from 28 percent in 1974 to 61 percent in 1998. This increase suggests a substantial move toward democracy; at the same time it confirms that this is a new movement. Thus, many countries classified as democracies in this context are still in the formative stages of implementing democratic principles. Prior to World War II, most of the poorer countries were colonies of the richer countries. In the thirty years after the war, most of these countries became independent.

From 2010 to 2012, the "Arab Spring" revolutions in North Africa and the Middle East seemed to encourage the possibility of democracy, although what this actually means is still a significant question. Similarly in Africa, there were movements toward democracy in a variety of countries that were previously not democracies, but again with questions as to the eventual outcomes.

Democracy emphasizes individualism and equality, a low power distance in Hofstede's terminology. "One person, one vote" exemplifies these values. Non-democratic states clearly do not subscribe to these values. In such states, power is usually vested in a few powerful people who consider those belonging to their in-group as particularly deserving. New democracies may nominally subscribe to democratic values, but seldom have these values had time to become an ingrained part of the society. Differences in political values show up in the "rule of law" in developed countries and the "rule of man" in many developing countries. The rule of law suggests that there should be a clear statement of what is right or wrong and that it should be applied equally to all people. The rule of man suggests that what is right or wrong may depend on the situation and that each situation should be interpreted by those in positions of power. Some societies believe that rules apply the same way to all people, others that rules change depending on circumstances. Democracies typically subscribe to the rule of law philosophy.

Democracy, although it often means regular changes in government, implies order and a certain amount of predictability. When elections will take place, who can be elected, and the platforms of those vying to be elected are clearly set out. Newly formed democracies aspire to the same ideals but are often unable to implement them effectively. Thus, changes of government may combine democratic ideals with those in positions of power seeking to retain their power by any means, or people demonstrating en masse to change governments before the appointed time. Non-democracies are stable because the people in power are expected to remain for the long term and their views are known; however, those in power can be overthrown or die, and the leadership can change suddenly and unexpectedly.

In the developed world, there is a substantial separation between government and business and, by and large, there is support for free markets and free enterprise. In the developing world, there is generally a closer link between government and business, and this link is considered appropriate. Conflict of interest is not seen as a concern, and businesspeople may continue to run their businesses while serving in top government posts as minister of trade or minister of finance, for example. In many developing countries, the state is also seen as the agent of economic change, and state planning is believed to be essential for the economy as well as for a fair distribution of resources.

The state is paramount in centrally planned communist countries such as the People's Republic of China, Cuba, North Korea, and Vietnam, but even where developing countries have free-market economies, they are more likely to look to the state to play an important role in overcoming the failures or excesses of the free market system. For example, in the kingdoms of the Middle East (Bahrain, Kuwait, Oman, Qatar, Saudi Arabia, the United Arab Emirates), the monarchs still rule and therefore have substantial influence on how business is carried out; at the same time foreign investment can be welcomed, and some kingdoms have laws to protect these investments ("Time Travelers" 2002, 12). We live in changing times, however, and the world of 2020 may look quite different from the world of 2002.

There is an interesting link between economic freedom and income levels as well. The Fraser Institute described economic freedom as encompassing personal choice, voluntary exchange, freedom to compete, protection of person and property, and "institutions and policies as consistent with economic freedom when they provide an infrastructure for voluntary exchange, and protect individuals and their property from aggressors seeking to use violence, coercion and fraud to seize things that do not belong to them" (this description includes much of what we associate with democracy) (Gwartney and Lawson 2002). The Institute reported that countries in the top quintile of economic freedom had a per capita gross national income on average of US$23,450, those in the next quintile drop to US$12,390, then US$6,235, US$4,365, and US$2,556 for those in the lowest quintile. As incomes increase, economic freedom also increases (2002, 20). In 2008, the top ten countries in terms of economic freedom were Hong Kong,* Singapore, Ireland, Australia, the United States, New Zealand, Canada, Chile, Switzerland, United Kingdom; and the bottom ten were Venezuela, Bangladesh, Belarus, Iran, Turkmenistan, Burma, Libya, Zimbabwe, Cuba, North Korea (Heritage Foundation 2008).

A Canadian consultant tells the following story about a project in the People's Republic of China. The Canadian consultant met with a group of Chinese managers from the Chinese automotive parts industry. The Chinese asked what they needed to do to sell their products in Canada. The consultant responded that the requirements were the right product, consistent high quality at a competitive price, with reliable, on-time delivery. The consultant expected the Chinese managers to accept this as a challenge, but something they could address. Instead, the Chinese expressed surprise. "Why?" they asked. It became clear with further discussion that because the consultant's client was the Canadian government

---

* Hong Kong is part of the People's Republic of China (PRC), but it is often treated as a "country" because of its status as a Special Administrative Region, which allows for an economic system different from that of the rest of China.

and the consultant was accompanied by the Canadian trade commissioner, the Chinese managers had assumed that the Canadian government could simply require Canadian auto companies to buy Chinese parts. The consultant's assumption was that these business arrangements were made on a company-to-company basis; the Chinese managers' assumption was that these would be government-to-government arrangements. These different assumptions about the political environment were based on the different structures and attitudes to which each party was accustomed in its respective home location.

Another interesting point is that most of the countries currently listed as developing were, until quite recently (the 1950s), colonies of the European powers. This colonial heritage is likely to influence their business practices in a number of ways. For example:

- Colonies were traditionally producers for markets in the European countries. This means that for many colonies, the concept of marketing is largely ignored, with a focus on production instead.
- Colonies were in subordinate positions and instructed by the "colonial masters" (as the European powers were called) in matters of government, economics, and business. Decisions were made elsewhere, and in many of these countries, there is still a tendency to look to others for decisions.
- A top-down decision-making style was enforced and accepted. Decisions were made at the master level, with little input from the local level, and these decisions were not questioned. This remains in the management style of many companies in developing countries.

It is difficult to be certain of the influence of colonization in a post-colonial society, but one can be certain that there is an influence. And as countries move further from colonial times, we can expect their management practices and styles to change.

International managers are also interested in the degree of corruption that exists in different countries, and there is a perception that developing countries are more corrupt than developed ones. This is supported by Transparency International's Corruption Perceptions Index (Transparency International 2012). This index is prepared on the basis of information provided by an array of people with experience doing business in the various countries, and it ranks countries from least corrupt (#1) to most corrupt (#180). The index ranks Finland, Denmark, and New Zealand each as #1, followed by Sweden and Singapore, then Switzerland, Netherlands, Canada, Australia, and Norway (the top ten). At the other end of the scale, Myanmar (Burma) and Somalia are at the bottom, preceded by Iraq, Haiti, Uzbekistan, Tonga, Sudan, Chad, Afghanistan, Laos, and Guinea (the bottom eleven). The United States is not in the top ten but among the least corrupt. Not all developing countries rank low; for example, Chile, Barbados, and St. Lucia rank just below the United States.

Summary and Conclusions

This chapter has focused on differences between developed and developing countries that are well established and documented, illustrating some clear distinctions between the two categories. The primary distinction is that the world's developed countries are wealthier and have higher per capita incomes than the developing ones. Many other distinctions flow from this basic fact. While the distinctions allow a discussion of developed versus developing countries, we should not forget that the developing world itself is certainly not homogeneous. In fact, it is very diverse, and managers will find many and substantial variations among countries described as developing. China and India, for example, both very large and populous, have completely different languages, religions, politics, social structures, and so on. Singapore and Jamaica, both small islands, are equally different.

The developing world is often thought of in negative terms by those in the developed world. Yet the developing world provides many opportunities for international businesses. This 80 percent of the world is potentially a very large market and source of resources, it can provide new products and services, and it has a young labor force. If significant increases in income can be achieved among the majority of the world's population that lives in the developing world, the developing world can be the engine of world economic growth.

References

"Banyan: The Elusive Fruits of Inclusive Growth." 2010. *Economist,* May 13.
Baruch, Y. 2001. "Global or North American? A Geographical Based Comparative Analysis of Publications in Top Management Journals." *International Journal of Cross Cultural Management* 1(1): 109–126.
"Carmaking in India." 2006. *Economist* (December 16–22): 64–65.
"Dubai's Financial Center." 2006. *Economist* (December 16–22): 69–73.
Gwartney, J., and R. Lawson. 2002. *Economic Freedom of the World: 2002 Annual Report.* Vancouver, BC: The Fraser Institute.
Heritage Foundation Web Site. 2008. www.heritage.org (accessed January 28, 2008).
Hofstede, G. 1991. *Cultures and Organizations: Software of the Mind.* London: McGraw-Hill.
McClelland, D.C., and D.G. Winter. 1969. *Motivating Economic Achievement.* New York: Free Press.
Official Board. 2012. "Tata Group." February 13. http://www.theofficialboard.com/org-chart/tata-group# (accessed March 28, 2012).
"The New Titans." 2006. *Economist* (September 16–22): 1–28.
Organisation for Economic Co-operation and Development (OECD). 2012. "Members and Partners." http://www.oecd.org/pages/0,3417,en_36734052_36761800_1_1_1_1_1,00.html (accessed March 13, 2012).

Punnett, B.J. 1999. "Management in the Caribbean." In *IEBM Regional Set*, ed. M. Warner, 23–44. London: International Thomson Publishing.

———. 2008. "Management in Developing Countries." In *21st Century Management: A Reference Handbook*, ed. C. Wanke, 190–199. Los Angeles, CA: Sage.

———. 2012. *Management: A Developing Country Perspective* London: Routledge.

Punnett, B.J., J. Duffy, S. Fox, A. Gregory, T. Lituchy, S.I. Monserrat, M.R. Olivas Lujan, and N.M. Fernandes dos Santos. 2006. *Successful Professional Women of the Americas: From Polar Winds to Tropical Breezes*. London: Edward Elgar.

Segall, M., P. Dasen, R. Berry, and Y.P.E. Poortenga. 1990. *Human Behavior in Global Perspective*. Elmsford, NY: Pergamon Press.

"Steel the Prize." 2006. *Economist* (November 25–31): 64–65.

Thomas, A. 1996. "A Call for Research in Forgotten Locations." In *Handbook for International Management Research*, ed. B.J. Punnett and O. Shenkar, 485–506. Cambridge, MA: Blackwell.

"Time Travelers." 2002. *Economist* (March 23–29): 12.

Transparency International. 2012. www.infoplease.com (accessed April 12, 2012).

United Nations. 1998. *World Population Prospects*. New York: United Nations, 1998.

———. 2000. "Entering the 21st Century." *World Development Report*. Oxford: Oxford University Press.

———. 2007/2008. *Human Development Report*. Oxford: Oxford University Press.

———. 2012. "Least Developed Countries: About LDCs." UN-OHRLLS. http://www. unohrlls.org/en/ldc/25/ (accessed March 13, 2012).

United Nations Population Fund. 2012. "Linking Population, Poverty and Development: Rapid Growth in Less Developed Regions." http://www.unfpa.org/pds/trends.htm (accessed March 13, 2012).

U.S. Council for International Business. 1985. *Corporate Handbook to International Economic Organizations and Terms*. New York.

World Bank. 2012. "Data: Indicators. GDP per Capita (Current US$)." Table. http:// data.worldbank.org/indicator/NY.GDP.PCAP.CD (accessed March 13, 2012).

7

Motivation in a Cross-National Context

Introduction

Motivation refers to the inner urges that cause people to behave in certain ways. In the workplace, we talk of people being highly motivated when they work hard to accomplish objectives that are consistent with the organization's goals. We talk of people being de-motivated on the job when they seem disinterested and need to be pushed to perform. What makes people motivated or de-motivated at work is complex because motivation is caused by a mix of psychological and personal characteristics.

It is not really accurate to talk of people being de-motivated. People are always motivated in some direction; the question is the direction of their motivation. When someone is de-motivated at work, it means that they are motivated in some nonwork direction; that is, they would rather be doing something other than work. Nevertheless, the terminology of de-motivation is used frequently in everyday language, so it will be used in this chapter. When we say that someone is de-motivated, then, we mean that they are not working very hard, and their performance is less than could be expected. This is why motivation and its causes are of such interest to managers. A firm's success and profitability are directly related, to a large extent, to the performance and productivity of the people who work for the firm; thus, a major component of a manager's role is to ensure that employees are performing at a peak level.

Within our own national confines, we can try to draw meaningful conclusions about the causes of motivation because there are certain basic values, attitudes, and beliefs that most people within the culture share. For example, if a coworker suddenly seems de-motivated, I might consider recent events and think, "Oh, she was passed over for that promotion that she thought she deserved, that's probably why." I am drawing on my own inner feelings and a general belief that when we think we have been treated unfairly (or inequitably) it is de-motivating. I may be right in my attribution regarding my coworker, or I may be wrong (e.g., she might have problems at home of which I am unaware that are affecting her work behavior), but I do have a basis on which to conjecture. Because outward behavior is caused by inner urges, however, I cannot be sure of my attribution. We cannot even be sure ourselves of what motivates us, and one hears people say things like "I don't know why I feel de-motivated."

Given the difficulties of understanding the inner urges that cause behavior in our own environment, where we do have a common base of values, attitudes, and beliefs, imagine how difficult it is to understand motivation in unfamiliar locations. For example, some African groups believe that rewards should be allocated according to need rather than performance—a person with several dependents should receive more pay than someone with none, even though the person with none works much harder and performs at a much higher level. An American manager might reward the high performer and expect this to be motivating. In the African circumstance, rewarding the high performer would be seen as inequitable and would de-motivate both parties. It would be difficult for the American manager to understand the causes of de-motivation in this situation.

When one works in a foreign environment, one needs to be very careful in attributing motivational causes. It is important to be aware of the variations in culture that can affect motivation. In addition, differences in political systems, history and geography, level of development, and so on, can all affect how people are motivated. In this chapter, we will explore a series of motivational theories that were largely developed and tested in North America, and we will ask the questions "To what extent are they likely to be valid outside of North America?" and "What would affect their relevance in other locations?"

North American Theories of Motivation

The major theories of motivation that we consider here encompass:

- the role of needs in motivation;
- the role of equity in motivation;
- the role of rewards in motivation;
- the role of goals and expectations in motivation; and
- the role of delegation and participation in motivation.

Each of these will be explained briefly from a North American perspective. We will then look at some country variations that might make the North American perspective inappropriate, in order to see whether the various theories can be applied across countries. In other words, we are asking whether the theories apply universally in all countries or whether they are culture bound and apply differentially across countries and cultures. To a large extent the links between country factors and motivation are conceptual rather than empirical.

The Role of Needs in Motivation

Need theories are based on the idea that people have certain needs, and their behaviors are designed to help them fulfill these needs. Simply stated, we act in ways that we believe will result in our needs being met. At a basic level, if someone has a need for food (they are hungry), they will seek a means to satisfy this need (for example, in New York City, they might look for a restaurant). Behavior (looking for a restaurant) thus reflects the need (being hungry).

Perhaps the best known of the need theories is presented in Maslow's *hierarchy of needs* (Maslow 1954). Maslow proposed a hierarchy of needs going from the most basic needs at the bottom of the hierarchy to the highest-level ones at the top. In this model, there are five levels:

1. Most basic: The physiological level deals with survival of the individual and the human race, that is, the need for food, water, shelter, and sex.
2. Next most basic: The security level deals with continued survival, that is, the need for some assurance that food, water, shelter, and sex will be available in the foreseeable future.
3. Mid level: The social level deals with interactions with others, that is, the need for friendships, relationships, and communication with others.
4. Higher level: The esteem level deals with feeling positive about what one does; that is, the need for praise, recognition, and self-esteem.
5. Highest level: The self-actualization level deals with being the best one can be, that is, the need to do things that are important to us, and to accomplish difficult goals that we set for ourselves.

Maslow proposed that each level of need became important, and thus a motivating force, only when the previous level had been satisfied. The basic, physiological needs were paramount until satisfied. Once someone's most basic needs were filled, they would then focus on security. Once security was achieved, social needs would come to the fore. Once social needs were met, esteem would become important, and finally, when the other needs were met, self-actualization would be the motivating force.

If one examines the hierarchy, it is clear that the needs move from concrete to abstract as one goes up the hierarchy. At the basic level, the survival needs can be clearly defined and delineated for all people. At the highest level, the self-actualization needs are unclear and vary from person to person (e.g., one person may aspire to being CEO of his own company and making a billion dollars, where another sees self-actualization as being an ascetic and leading an exemplary spiritual life). The basic physiological needs, as well as the security needs, are likely to be essentially universal—that is, people every-where share these needs, and they will be the dominant motivational force until they are satisfied. So people who do not have enough to eat, whether they are in Arkansas or Zimbabwe, will be motivated primarily by the need to find food and will behave accordingly. There have been several empirical studies of Maslow's hierarchy in countries around the world, and these have suggested that the idea of a hierarchy of needs is universal, but that the order of the hierarchy can vary. As the need categories become more abstract, they also seem to become more culturally and nationally contingent.

Even with the most basic need, there are also cultural variations. For example, in Arkansas the chosen foods may be quite different from those in Zimbabwe. In some locations, certain foods will be prohibited, in others, cooking methods prescribed, and so on. These differences in how basic needs are satisfied may actually, however, be related to higher-order needs. For example, religious customs often dictate what, how, and when we eat.

The order of the needs may also vary. For example, it is possible that in some locations social needs are at the pinnacle because of cultural character-istics. Alternatively, geography may help determine the importance of vari-ous needs. In locations subject to natural disasters, security could be an even more basic need than food and water. The expression of the needs may vary, and the way in which the needs are satisfied may also differ from location to location. As noted above, even at the basic level, food choices vary from country to country and within countries, often for religious reasons. Culture can influence how and when basic needs are satisfied—for example, most cultures have relatively strict rules regarding sex (including when and with whom sex may take place), and these are often tied to religious beliefs. At the higher levels, everyone would agree that culture influences what is meant by esteem or self-actualization; how people choose to meet these needs, as well as their social needs, can vary dramatically. The expression of needs can also vary because of other national characteristics. In communist countries, basic needs are provided for by the government, and if the government can provide for only a limited level of these, people may accept this minimal level as the norm. In the Chinese languages there is no word for *privacy,* so fulfilling social needs would not include this concept. It is also possible that some needs may not be manifested in certain places. Self-actualization, for example, could be inimical to certain religious beliefs because God is the only one able to determine one's fate.

We can agree that people everywhere have needs and that these needs motivate behavior, so in this sense need theories are universal. We should not assume, however, that the importance of these needs is the same everywhere or that people will choose to satisfy their needs in similar ways. Managers can use the concept of needs to help motivate those with whom they work, wherever they are. To do so effectively, however, means that managers need to figure out which needs are most important and how a particular person or group prefers to satisfy them. Political systems, economics, language, religion, history, geography, and culture all have an impact on needs and their importance and satisfaction.

The need theory literature in North America has another side that should be recognized by international managers. Generally, in North America, Maslow's hierarchy is used to illustrate the need to give employees opportunities to meet their higher-level needs on the job in order to motivate them. Providing opportunities for esteem and self-actualization is deemed to be relevant to motivating employees, while their lower-level needs are assumed to have already been adequately met. This may be less the case, however, in other parts of the world. As chapter 6 pointed out, 80 percent of the world's population lives in the developing world. For a substantial portion of these people, basic needs have not been met, and they have little sense of security in the future. In such situations, employees may well be motivated by basic needs, and providing lunch on the job could be more motivating than giving someone more responsibility or making a job more intrinsically interesting.

Another theory based on needs, but without the hierarchy, is McClelland's. McClelland (1967) suggested that different needs manifest themselves more or less strongly in different people. McClelland focused on the needs for achievement, affiliation, and power as being most relevant in the organizational context. These needs have been investigated cross-culturally, and there is some evidence that they may all be important components of motivation, but there is also reason to question this. Hofstede (1980), for example, noted that the achievement construct is peculiar to the English language. In a study of a larger number of needs (but including achievement, affiliation, and power), this author compared China with North America and found that Chinese respondents scored uniformly lower on all the needs measured. The best explanation of these results was that the more important needs from a Chinese perspective were not being captured in the North American framework. In other words, our North American–based theory may well exclude needs that are important in another location. Exhibit 7.1 illustrates the differences in need category scores between two Chinese scores and North American norms (Punnett 1999).

As with the upper-level needs of Maslow's hierarchy, the needs studied by McClelland may be exhibited in a variety of ways and can be satisfied by many means. For example, a high need for achievement means that a person has a drive to do tasks that are difficult and to accomplish objectives that are seen

Exhibit 7.1 **Comparison of U.S. and PRC Scores on Selected Personality Variables**

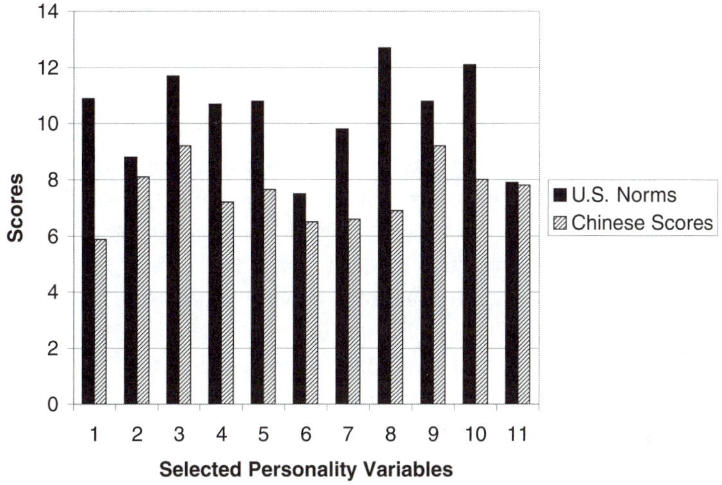

1=Achievement 2=Affiliation 3=Cognitive Structure 4=Dependence 5=Dominance
6=Endurance 7=Exhibition 8=Harm Avoidance 9=Nurturance 10=Social Recognition
11=Succorance

Source: Punnett 1999.

as worthwhile. What is relatively difficult in one location may be somewhat easy in another, and what is considered worthwhile can vary substantially. Thus, even if we accept that people everywhere exhibit a need for achievement, the expression of this need is likely to vary from place to place. For example, in some locations, people value autonomy and will seek to achieve goals on their own. In other locations, structure is valued, and people seek to achieve what their superiors deem important. Historical and geographic factors play an important role in how needs are exhibited and satisfied. In India, achievement often comes by rising in the bureaucracy, which has been perpetuated from the colonial system. This is quite different from the achievement of the Australian working independently in the outback. The two countries share a British colonial heritage, but India had well-developed systems in place when it was colonized, while Australia was largely uninhabited. The intertwining of various forces leads to infinite variations in what we experience around the world.

One can conclude that the general concept of needs is universal and that people everywhere have needs that motivate them. The existence of manifest needs is also likely universal—some needs will be more important to some people and will be manifest in their behavior. International managers have to be alert to which needs seem to be most relevant in different locations, and they also have to be aware of needs that might not be familiar from the home context. Using manifest needs to motivate people is a valid strategy around the world, but figuring out which needs are manifest and how they can be best satisfied requires substantial cross-national and cross-cultural sensitivity.

Herzberg's two factor theory and a lot of subsequent work on intrinsic and extrinsic motivational factors, as well as job design, followed from earlier need theories. Herzberg (1959) argued that there are two sets of factors associated with any job and with a person's motivation relative to the job. One set was intrinsic to the job itself—how interesting, challenging, and rewarding the job was—and these were the factors that motivated a person. The second set was extrinsic to the job—physical conditions, money, supervision, coworkers, and so on—and these had to be met for a person to be satisfied, but they did not actually motivate a person. The absence of extrinsic factors could, however, de-motivate even though their presence did not motivate. These concepts are appealing because they separate what makes us want to do a job from the conditions in which we do it. This theory is also interesting because, in essence, it separates satisfaction from motivation—that is, because someone is satisfied with their working conditions, it does not necessarily mean that they will be motivated to work hard and perform well. The outcome of Herzberg's theory was literature that focused on designing jobs to be intrinsically motivating. Such jobs incorporated variety and autonomy (making one's own decisions) as well as feedback and understanding of the importance of the tasks one performed (often termed *task significance*).

The distinction between intrinsic and extrinsic job aspects may well be universal, and these aspects may have different roles to play in motivation. The relationship to motivation is not necessarily the same around the world, however. Extrinsic factors essentially relate to the lower-order needs on Maslow's hierarchy, and intrinsic factors to the higher-order needs. It has been this author's experience that in poorer countries the extrinsic factors are often valued as motivators more than the intrinsic ones. Workers in these countries often want jobs with little variety and autonomy, and speak of the importance of pay, supervision, working conditions, and other extrinsic factors.

The author worked on a project in a small, developing island country. The project took place at a factory where electronic parts were assembled. Part of the project looked at ways to increase motivation. When asked why they continued to work with the firm, long-time employees said that it was because they could do their particular task with little thought while conversing with their coworker friends, that their supervisor helped them to do their jobs, and that the factory was clean. When asked if rotating jobs would make the work more interesting, the answer was that they preferred to do the job they already knew well. When it was suggested that each person should check his or her own quality, the response was that the quality people knew that aspect and should continue to do their specialized job. Job variety, autonomy, and feedback were essentially seen as being inefficient and would likely have been de-motivating. Job significance did seem to provide a potential motivating tool; employees were most interested to know, and see physical evidence, that the electronic parts they made were used in computers.

The relationship between satisfaction and motivation can also differ from place to place. One can imagine that in some locations a satisfied employee will feel an obligation to work hard and perform well. In other places, it is possible that being satisfied would result in a relaxed attitude, which would affect performance negatively—anecdotes suggest that in the tropics, people work less once they are satisfied. One can conjecture that if employees were dissatisfied, they might be motivated to work hard, feeling that if they performed well, they could change the situation. Alternatively, hard work could take one's mind off one's dissatisfaction, and so on. There are many potential relationships, and, again, the effective international manager needs to be aware that the relationships will not necessarily be the same everywhere.

The Role of Equity in Motivation

Equity refers to the fairness that people perceive in a situation. Basically, equity theory proposes that individuals consider what they put into a given situation relative to what they get out of the situation and then compare this with the inputs and outcomes of some other(s). If the relationships are judged to be fair or equitable, then the person will seek to maintain the current situation. If they are deemed to be unfair or inequitable, the person will seek to change the situation in the future. An example will serve to illustrate these relationships:

If a student works hard in a particular course, goes to classes, and hands in all the assignments (these are her inputs in this situation) and ends up with a grade of "B" (her outcome), she will then compare this input–output ratio to that of others in the class. If the comparison seems fair, she will continue to work hard. If, in contrast, others seem to have done little work but ended up with higher marks, the comparison will seem unfair. In this case the student will try to change some of the inputs or outcomes. It is difficult to change other people's inputs or outcomes, so it is most likely the student will try to change her own inputs or outcomes. The student may ask the professor for a better grade (outcome), but if that does not work, the student may lower her inputs in the future. The impact of a perception of inequity may be to de-motivate the student.

Equity theory stresses the importance of evaluating and rewarding people fairly so that hard work is rewarded equitably. Equitable treatment is thus seen to encourage hard work. At first inspection, it is hard to see how equity translates cross-nationally. An earlier example talked of a group in Africa that believes need should be rewarded over performance. This would certainly seem inequitable in the North American context. In the previous student example, suppose the professor only gave As to those from a certain social class—would this be fair? Certainly not in North America, but conceivably elsewhere, where society respects and values a class system, this could be the norm.

Concepts of equity seem to vary quite a lot depending on location, therefore the North American concepts can be transferred only with careful thought. If one understands what are considered inputs in different locations and what outcomes are valued, it may still be possible to use equity to motivate employees. For example, in a location where the number of dependents is believed to entitle someone to greater rewards, the number of dependents could be considered a valid input; where status because of birth is accepted as giving rights to certain rewards, this may be a normal input.

Interestingly, the author was involved in a major research project in the Caribbean examining absenteeism and its potential causes (Punnett, Greenidge, and Ramsey 2007). Absenteeism may be thought of as, at least partially, absences due to de-motivation. One of the strongest links that this research identified is absences related to perceived inequity and lack of justice.

A challenge arises for international managers when they believe it unethical to consider certain inputs. For example, in some places, men and women doing the same work are paid differentially because women are deemed to be less valuable than men, or because it is believed they need less compensation. Discrimination on the basis of gender, age, race, religion, language, physical ability, sexual preference, and other similar factors is unlawful in North America and Western Europe, but accepted in many other locations. In these situations, deciding what is equitable is very difficult. Foreign managers have to weigh their own beliefs in the context of the local values. If they decide to enforce what they see as nondiscrimination, they need to recognize that they may face negative reactions and will have to manage these.

The Role of Rewards in Motivation

Equity theory incorporates the idea of rewards as a means for motivating employees, assuming the rewards are distributed fairly. More basically, reinforcement theory ties rewards to behavior as a means of encouraging desired behavior and discouraging and eliminating undesired behavior. The idea of reinforcing desired behavior through rewards is that people will repeat behaviors that are rewarded, and behavior that is not rewarded will eventually not be repeated. People often use reinforcement in daily life; for example, mothers promise children ice cream when they finish their homework (and withhold the ice cream if the homework is not completed); pet owners give their dogs treats when they obey commands (and withhold them when they do not). Reinforcement theory does not incorporate ideas of equity; in fact, to encourage a particular person to change behavior, one might reward them in what would seem to be an inequitable manner. Reinforcement theory generally avoids punishment, as punishment is believed to have undesired side effects.

Encouraging desired behavior through the use of rewards is probably effective in a wide variety of locations. Rewards must be desired in order to be motivating, and this means that they should provide a means to satisfy needs. Needs seem to be a universal concept, so reinforcement likely is as well. Reinforcement is also culturally contingent in terms of understanding which rewards will be most effective, when to give rewards, how to give them, and so on.

Consider *what* we use as rewards:

- Typically, in North America, money is considered a valued reward, and increased compensation is used to motivate employees who perform well. In other locations, people work until they have enough money to pay for necessities, and additional compensation means that they are likely to stop working.
- In North America, it is considered appropriate to single out individuals who have done a good job. In Japan and other Eastern countries, singling out is used to indicate that an individual has not been performing up to standard. In North America, there is the expression "the squeaky wheel gets the grease"—meaning that if you stand out, you will be rewarded. The parallel expression in Japan is "the nail that sticks up gets hammered down"—meaning that if you stand out, it will be seen as negative.
- Typically, in North America, coaching—where the positive aspects of work are recognized and suggestions for improvement given—is considered a valuable approach. In India, straightforward criticism is preferred, and people expect to be told that they have made mistakes and to be punished for these mistakes.

Consider *when* we give rewards:

- Some societies believe in giving rewards often and as soon as desired behavior occurs; others see rewards as appropriate only occasionally. North Americans typically believe that rewards should be frequent.
- Some societies set short-term objectives and tie rewards to these; others favor long-term objectives and link rewards only generally to achiev-

ing objectives. North Americans typically focus on short-term, specific objectives and tie rewards to these.
- Some societies give small rewards; others believe in substantial ones. North Americans typically believe that rewards should be substantial.

Consider *how* we give rewards:

- Rewards can be given to individuals or they can be given to groups. North Americans generally favor individual rewards.
- Rewards can be given by a superior, by coworkers, or by subordinates. North American rewards are usually allocated by superiors, sometimes by coworkers.
- Rewards can be given formally or informally, publicly or privately. In North America, rewards are given both formally and informally, almost always in public. (In contrast, where discipline is used, it is usually formal and done in private.)

Exhibit 7.2 summarizes these potential variations. The examples illustrate the importance of cultural understanding in using reinforcement. Reinforcing desired behavior appropriately relies on knowing what, when, and how to give rewards.

In addition, many societies feel that punishment is an important part of motivation. In chapter 2, a model of culture was discussed that included people's belief about basic human nature—that individuals are either changeable or fixed bad/good. The reinforcement theory endorsed by North American theorists focuses on rewards and inherently incorporates a belief that people are changeable. North American reinforcement theory stresses the potential negative impact of punishment, which is suggested only as a last resort. In many societies, the prevalent belief is that if someone behaves in undesirable ways, it is because they are "bad," and that punishment is the only possible way to stop the undesirable behavior. In some Islamic societies the punishment for stealing is amputation of the guilty hand; consequently, theft in these countries is extremely rare, and the idea of rehabilitation is considered essentially ludicrous.

In order to use reinforcement well in cross-national situations, managers need to focus on the local environment and match rewards to local expectations. Reinforcement can be effective, but only when rewards are appropriate from the perspective of those receiving the reinforcement. Where public criticism and discipline are the norm, managers will have to consider carefully how to administer such criticism and discipline, as it can make some managers uncomfortable.

Exhibit 7.2

Potential Variations in Rewards

	North American view	Contrasting view
What	Additional compensation	Just enough compensation
	Single out good performance	Accept good performance
	Coaching	Criticism and punishment
When	Short-term, often	Long-term, occasional
	Related to specific outcomes	Related to general outcomes
	Substantial	Small tokens
How	Individually	Group
	By superior, co-workers	By subordinates
	Formal and informal, public	Only formal, private

The Role of Goals and Expectations in Motivation

Goal Setting

There is substantial evidence that goals help people focus their energies and serve to improve performance. The North American literature on goals has clearly linked specific and challenging goals, once they are accepted, to higher outputs (Locke and Latham 1990). Goal acceptance is often linked to participation in goal setting, and participatively set goals are generally believed to be more effective than assigned goals. Goals on their own appear to stimulate productivity, but they are especially effective when they are linked with desired rewards.

The studies of goal setting cross-nationally indicate that goals are effective under a wide array of national conditions. The author's own work in the Caribbean (Punnett 1986; Punnett, Corbin, and Greenidge 2007) found that specific and difficult goals increased performance significantly compared to asking employees to "do their best." Studies in countries as varied as Australia (Niles 1998), Israel (Erez 1986; Erez and Earley 1987), and Sri Lanka (Niles 1998) have similarly found that goals improved performance. Based on this body of research, it seems that goals may have a universal effect on performance.

We cannot be sure of this, however, as the international research is still relatively limited. There are also national and cultural factors that might mitigate against the usefulness of goals. Using Hofstede's (1980) dimensions, for example:

- A very feminine society might see specific and difficult goals as encouraging competition and regard them negatively.

- A collective society would likely see group goals as appropriate but would not react positively to the individual goals that are typical in North America.
- A society where people avoid uncertainty might find difficult goals stressful because of the fear that the goals could not be achieved.

Other factors could also affect how goals work to improve performance. For example:

- People in postcolonial societies may associate goals with the previous colonial masters and may resent specific and difficult goals.
- People in tropical locations often have a "mañana," "soon come," or "jus' now" approach to life, which implies that immediate desires/needs are more important than plans. This approach could make goal accomplishment difficult.
- People who have a high need for achievement may benefit particularly from reaching a challenging goal, but those with a low need for achievement may see little value in reaching such a goal.
- Where people feel that they have little control over their environment, the idea of setting a specific target may seem foolish at best and possibly thought of as going against God's will.
- In very hierarchical societies, goals would have to be set by those in a position of power, whereas in more egalitarian societies, participative goal setting would be more appropriate.
- Where people have a short-term orientation, immediate goals will be best, with rewards tied closely to performance; where orientations are longer-term, goals projected well into the future may be used.

Overall, goals likely play an important motivational role in a variety of settings. At the same time, as with other motivational approaches, managers will want to experiment with different types of goals to determine what works well in different locations. In particular, there is some evidence that the effectiveness of participation in goal setting varies from culture to culture, as does the nature of appropriate feedback (Audia and Tams 2002).

Expectations

Expectancy theory, as it is usually called, is based on people's expectations about the outcome of their actions. Expectancy theory, simply, proposes that a person looks at a situation and asks:

1. "If I try/work harder (put in a lot of effort) will my performance improve?" (expectancy 1)
2. "If my performance improves, will my rewards increase?" (expectancy 2)
3. "How much do I value these rewards? (valence of rewards)

We can imagine the answers to these questions ranging from zero to one. If the answer is clearly no, one's score would be a zero, if clearly yes, it would be a one, and if in-between, the score would be some fraction to indicate how close to no or yes; for example, a 0.1 is close to no and a 0.9 close to yes. If the answer to any of the three questions is a no, then the person will not put in a great deal of effort. So, if I do not think increased effort will result in increased performance, there is no point in increasing effort. Similarly, if increased performance will not lead to greater rewards, there is no point to increasing efforts. Finally, if I do not value the rewards, there is no point to increasing efforts. Rewards, of course, are not simply extrinsic (pay, time off, and so on), but may be intrinsic as well (the pleasure of doing a good job, a sense of achievement). In expectancy theory, motivation is believed to be a multiplicative relationship; that is, motivation = expectancy 1 × expectancy 2 × valence. The higher (closer to 1) the score, the higher a person's motivation will be, and, conversely, the lower (closer to 0), the less motivated the person will be.

Using expectancy theory to motivate employees in North America entails ensuring that people feel they can perform well if they put in the effort and that they have appropriate goals (this links to goal setting), ensuring that performance is rewarded fairly (this links to equity), and ensuring that rewards are valued (this links to needs and reinforcement). Since expectancy theory incorporates aspects of the other theories, it is considered somewhat holistic.

Expectancy theory as described clearly illustrates a Western, or North American, bias. Expectancy is built around the individual; it integrates individual performance and rewards. Expectancy incorporates rational, linear thinking and control of one's environment; that is, the individual logically evaluates the likelihood of various outcomes and chooses on this basis whether to exert effort or not. It is based on egalitarian beliefs and the sense that individuals have options; thus, the individual is not bound to do what a superior wants or expects, and can seek alternatives rather than accept a situation that is seen as unfair or unpleasant. Individualism, control of one's environment, and rational, linear thinking are all part of the North American cultural context; described thus, expectancy is peculiarly North American.

In many parts of the world, the context is essentially the reverse: the group is more important than any individual, the world is controlled by those in positions of power and by the spirit realm, and people's thinking is circular. Under these conditions, the logic of the expectancy model no longer holds up. It may be appropriate, nevertheless, to use aspects of the expectancy model even in these locations; that is, it seems appropriate, anywhere, to ensure that an employee's increased effort will result in increased performance, that performance is appropriately rewarded, and that rewards are in fact desired. It is particularly relevant to note that one reviewer of this text felt that expectancy theory was the most universal of the theories discussed.

The caveats previously discussed apply here as well: the effective manager needs to understand the cultural and national context and to adapt the how and when of rewards appropriately.

The Role of Delegation and Participation in Motivation

The North American management literature is built around the belief that delegation and participation are important positive aspects of effective management. Managers delegate responsibilities to their subordinates and provide subordinates with the authority necessary to carry out the delegated responsibilities. This is based on the idea that employees want to have responsibility and that they appreciate the implicit trust in their abilities and attitudes that accompanies delegation. Further, delegation is seen as an effective means to develop employees' abilities and decision-making capabilities. In addition, participation in decision making is seen as essential to acceptance of decisions and, consequently, willingness to carry out decisions.

The North American goal-setting literature, for example, suggests that participative goal setting is more effective than assigning goals and that individuals accept responsibility for achieving their own goals. The reinforcement literature similarly incorporates employee involvement in designing appraisal and reward systems. Expectancy and equity implicitly assume delegation. Delegation and participation essentially go hand in hand because effective delegation relies on employees accepting the responsibility that is delegated, and acceptance of responsibility is enhanced by participation in decisions, including decisions regarding delegation. Together, delegation and participation provide a work environment conducive to hard work and good performance. This environment thus contributes to individual motivation.

The universal effectiveness of delegation and participation is not at all clear. Many cultures do not have a tradition of either delegation or participation. In these cultures, it is assumed that the manager's job is to make decisions and the subordinate's job is to receive instructions and carry out those instructions. Further, managers are expected to monitor subordinates closely to ensure that instructions are being carried out properly and to correct subordinates immediately if they deviate.

People from societies that do not have a tradition of delegation and participation believe that managers have the ability to make decisions and that is why they are managers. Equally, they believe subordinates do not have these abilities. Subordinates, therefore, are more comfortable with their managers making decisions and giving instructions. They are uncomfortable if asked to participate in making decisions and take on responsibility beyond the simple performance of assigned tasks. The author's work on goal setting mentioned earlier did not include participation—employees were assigned difficult goals, and this was effective in increasing productivity.

The author's work in the English-speaking Caribbean[1] has included aspects of delegation and participation. In the Caribbean context, it seems that a tradition of nondelegation and nonparticipation makes it difficult for managers and their subordinates to accept and implement delegation and participation. To do so effectively involves changing perceptions, attitudes, and behaviors. At the same time, where managers are willing to delegate and encourage participation, and where subordinates are appropriately trained and coached, it seems to have a positive impact on motivation and performance. Whether the same would hold elsewhere is not clear.

In addition to cultural forces that mitigate against delegation and participation, a variety of other factors need to be considered. For example, historically, colonies have been governed from the homeland, and delegation and participation have been discouraged. In colonies and recently independent countries, people may be reluctant to delegate or accept delegation, and they may be uncomfortable with participative practices. Similarly, in communist countries, decisions tend to be made by the Communist Party leaders, with others accepting these decisions with few questions. Participation from lower levels is not sought for major decisions, and this pattern has become accepted. In organizations the same is likely to be the case.

It is clear that delegation and participation are not currently universally accepted as effective management practices. Managers wishing to experiment with delegation and participation in locations where these are not the norm will need to implement these approaches cautiously and examine the results carefully.

Is Motivation Universal or Culture Bound?

The previous discussion suggests that there are aspects to North American theories of motivation that can be applied in spite of national and cultural differences, and that other aspects are definitely affected by culture as well as other national characteristics. Many of the theories apply at a "global" level; that is, the big picture is probably universal. People everywhere have needs, people probably seek some kind of equity, people react to rewards, they work toward goals and have expectations about performance. The details of all the theories, the how and the when of implementing them, are likely to be culturally bound and will have to change cross-nationally. Rewards are an integral part of all the theories of motivation discussed. They provide a good illustration of the need to change the "how and when" of motivation. Consider the following:

- Some groups consider additional pay a valuable reward;
- Some groups work to get just enough for basic necessities;
- Some people want rewards closely tied to individual performance;
- Some people want rewards based on overall group performance;
- Some groups tie rewards to outcomes;
- Some groups tie rewards to behaviors;
- Some nationalities have long-time horizons, and rewards are related to long-term performance; and
- Some nationalities have short-time horizons and rewards are frequent and immediate.

One can conclude that when managers move cross-nationally they face challenges in motivating employees. Effective managers will be sensitive to the cultural and national context that is likely to affect employee motivation. Good managers will try a variety of approaches to motivate their employees and will watch the results closely to find those that work best.

Smith, Peterson, and Schwartz's (2002) work, in conjunction with local researchers in a variety of countries, provides some information that can be helpful in assessing motivation in different cultural situations. The following discussion is based on their findings regarding the sources that people use to guide decision making and behavior in forty-seven countries around the world.

They found that:

• Nations that used participatively oriented guidance sources were those characterized by high individualism as well as autonomy, egalitarianism, low power distance, harmony, and femininity. These values are most typical in the nations of Western Europe. Nations that relied on superiors and rules were those that were collective as well as high on embeddedness, hierarchy, power distance, mastery, and masculinity. Most of the nations of Africa fit this profile. High power distance and mastery were also related to reliance on hierarchical sources. The authors comment that the cultural contrast between hierarchy and participation can be enriched by understanding this fuller range of value dimensions.

• Reliance on "beliefs that are widespread in my nation as to what is right" was one of the least frequently reported of the eight sources of guidance, and variance across nations in scores on this measure was greater than it was for the other indices. Widespread beliefs were important in nations such as China, Bulgaria, and Romania, but were discounted in others, particularly Hungary and Portugal. The authors note that these nations had all relatively recently experienced a prolonged period of state enterprise, with the latter group having moved away from this pattern more rapidly than the former group. The measure of conservatism was related to embeddedness and power distance. Conservatism proved the stronger predictor of reliance on widespread beliefs. Smith, Peterson, and Schwartz (2002) showed that items related to this dimension reflected endorsement of paternalism, and it may be that acceptance or rejection of this aspect differentiates the nations scoring particularly high or low from other nations that have much state enterprise.

• Reliance on unwritten rules was related to Smith, Peterson, and Wang's (1996) loyal involvement (based on Trompenaars and Hampden-Turner's 1998 data). The authors indicated that the items that were most closely linked to loyal involvement refer to loyalty to one's work team and to one's organization, rather than making any specific reference to one's superiors. These values thus appear to tap a generalized endorsement of commitment to the organization, as contrasted with an individualistic calculation of one's own benefits. Unwritten rules will be important in organizations where informal agreements have emerged from long-established interactions between organization members. They express a local wisdom distilled from continuing dialogue among those who have worked together undisturbed for a long time. In this context, reference to superiors would be unnecessary because there would be a shared understanding of what is desirable. Loyal involvement involves a substantial commitment to one's organization. In nations scoring highest on reliance on unwritten rules (Israel, Korea, and the Philippines), where more collective values prevail, commitment is likely to be more contextualized and less calculative.

• Reliance on specialists varied across nations, in terms of the types of specialists likely to be used and in terms of the financial resources available for their services. Similar to reliance on unwritten rules, the Trompenaars dimension contrasting utilitarian with loyal involvement provided the strongest predictor of reliance on specialists. The questionnaire described specialists as "outside my department," thereby giving some suggestion as to the affiliation of the specialist in question. The results suggest that outsiders are mostly likely to be hired where utilitarian values prevail.

The authors caution that the eight sources of guidance selected for their study were those that are driven by the basic nature of formal organizations, and that these organizations may be a Western innovation that has spread globally. Studying these organizations, rather than primary groups such as families, as economic units reflects a Western bias. Formal organizations cover only a modest proportion of the economic process in many countries. Family members would probably have proved an important source of guidance in some countries, as other groups, such as trade unions might have in others.

Summary and Conclusions

Motivation is complex and difficult to understand even within familiar settings. It is thus especially tricky to motivate people in unfamiliar contexts. In this chapter a variety of familiar North American motivational approaches have been explored against the background of national/cultural variations. It seems that some aspects of motivation may be universal, while others are clearly culture bound. Managers can use the broad concepts of motivation—needs, equity, expectancy, and so on—as a base for understanding motivation cross-culturally. They will find that the details of how these broad concepts apply are likely to differ from place to place.

Motivation itself remains a critical aspect of management no matter where one is. Managers everywhere need to find ways to ensure that employees work hard and perform at peak levels. Especially in today's globally competitive environment, maximum performance can give a firm its competitive edge. Taking the time and making the effort to understand motivation is, thus, central to effective international management.

Note

1. The author has worked on research relating culture to effective management in the English-speaking Caribbean. This research was partially funded by the Ford Foundation and the University of the West Indies.

References

Audia, P.G., and S. Tams. 2002. "Goal Setting, Performance Appraisal, and Feedback Across Cultures." In *Handbook of Cross-Cultural Management*, ed. M.J. Gannon and K.L. Newman, 142–154. London: Blackwell.
Erez, M. 1986. "The Congruence of Goal-setting Strategies with Sociocultural Values and Its Effects on Performance." *Journal of Management* 12: 83–90.
Erez, M., and P.C. Earley. 1987. "Comparative Analysis of Goal-setting Strategies Across Cultures." *Journal of Applied Psychology* 72(4): 658–665.
Herzberg, F. 1959. *The Motivation to Work*. New York: John Wiley.

Hofstede, G. 1980. *Culture's Consequences: International Differences in Work Related Values.* Beverly Hills, CA: Sage.

Locke, E.A., and G.P. Latham. 1990. *A Theory of Goal Setting and Task Performance.* Englewood Cliffs, NJ: Prentice-Hall.

Maslow, A.H. 1954. *Motivation and Personality.* New York: Harper.

McClelland, D.C. 1967. *The Achieving Society.* New York: Free Press.

Niles, F.S. 1998. "Achievement Goals and Means: A Cultural Comparison." *Journal of Cross-Cultural Psychology* 29(5): 656–667.

Punnett, B.J. 1986. "Goal-setting: An Extension of the Research." *Journal of Applied Psychology* (February): 171–172.

———. 1999. "The Impact of Individual Needs on Work Behavior: China and North America." *Journal of Asia-Pacific Business* 2(3): 23–44.

Punnett, B.J., E. Corbin, and D. Greenidge. 2007. "Assigned Goals and Task Performance in a Caribbean Context: Extending Management Research to an Emerging Economy." *International Journal of Emerging Markets* 2(3): 215–235.

Punnett, B.J., D. Greenidge, and J. Ramsey. 2007. "Job Attitudes and Absenteeism: A Study in the English speaking Caribbean." *Journal of World Business* 42(2): 214–227.

Smith, P.B., M.F. Peterson, and Z.M. Wang. 1996. "The Manager as Mediator of Alternative Meanings." *Journal of International Business Studies* 27, 115–137.

Smith, P.B., M.F. Peterson, S.H. Schwartz. 2002. (With Abd Halim Ahmad, Debo Akande, Vladimir Anchuk, Jon Aarum Andersen, Sabino Ayestaran, Stephen Bochner, Victor Callan, Carlos Davila, Bjorn Ekelund, Pierre-Henri François, Gert Graversen, Charles Harb, Jorge Jesuino, Aristotle Kantas, Lyudmila Karamushka, Paul Koopman, Pavla Kruzela, Kwok Leung, Sigmar Malvezzi, Andrew Mogaji, Shahrenaz Mortazavi, John Munene, Ken Parry, Betty Jane Punnett, Mark Radford, Arja Ropo, Jose Saiz, Grant Savage, Bernadette Setiadi, Ritch Sorenson, Erna Szabo, Punyacha Teparakul, Aqeel Tirmizi, Sevda Tsvetanova, Conrad Viedge, and Carolyn Wall). "Cultural Values, Sources of Guidance and Their Relevance to Managerial Behavior." *Journal of Cross-Cultural Psychology* 33(2) (March): 188–208.

Trompenaars, F., and C. Hampden-Turner. 1998. *Riding the Waves of Culture: Understanding Diversity in Global Business.* 2nd ed. New York: McGraw-Hill.

8

Leadership in a Cross-National Context

Introduction

Leadership, broadly defined, is the ability to get others to behave as the leader wishes them to behave. Leadership is thus a key component of all organizations. Organizational functioning depends on people within the organization working toward goals that benefit the organization as a whole. There are many processes and structures that enhance organizational functioning, but in the final analysis, organizations succeed or fail because of leadership, and they cannot function well without effective leaders. This does not mean that all good leaders will be visible in their capacity as leaders. Leadership means different things in different situations, and sometimes the most effective leader is one who appears not to lead in any active sense.

Being an effective leader is difficult even in a familiar environment. The challenge of getting leadership right is multiplied many times in unfamiliar environments. Appropriate leadership is influenced by a variety of factors, especially those discussed in earlier chapters: culture, politics, religion, history, geography, and so on. The successful leader takes all of these into account and adapts her/his leadership style accordingly. In this chapter, we will explore various theories of leadership that are commonly accepted in North America and ask if and how these can be transferred to other locations. In addition we will examine some non–North American beliefs about effective leadership, as well as what we know about cross-cultural leadership characteristics.

Leadership is a function of the person who acts as leader to a group of followers, as well as a function of the position or role that a person occupies. For example, a group of people may meet to decide where to go on vacation, and no one is assigned or appointed as leader of the group. Nevertheless, a leader or leaders may emerge and take on the role of ensuring that the decision is made in a timely manner and within the appropriate parameters. Similarly, in organizations, leaders may emerge even though they do not hold leadership positions. These can be leaders who encourage others to perform at a certain level, or they can be leaders who are more concerned with social issues and ensuring that the group functions harmoniously. Leadership can also be associated with negative organizational outcomes, for example, a slowdown in production or a conflict between certain groups.

Leadership is often associated with particular positions; for example, the head of an academic department in a university is expected to provide leadership for the department; the chief executive of a firm is the leader for the firm. As one examines the nature of leadership, one needs to keep these dual aspects of leadership in mind.

Many authors differentiate between leadership and management. Clearly the two concepts are different, and the roles of manager and leader can be separated. Managers are responsible for the running of a unit (department, function, organization, and so on), so they do the necessary planning for their unit, ensure that an organization structure is in place, that the resources are available to achieve plans, and monitor performance and take corrective action to reach desired goals (the traditional management model identifies planning, organizing, staffing, directing, and controlling as the activities of management). Leadership is more than management, however, as it incorporates developing a shared vision throughout a group and stimulating others to behave in desired ways. While the differences between management and leadership are valid and important, many writers also use the terms largely interchangeably. In this chapter, although the focus is on leadership rather than management, we will often refer to leadership in the context of management and as a function that managers seek to perform along with their other activities.

Theories of Leadership

Leadership has been studied throughout history (often from the viewpoint of state or military leadership). Discussions of the practice and philosophy of leadership can be found in a range of early writing from Homer's *Iliad* to the Old Testament and the essays of Confucius in China. Much of these early discussions, including those relating to the state or the military, have been incorporated into the literature on leadership in an organizational setting. Unfortunately for international managers, much of the existing English-language literature on leadership in an organizational setting is based on Western theories and practices of leadership. This base needs to be kept in mind in the following discussion of leadership theories:

1. Organizational researchers, in the early parts of the twentieth century, looked at leadership from a *trait* perspective; that is, they sought to identify

personal traits or characteristics that could generally be associated with effective leaders. Both physical traits (e.g., height or attractiveness) and psychological traits (e.g., intelligence or emotional stability) were investigated by researchers, but no consistent relationship between traits and good leadership were identified. Today, people seldom consider traits of this kind in Western leadership studies, but we have little evidence from non-Western societies regarding the role of physical or psychological traits in leadership effectiveness. It is possible that certain traits may be relevant in some societies. For example, people refer to the "bearing" (height, stance, and so on) of Nelson Mandela as marking him as a leader even after many years of imprisonment. It is equally likely that certain traits may be considered inappropriate in some locations. For example, if leaders have traditionally come from a tribe, or other group, that is relatively short, then tall people might be frowned on in leadership roles.

While Western research linking traits to effective leadership has not been very helpful in identifying and predicting successful leaders, we must recognize that there are biases in the world that make certain traits salient in spite of this. In many parts of the world, formal leadership revolves around males; in others, status or caste is a prerequisite for leadership; in still others, race or ethnicity determines leadership eligibility. In Africa, for example, there seem to be two streams of findings: one is the powerful leader, who uses his place at the top of the hierarchy to accomplish his objectives; the other is the communal, servant leader, who sees his role as leading for the good of others. Some readers may wish this were not the case, but it is the reality in many parts of the world and therefore cannot be ignored. International managers need to be aware of these preferences or dislikes because they are required to work within the systems that exist in different parts of the world.

Imagine a manager who has always lived and worked in a country where women are not permitted to work for economic returns (they may carry out such work as raising crops, teaching children, caring for the sick, and so on). If this manager is assigned to work in Canada, he will find working with women difficult. Associating closely with female colleagues will make him uncomfortable. It will be difficult for this manager to accept female colleagues as equals or to report to a female superior. Nevertheless, this manager will have to adjust to the Canadian norms because he will be required to work within a system that strives to treat males and females relatively equally. Similarly, in the reverse situation, a Canadian manager will find it uncomfortable to work in a country where women are not in the visible workforce, and it may be impossible for a female manager from Canada to undertake an assignment in this country.

2. Leadership research in the mid-twentieth century focused on leadership *style*. The prevalent dichotomy was between a task-oriented style and a

people-oriented style. In Herzberg's (1968) well-known characterization, the task-oriented style was termed *theory x,* while the people-oriented style was termed *theory y.* Herzberg argued that most managers were *theory x* managers who believed that people did not want to work and worked only for economic rewards, thus subordinates could not be trusted or given responsibility; managers focused on the task to be performed and provided discipline if performance was not forthcoming. In contrast, Herzberg believed that people want to work and would respond favorably to responsibility if they were trusted. He argued that *theory y* managers, who recognized this and paid attention to people issues, would have satisfied employees who would perform at higher levels. Current research has moved beyond this simple *theory x/theory y* paradigm, but the concept is still relevant for today's managers. Many people still describe managers as falling into these two broad categories. More importantly, from an international perspective, many countries seem to favor the *theory x* approach, while others favor the *theory y* approach. Leadership and management are clearly more complex in reality, but this division may provide a simple initial way to categorize leadership and management in different locations.

A *theory x* management style (i.e., a style that focuses on the task, includes close supervision, provides task-related payments, and enforces discipline for infractions) will likely be effective so long as employees, as well as managers, favor this approach. A *theory y* management style (i.e., a style that focuses on people and their satisfaction, delegates responsibility and authority, and encourages performance through rewards) will be most effective when employees are willing to accept responsibility and authority, and managers are comfortable with this approach. Challenges and problems arise when the management style is incongruent with the employees' preferences, as described in the following two scenarios:

> A Canadian consultant was engaged to carry out a series of training programs in India for academics that wished to be able to undertake management consulting assignments. The programs were well received, but some of the Indian participants expressed a wish for harsher discipline. The Canadian normally focused his comments on how participants could improve performance, but some participants expressed a wish that he focus on what they had done wrong. The Canadian was concerned with ensuring that the participants felt good about their experience in the training sessions and believed that focusing on improvement was the best approach. Some of the participants believed that more direct criticism of their performance was needed. To some extent, the Canadian style can be seen as reflecting a *theory y* approach, while the participants were expecting more *theory x.*
>
> In the Caribbean, it may be that employees prefer a *theory y* approach (this is supported by the author's research, which indicates a relatively low

level of power distance in the English-speaking Caribbean). Yet the colonial and plantation heritage in the Caribbean has resulted in a top-down, directive management style that is more *theory x* in nature. The consequence of this mismatch is workers who are often uninterested and unproductive and who essentially "won't work."

The lesson, internationally, is that we cannot assume that one style or another is "the best" in some sense. This, of course, is also the case within a given country, and research has recognized this by developing leadership theories known as contingency theories.

3. *Contingency* leadership theories recognize that the best leadership style depends on the situation. These theories suggest that there is no one best approach, but that aspects of the environment, as well as the nature of the leader and followers, need to be taken into account to determine the most effective leadership approach. North American contingency theories initially focused on the task/people dimensions.

Early contingency researchers (e.g., Fiedler 1967) pointed out that there are situations where task orientation is required; for example, where urgent action is needed (say in a fire), where subordinates do not have much experience, or where superior–subordinate interactions are not very friendly. In other situations, a people or relationship orientation is more appropriate; for example, where time is available for developmental activities, where subordinates are familiar with the task, and where superior–subordinate interactions are cordial. These theories essentially treated leadership style as either task-oriented or people-oriented. A further development in the field was the realization that leaders could be both task-oriented and people-oriented at the same time. The model in Exhibit 8.1 is based on one proposed by Hershey and Blanchard (1969) and Blake and Mouton (1964). Each of the four styles portrayed in the model can be effective depending on the situation, and good leaders vary their choice of style to suit the situation. Aspects of the situation that affect choice of style include characteristics of the leader, characteristics of the followers, the nature of the task, the culture of the group, and so on.

In one discussion of the model, in order to illustrate how leadership style should vary, Hershey and Blanchard related these styles to a subordinate's stage of maturity at work and argued that:

- new employees need a leader who is task oriented to help them succeed with their new job (bottom right: high task/low people);
- as employees mature, they need continued task orientation combined with a people orientation to develop work-group relationships (top right: high on both);

Exhibit 8.1   **People/Task Orientation**

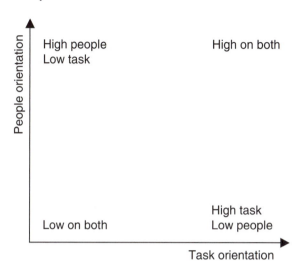

- employees who are familiar with their jobs no longer need a task orientation but continue to need a people orientation for personal development,
  career progress, and so on (top left: high people/low task); and
- finally, employees who are thoroughly familiar with their job and the
  organization need little support in terms of task or people/relationships
  and prefer a leader who leaves them essentially on their own (bottom
  left: low on both).

According to Dorfman (2004), studies done in different parts of the
world suggest that considerate, supportive leaders are generally preferred
throughout, but reactions to task orientation are more complex. Interestingly, Dorfman (2004) reports that managers from all countries espoused
democratic and participatory styles, but they also had a low opinion of
their subordinates' ability to take initiative. These concepts are especially
helpful internationally, because they encourage people to think about the
varied contextual factors that influence the leadership style that is effective
in different situations. Different styles work in different environments; this
means that in another country, it is very likely that you cannot rely on what
you might consider an effective style at home. Understanding cultural, political, historical, and other environmental factors, as well as their impact on
effective leadership, is key to managing and leadership around the world.
There is relatively little specific research information on different countries
and the appropriate leadership in each of these environments; therefore, the

challenge for international managers is to observe diverse environments and identify what seems to work in each one.

4. *Participation* is also an important component of superior–subordinate relationships. Managers who are task oriented are sometimes described as autocratic, those who are people oriented as democratic. Democratic leaders, however, are not just people oriented, rather they are leaders who involve their subordinates in making decisions. In the West it has been argued that people are more committed to decisions when they have participated in making those decisions, thus participation in decision making is often promoted as a positive aspect of leadership. Of course, even in the West, participation has its limitations. For example, subordinates can only participate effectively if they have the ability and the desire to do so, and subordinates may be interested in participating when they believe a decision will directly affect their work/life.

One can picture a range of decision-making styles from autocratic (decisions made by the leader) to democratic (made by the leader and subordinates together) with various levels of subordinate input in between. The appropriate choice would then depend on the situation—the time available, the leader's expertise and experience, the subordinates' expertise and experience, the importance of the decision, the need for subordinates' commitment, and so on. Vroom and Yetton (1973) developed a decision tree that allowed managers to select among different decision-making styles based on aspects of a situation. The styles ranged from the leader's making the decision to the decision made by leader and subordinates together, with equal input from all. The variables included in the decision tree are the requirement for quality, the importance of subordinate commitment to the decision, the likelihood of subordinate commitment, the manager's information base, the structure of the problem, the degree to which goals are shared, and the likelihood of conflict among subordinates. For example, a very participative style is suggested if quality requirements are low, commitment requirements high, and participation is likely to increase commitment. In a similar situation, where participation is not likely to increase commitment, a more autocratic style is suggested.

Just as various levels of participation are appropriate according to the characteristics of the situation, one can imagine that in different societies the levels of participation that are expected and accepted would vary. If participation in decision making is the norm, then a very autocratic leader is likely to be resented. In contrast, where participation is not the norm, an autocratic leader will be accepted and a democratic one would be resented. For example, in the movie *Going International,* there is a scene in which a manager from the UK, working in India, attempts unsuccessfully to get his Indian subordinate to take responsibility for making a decision. The UK manager is frustrated by his subordinate's unwillingness to do so, and the Indian subordinate comments that it is the manager's job to make decisions (that's why he is a manager, and that's what he gets paid for) and does not understand why the manager wants him, his subordinate, to do the manager's job.

Colin Morrison, president of Business Fit International, gave the following account of a situation that illustrates how leadership styles need to vary (Punnett and Greenidge 2009): In the facilitation of a national program in St. Lucia, the leadership practice developed was congruent with a top-down, hierarchical leadership system with little information sharing or empowerment of subordinates. This style emerged in spite of efforts on the part of the consultants to flatten the hierarchy and share the power. It appeared that leaders and subordinates supported and felt more comfortable with the clearly defined hierarchy. A significant factor was the personality of the manager, which made the style more palatable for everyone. This comfort is not present with a Caribbean manager and her team in my Canadian company. In St. Lucia, this style worked because it was accepted. In Canada, it is not working, and tricksters continually try to undermine the manager's authority. The more this happens, the less she trusts them, and her dictatorial stance increases accordingly. We are currently initiating training and mentoring for this manager and team. The concepts in this chapter will be helpful in increasing the manager's understanding of the issues and their origins, and we are hopeful they will point the way to a successful shift in style.

Perhaps cross-national decision trees can be developed to identify, based on national characteristics, the appropriate degree of participation in a given situation. Such an approach has not currently been developed, but it could be a helpful way for managers to think about the question of how best to make decisions.

Both autocratic and democratic leaders play an active leadership role and are intimately involved in the decision-making process. A third possibility has also been suggested—that of a laissez-faire leader, one who does not appear to be actively involved. On the surface, one might feel that such an approach is tantamount to abdication of the leadership role. There are, however, situations where this may be the most appropriate approach. Consider a group of highly skilled and motivated scientists working to find a cure for a major disease. This group likely wants simply to be left alone to get on with their work. A good leader for such a group is one who ensures that needed resources are in place and stands ready to provide guidance or act as intermediary if this becomes necessary. In some cultures this approach, under the right circumstances, would be readily accepted; in others, it may be less acceptable.

Leadership is clearly more than a choice between a focus on task or a focus on people and relationships, or a matter of autocracy and democracy.

Additional leadership models and theories have been developed to explain why some leaders are more effective than others. Some other models are described below.

Supports/Substitutes for Leadership

Although the initial paragraphs of this chapter state that there are no substitutes for leadership, there are various systems and procedures that support the leadership process, and in certain circumstances they do substitute for leadership. For example, a substantial part of an organization's activities are carried out because there are rules and regulations, policies and procedures; in addition, there are self-managed teams, quality circles, and highly motivated individuals who ensure that an organization reaches its goals. All of these, to some extent, can be thought of as substitutes for leadership. They do not truly substitute for leadership, however, because leadership is needed to put these into place and to go beyond them. I prefer to think of these as supports for leadership. Various leadership supports are likely important around the world, but the nature of these supports, and how and when they are used, may differ from place to place. For example:

• In some countries, job descriptions are extensive and detailed, giving step-by-step and hour-by-hour explanations of what an employee needs to do. Job descriptions of this kind can be seen as ensuring that the everyday work of the organization gets accomplished without managers/leaders having to be actively concerned with routine activities. In other countries, job descriptions may not exist, and where they do, they are general explanations of the work to be performed. This may be seen as giving employees the flexibility to accomplish the work that needs to be done. In this situation, managers/leaders may have to be at least somewhat involved in monitoring routine activities.

• In some locations, decisions are based on rules, policies, and procedures. People in these societies refer to "the book" and are very uncomfortable with decisions that ignore or contravene the rules. Managers/leaders are expected to enforce the rules and to follow them as well. In other locations, policies are seen as general guidelines, and specific decisions are made based on what seems appropriate in any given circumstance. In these locations, managers/leaders are expected to interpret the rules.

As reported in the earlier chapter on culture, the author conducted a cross-cultural workshop in Barbados in an organization that included local, long-serving Barbadians and expatriate newcomers from the UK. She presented some empirical evidence (Peterson, Smith, and Schwartz 2002), suggesting that Barbadians made decisions based on rules, while people from the UK made decisions based on personal experience. The participants found this information especially relevant to their situation—the Barbadians had complained that their UK counterparts wouldn't "follow the rules," while the UK expatriates had complained that the Barbadians wouldn't "do what was needed." Clearly each group had a different perspective on how to make decisions.

Some organizations have clearly defined structures and reporting relationships, and these determine who makes what kind of decisions. Other organizations are loosely structured, with similar decisions being made at a variety of levels in the organization. Managers/leaders in the first type of organization need to be clearly aware of their role and which decisions they are responsible for making. In the second type, managers/leaders have more flexibility, but they also need to be more in touch with the decisions that are being made by others.

These examples illustrate how supports for leadership can differ using traditional Western concepts of organization. Organizations that originate from non-Western locations have different support mechanisms. For example, in many developing countries, organizations are family-owned and employ family members in key positions. These family members are often employed not because of their expertise or experience, but because they can be trusted to look out for the family's interests. In the West, employing family members is often depicted negatively as nepotism or favoritism, but in other societies, it is considered the safe, prudent way to ensure the best for the organization. The manager's challenge is to figure out and evaluate varying support mechanisms in order to decide how to use supports effectively.

Charismatic and Transformational Leadership and the GLOBE Project

Some leaders seem to have an innate ability to attract followers, which we call charisma. Some leaders also seem to have the ability to go beyond sustaining the normal functioning of a company to transforming it and enabling it to operate at new levels. Both charismatic and transformational leadership received substantial attention in the late-twentieth-century literature. There seems to be a general consensus around the world that some people possess charisma that attracts others to them and encourages their followers to behave as the leader wants. Similarly, there seem to be leaders in all locations who can go beyond operational activities, or even strategic ones, and actually engage their followers to transform organizations.

Charismatic and transformational leadership seems to be a universal concept, and such leaders are found around the world, but what makes someone charismatic or transformational is not clear. More importantly, from an international manager's perspective, characteristics of charismatic and transformational leadership are likely to differ from place to place. For example, Mahatma Gandhi and Adolf Hitler (the former seen positively and the latter negatively) are both considered charismatic leaders, yet they represent totally opposing worldviews and approaches to society.

It is also important to recognize that charismatic or transformational leadership is not necessarily good, in a moral sense. State leaders such as Ghengis Khan, Adolf Hitler, and, more recently, Saddam Hussein might be described as charismatic or transformational, but they would be reviled by most students of moral good. Adler (1991) noted that in Germany, because of Hitler, the idea of charisma in leaders has a negative, rather than positive, connotation. Further, in the early twenty-first century, organizational collapses of corporations such as WorldCom and Enron reminded the world that charismatic and transformational leaders are not always good leaders.

A major worldwide leadership project (the GLOBE study, whose acronym stands for Global Leadership and Organizational Behavior Effectiveness) undertaken by House (1971), with a large number of co-researchers, provides some evidence that the charismatic and transformational concepts are valid ones around the world (Dorfman 2004). The research, which is still in progress, suggests that leadership is more than an exchange of rewards for effort. Effective leaders share a sense of purpose with their subordinates that embodies charisma and transformation, and this results in superior performance. Although the concepts may be valid worldwide, they may still be expressed quite differently. Mother Teresa in India was certainly both charismatic and transformational but in an entirely different way from the former, rather flamboyant, Canadian prime minister Pierre Trudeau, who has also been described as charismatic and transformational.

The GLOBE project is a landmark study of leadership internationally. The resulting book, *Culture, Leadership, and Organizations—The GLOBE Study of 62 Societies* (House et al. 2004), is an extensive discussion of leadership around the world and how leadership is influenced by culture. This project identified six leadership dimensions, described as (Dorfman, Hanges, and Brodbeck 2004):

1. Charismatic/Value-Based—reflects the ability to inspire, motivate, and expect high performance from others based on core values (subscales identified were visionary, inspirational, self-sacrifice, decisive, performance oriented)
2. Team Oriented—reflects emphasis on team building and common purpose (subscales identified were collaborative team orientation, team integrator, diplomatic, not malevolent, administratively competent)

3. Participative—reflects involvement of others in making and implementing decisions (subscales identified were nonautocratic and participative)
4. Humane Oriented—reflects support and consideration, including compassion and generosity (subscales identified were modesty and humaneness)
5. Autonomous—reflects independent and individualistic approaches (subscale identified was autonomous)
6. Self-Protective—reflects a focus on the safety and security of the individual (subscales identified were self-centered, status conscious, conflict inducer, face saver, procedural).

The researchers report that the visionary and inspirational leadership dimensions that were critical aspects of Charismatic/Value-Based leadership were universally endorsed as contributing to effective leadership. In contrast, the self-sacrificing dimension was not universally endorsed. The team-oriented dimension was also considered important. They conclude "the portrait of a leader who is universally viewed as effective is clear: the person should possess the highest levels of integrity and engage in Charismatic/Value-Based behaviors while building effective teams" (Dorfman, Hanges, and Brodbeck 2004, 678). On the other side, the criteria universally perceived to inhibit effective leadership related to the dimensions labeled as self-protective and malevolent.

Other dimensions of leadership were found to be culturally contingent. For example, the authors reported that individualistic scores ranged from "somewhat inhibits" to "slightly contributes" to effective leadership (1.67 to 5.10), status conscious ranged from somewhat inhibits to moderately contributes (1.92 to 5.77), and risk taker ranged from somewhat inhibits to contributes somewhat (2.14 to 5.96).

The GLOBE project clearly indicates that there are universal aspects to effective leadership, as well as culturally contingent aspects. The challenge for the international manager is to emulate the globally effective style, while adapting in those areas that are culturally contingent.

Path/Goal Clarification

An integral aspect of leadership and organizational accomplishment is facilitating organizational members' attainment of goals. Models and theories that deal with this aspect of leadership stress the importance of a leader clarifying goals for followers and ensuring that followers understand the path, that is, how they can achieve these goals. Path/goal clarification is likely important in many cultures, but there are also aspects that seem peculiarly Western. For example, the concept of setting specific goals and working to achieve them relies on Western ideas of control of the environment and a causal relationship between a person's activities and the outcomes. Some cultures believe that outside forces control events, and they do not see a necessary relationship between an individual's actions and outcomes—in such a society, path/goal clarification may not work or may work in a completely different way than we envisage in the West. People in these cultures may perform better with vague directions (goals) and a general sense of how to get there rather than the specific approach identified in Western literature.

It seems likely that people everywhere need a sense of what they want to accomplish (goal) and how they can reach this goal (path), but the types of goals that will be acceptable, the specificity of these goals, and the means for accomplishing goals may well differ from location to location. We can speculate that in some locations, employees will prefer goals that incorporate specific objectives (e.g., "complete x sales by y date") and in others, employees will prefer more general objectives (e.g., "increase sales"). An effective leader needs to identify which goals are most likely to be attainable in a particular environment and which paths will work in that same environment.

This discussion has given a basic overview of the leadership research in North America in the twentieth century. It has also outlined some issues regarding whether and how these theories may apply elsewhere. Much of this discussion is in effect conjecture, because there is relatively little empirical information available to English speakers on non-Western societies. In the following discussion, we look briefly at some non-Western conceptualizations of leadership.

Variation in Leadership Concepts

A fundamental issue in any discussion of leadership is the relative importance of leaders. Leadership in the North American context has a positive connotation; that is, having the quality of a leader is considered a desirable characteristic. Dorfman (2004) explains that this view of leadership is not universal. Europeans are less positive about leadership, and in some countries, such as Holland, people believe that leadership should be downplayed. In Japan, CEOs of large, successful corporations credit subordinates with organizational accomplishments and deemphasize their own roles. The author found that, in China, leaders played a pivotal role, as the following examples illustrates:

During the 1989 student demonstrations in China, which eventually resulted in the deaths of a substantial number of students at Tiananmen Square, I was teaching at the Huashong University of Science and Technology in Wuhan, Hubei Province. The students on my campus were well aware of the general student unrest throughout the country, and there was a sense of excitement as demonstrations started on the campus. These demonstrations were initially rather small and sporadic. I talked to my students about the situation, and their responses were supportive of the "democracy movement," but they had not yet actively joined the demonstrations. After some time, as the demonstrations were growing, I was in conversation with a group of students and asked, "Are you going to join the demonstrators?" In typical Western fashion, I expected that some students would say "yes," some "maybe," and possibly some would say "no." The answer I got was, of course, typically Chinese: "We wait to see what our leaders say." As I sought to understand the situation better, I learned that each unit (e.g., the students studying business) had designated leaders, and these leaders made the decision regarding the unit's joining or not joining the demonstrations and student strike. Two days later, I went to class and was politely informed by the students that there would be no class because "our leaders have decided to join the student strike." I had a test to return, and I offered to informally sit in the class so that students could come and get their graded tests; I was again politely told "our leaders have decided to join the strike. There will be no class."

These examples clearly indicate that not only does leadership style vary, but that the fundamental view of what leadership is, and its importance, varies among cultures. In the following discussion, we consider some research that looks at specific locations.

In the 1980s, there was a substantial interest in Japanese management practices, and these practices have been studied and described in some detail. Many researchers identified the Japanese national and cultural environment as substantially different from that of the United States, and Japanese management practices were found to be very different as well. In broad terms, the following contrasts were identified (Punnett and Jain 1989):

Japan	United States
Generalists	Specialists
Lifetime employment	Frequent job changes
Job rotation	Upward mobility
Promote from within	Fill from outside
Promote based on seniority	Promote based on performance
Group orientation	Individual orientation
Cooperation	Competition
Long-term perspective	Short-term perspective
Emphasis on personal matters	Emphasis on task and performance
Emphasis on status	Emphasis on profits

These differences suggest different leadership styles. A Japanese leader will be more concerned with the well-being of his subordinates and will seek to help them develop gradually. A U.S. leader will focus on individual productivity and seek to identify high performers to promote. A Japanese leader will take a holistic, long-term view of the organization's progress. A U.S. leader will likely focus on her/his specialty and look for quick results. A typical Japanese leader might be thought of as paternalistic; that is, like a father, knowing best and wanting the best for everyone in the organization. The Japanese management approach has been described as *theory z* (in contrast to *theory x* or *theory y*), and it has been argued that *theory z* organizations were more effective than either of the others because they emphasized trust in subordinates, a less hierarchical and bureaucratic structure, and higher levels of worker involvement, all of which created a distinctive corporate style and culture that was conducive to high performance (both in terms of productivity and quality). A Japanese scholar (Misumi 1985) described two functions for effective leaders in Japan: performance and maintenance. Interestingly, these are similar to the task and people orientations that we find in the North American literature. The performance function has to do with task accomplishment, and the maintenance function relates to maintaining good working relations among group members. In the Japanese context, these are not seen as independent functions but complementary ones; both are important and necessary. Misumi also considers that while both are always important and necessary, the way in which they are carried out varies from situation to situation.

Even within a relatively homogenous society such as Japan, the effective leadership approach is described as being contingent on the environment. It seems clear that the national environment will affect what works in terms of leadership, but it also seems that the situation within the country will influence the best choice of leadership approach.

A substantial amount of research on leadership has been done in India as well. According to Hofstede's (1980) model, Indian society is high on power distance and relatively low on individualism in contrast to the United States and Canada, which are high on individualism and relatively low on power distance. We would expect these differences to be reflected in management and leadership styles. The Indian culture has been described as vertical collectivist, characterized by familialism, patronage, personalized relationships, and obedience to authority (Sinha 1984).

Sinha (1994) has suggested two key dimensions of leadership in the Indian context—nurturance and task. He described the relatively hierarchical Indian leader as emphasizing task aspects. Further, some studies show that Indian subordinates prefer this autocratic type of leadership. Sinha's research suggests, however, that the most effective Indian leaders were those who emphasized both nurturance and task. He found that encouraging subordinate participation was valuable and contributed to performance, but that the leader had to work closely with subordinates to nurture their willingness to take responsibility. In essence, a good leader benevolently guides the subordinate, and the subordinate reciprocates with obedience and loyalty.

The two dimensions from the Indian literature, nurturance and task, are similar to the people/task dimensions discussed in the North American literature as well as the dimensions of performance and maintenance described by Misumi in Japan. In three very different locations, then, we find that similar dimensions of leadership have been identified. This suggests that in any location it may be helpful for managers and leaders to assess their behavior along these two dimensions.

In Arab countries, management and leadership practice have been influenced by Islam, tribal and family traditions, and colonial bureaucracies, as well as contact with the West (Ali 1990). The traditional leader was based on a great hero who leads warriors into battle. In addition, leaders are expected to act as fathers and to look after their subordinates, providing and caring for them. Dorfman (2004) describes "the complex world of Arab management (viewed from an American perspective)" as promoting "a duality of managerial thinking and practice that values modernity while maintaining traditional values." He describes the following as likely to be confusing to a Western manager:

- Establishing a large number of rules and regulations with no attempt to implement them.
- Designing selection and promotion systems based on merit, while hiring and rewarding according to social ties and personal relations.
- Paying employees in the public sector but not requiring them to report for work.

Khadra (1990) described Arab leadership in terms of the prophetic-caliphal model. One type of leader is the prophetic type who is seen to have performed extraordinary actions. Followers revere and love such a leader, and this results in strong attachment to the leader, unity of purpose, and submission to his authority. The second kind of leader is an ordinary or caliphal man. Followers do not have the same attachment to this type of leader, and this can result in conflicts. To avoid that outcome, the leader uses coercion and fear to keep his subordinates in line.

There is relatively little empirical evidence to support these descriptions of leadership in Arab countries, but there does seem to be a preference for strong and decisive leaders. Undoubtedly, American and Western managers are likely to find management and leadership in the Arab countries substantially unlike what is typical at home.

In Africa, there are a variety of results relating to leadership. Some authors have proposed that an effective leadership model for Africa is a blending of transformational leadership theory with servant leadership. However, along somewhat different lines, Walumbwa, Orwa, Wang, and Lawler (2005) compared the relationship of transformational leadership to organizational commitment and job satisfaction and identified African leadership as authoritarian due to high power distance, and they hypothesized that this may negate the positive impact of transformational leadership. In contrast to the studies that indicated the importance of hierarchy and power in Africa, Smith (2002) identified spirituality, time as eternal, importance of ancestors and the connection of ancestors and land, strong relationships, and communalism as important. He concluded that leaders are expected to be tough, but decisions are holistic and collective. Mangaliso (2001) and Newenham-Kahindi (2009) stressed indigenous leadership styles such as Ubuntu and Indaba—endorsing factors such as supportiveness, relationships, and extended networks, as well as spiritualism and tribal destiny, and suggested that trust is based on interpersonal relationships, open discussions involving participation from all employees, and discipline based on how the individual affects the group.

My research in the Caribbean suggests that people are generally low on power distance, that is, they do not like power differences and hierarchies (Punnett and Greenidge 2009). The postcolonial management structure is, however, founded on a belief in power at the top, little sharing of information, and little trust or participation. This lack of fit between leadership style and cultural values results in lower motivation, lower productivity, higher absenteeism, and a range of negative outcomes.

This review of management practices in Japan, India, Arab and African countries, and the Caribbean is only the tip of the iceberg. There is much that we do not know about what is effective in these locations, and clearly there are many parts of the world about which we know virtually nothing. Nevertheless, this discussion should further emphasize the need for managers to be aware of the potential for variation in leadership practices and to be sensitive to reactions to any particular leadership approach.

Some Cultural Interactions

Clearly, cultural dimensions are intricately interwoven with effective leadership. Hofstede's cultural dimensions, described in chapter 2, are a good starting point to examine how culture is likely to influence leadership.

Power Distance

In high power-distance (PDI) societies, it is believed that there should be an order of inequality where each person has a rightful place. This is seen in organizations and leadership in a number of ways. For example:

- Organizations have clear hierarchies where those at the top are powerful and those at lower levels have little power. Consequently, those at the top are expected to make the decisions and those at lower levels simply carry out these decisions.
- Powerful people are expected to look powerful and are entitled to privileges, thus leaders should have the trappings that come with leadership (large offices, cars, and so on).
- Others are a threat to one's power and can rarely be trusted, so information is not shared and input is not sought from subordinates.
- Those in positions of power are independent and those at lower levels are dependent, thus subordinates are loyal to leaders, follow instructions, and accept what the leader says as right.

Approaches such as participative management, industrial democracy, and similar movements aimed at creating equality among organizational members may not work in high PDI countries because the value system of both the powerful and their subordinates is against such approaches. A system like management by objectives depersonalizes the authority of the manager. Aycan (2004) has described leadership in developing countries as a reciprocal relationship between the leader and her/his subordinates based on relatively high power distance (as well as high uncertainty avoidance and collectivism). Leaders are expected to take responsibility for the welfare of their subordinates, and, in turn, subordinates are loyal to their leaders and perform the tasks they are assigned. Leadership in this context is essentially autocratic—subordinates believe that leaders know what needs to be done, and they look up to the leaders simply because they are leaders. But it is benignly autocratic—leaders are concerned for the welfare of their subordinates and make decisions that take this into account.

Individualism and Collectivism

In individualistic societies, people are expected to take care of themselves and their immediate family. This is seen in organizations and leadership in a number of ways. For example:

- Individuals are expected to make decisions, and everyone has a right to an opinion, thus leaders will be decisive but will also accept input from subordinates.
- Individual achievement is valued, and leaders need to demonstrate their ability through performance.
- Autonomy is valued, so subordinates expect leaders to delegate responsibility and authority, and to value initiative.
- Personal financial security is necessary, thus leaders cannot expect loyalty from subordinates.
- Employees are independent of the organization and will change jobs if they find a better one, therefore leaders have to find ways to make subordinates' jobs attractive to avoid excessive turnover.

It seems that in collective societies people pay more attention to the social context than do those in more individualistic societies. In collective societies, leaders are not seen as apart from the social context; their role is integral to the social fabric. The result is that subordinates react on the basis of the leader's role rather than because of the leader's behavior or style. In addition, in these societies, the maintenance of harmonious leader–follower relationships is important, and subordinates will describe leaders in positive terms simply because they have reverence for the position. Labor relations are also affected in that in collective societies contracts are seen to be aimed at the good of all.

Uncertainty Avoidance

In societies that are high on uncertainty avoidance, people are concerned about the uncertainty that is seen as inherent in life, and they seek certainty. This is seen in organizations and leadership in a number of ways:

- Uncertainty produces anxiety and stress, and leaders can alleviate this by providing security for their subordinates.
- Expertise is valued because it reduces uncertainty, and leaders will seek input from persons both inside and outside the organization who can provide valid and reliable information. Leaders will also be seen as experts.
- Consensus provides a sense of security, so leaders will spend time and effort to reach consensus among group members.
- Conservatism is preferred, therefore younger members and those with divergent ideas are suspect and not trusted.
- Achievement is defined in terms of security, and leaders are expected to provide a secure work environment for subordinates rather than one that is conducive to advancement within the organization.

- Rules and regulations, policies and procedures, are all important to stability, and leaders are expected to define these clearly and to ensure that all organizational members abide by them.

In the English-speaking Caribbean, people are high on uncertainty avoidance, and research has shown that employees seek jobs with a high degree of security (public sector jobs are preferred to private sector ones, even where the latter are better paid). Research has also shown a heavy reliance on rules for making decisions in both Barbados and Jamaica. More generally, developing countries tend to be high on uncertainty avoidance (UAI), and employees in these countries will be concerned with security. Laurent (1983) argued that flexible organizational policies and structures would not work in high UAI countries.

Masculinity and Femininity

Masculine societies are those that value competition, assertiveness, and achievement. Male and female work roles are often clearly delineated. Feminine societies are concerned with nurturance and the quality of life, and roles are more fluid. These characteristics are seen in organizations and leadership in a number of ways:

- In masculine societies, leaders will predominantly be male, and female leaders will embrace traditional male values.
- In masculine societies, leaders will focus on competing to achieve difficult performance goals, while in feminine societies, these goals will be tempered by concern for the quality of work life.
- In masculine societies, leaders will provide tangible rewards for high achievers, whereas in feminine societies, leaders will pay attention to the less fortunate, and rewards are likely to be more intangible and family-oriented, such as time off from work.
- In masculine societies, independence is respected, and leaders will encourage and reward independent thought and action, but in feminine societies, interdependence is seen as good, and rewards will focus on good interpersonal relationships.

In Hofstede's 1980 book, scores reported for Scandinavian countries were uniformly low on masculinity; that is, as a group they could be described as feminine societies. Interestingly, this was reflected in strict environmental and equal opportunity laws. As well, governments and organizations in the region were at the forefront of developing leave laws for new fathers as well as new mothers, in-organization day-care centers, flexible working hours, and other approaches that represent concern for the quality of life and a focus on nurturance and equality. Clearly, equal opportunity for men and women will be easier to pursue and achieve in more feminine societies, and we can expect more women in leadership roles in these countries.

Hofstede and colleagues in the Far East later expanded the research described previously and added a fifth dimension to the model. This dimension was called "Confucian Dynamism." Confucian Dynamism is a complex concept, but it is often simply described as a short-term orientation (low) versus a long-term orientation (high).

This brief discussion of cultural dimensions is intended only to illustrate some of the differences in leadership style that may arise because of culture. Many other variations can be associated with these cultural dimensions as well as others. This discussion provides a basis for readers to develop their own additional thoughts on adapting leadership approaches, practices, and styles to different cultural environments.

Summary and Conclusions

This chapter has given an overview of issues relating to effective leadership in varying national environments. The chapter reviewed various theories of leadership that have been well accepted in North America and the West, and explored national differences that might impact on the effectiveness of these approaches in other environments. The chapter also reviewed some non–North American thinking on leadership. The leadership literature available in English revolves largely around North America and Europe; therefore, the discussion on thinking outside of this sphere is necessarily limited. To broaden this area, the chapter considered the cultural dimensions proposed by Hofstede and briefly examined their potential impact on effective leadership.

The conclusion of the discussion in this chapter is that managers need to be aware that effective leadership will be affected by national and cultural variables. A contingency approach, matching leadership approaches to the situation, is clearly the order of the day for international managers. These managers must evaluate each situation in terms of national characteristics as well as other situational characteristics in order to find the best leadership approach.

This discussion underscores the challenge that multinational companies face as they operate in many different national and cultural environments. These firms may have global approaches that they wish to implement around the world, but at the same time, it is clear that where people are concerned, adaptation is required. Further, adapting leadership style is not simply a matter of behaving differently. Leadership style is reflected in, and supported by, a wide array of organizational processes and structures. These all have to be taken into account if leadership is to be effective. Operating a global business in a world made up of multiple leadership styles itself takes a special kind of leadership.

References

Adler, N.J. 1991. *International Dimensions of Organizational Behavior.* 2nd ed. Boston, MA: PWS-Kent Publishing.

Ali, A. 1990. "Management Theory in a Transitional Society: The Arab's Experience." *International Studies of Management and Organization* 20(3): 7–35.

Aycan, Z. 2004. "Leadership in Developing Countries." In *The Handbook of International Organizations*, ed. A. Bird, H. Lane, and M. Maznevski. Oxford: Blackwell.

Blake, R.R., and J.S. Mouton. 1964. *The Managerial Grid.* Houston: Gulf Publishing.

Dorfman, P. 2004. "International and Cross-Cultural Leadership." In *Handbook for International Management Research*, ed. B.J. Punnett and O. Shenkar, 265–354. Ann Arbor: University of Michigan Press.

Dorfman, P., P.J. Hanges, and F.C. Brodbeck. 2004. "Leadership and Cultural Variation." In *Culture, Leadership, and Organizations—The GLOBE Study of 62 Societies*, ed. R.J. House, P.J. Hanges, M. Javidian, P.W. Dorfman, and V. Gupta, 669–719. London: Sage Publications.

Fiedler, F. 1967. *A Theory of Leadership Effectiveness.* New York: McGraw-Hill.

Hershey, P., and K. Blanchard. 1969. *Management of Organizational Behavior: Utilizing Human Resources.* Englewood Cliffs, NJ: Prentice-Hall.

Herzberg, F. 1968. "One More Time: How Do You Motivate Employees?" *Harvard Business Review* (January–February): 53–62.

Hofstede, G. 1980. *Culture's Consequences: International Differences in Work Related Values.* Beverly Hills, CA: Sage.

House, R.J. 1971. "A Path–Goal Theory of Leadership Effectiveness." *Administrative Science Quarterly* (September 16): 321–339.

House, R.J., P.J. Hanges, M. Javidian, P.W. Dorfman, and V. Gupta, eds. 2004. *Culture, Leadership, and Organizations—The GLOBE Study of 62 Societies.* London: Sage.

Khadra, B. 1990. "The Prophetic-Caliphal Model of Leadership: An Empirical Study." *International Studies of Management and Organization* 20(3): 37–51.

Laurent, A. 1983. "The Cultural Diversity of Western Conceptions of Management." *International Studies of Management and Organization* 13(1–2): 75–96.

Mangaliso, M.P. 2001. "Building Competitive Advantage from Ubuntu: Management Lessons from South Africa. *Academy of Management Executive* 15(3): 23–33.

Misumi, 1985. *The Behavioral Science of Leadership: An Interdisciplinary Japanese Research Program.* Ann Arbor: Michigan University Press.

Newenham-Kahindi, A. 2009. "The Transfer of Ubuntu and Indaba Business Models Abroad: A Case of South African Multinational Banks and Telecommunication Services in Tanzania." *International Journal of Cross Cultural Management* 9(1): 87–108.

Peterson, M., P. Smith, and S. Schwartz. 2002. "Cultural Values as Sources of Guidance and Their Revelance to Managerial Behavior: A 47 Nation Study." *Journal of Cross-Cultural Psychology* 33(1): 188–208.

Punnett, B.J., and D. Greenidge. 2009. "Culture, Myth and Leadership in the Caribbean." In *Cultural Mythology and Leadership*, ed. E.H. Kessler and D.J. Wong-MingJi, 65–78. London: Edward Elgar.

Punnett, B.J., and Jain, A. 1989. "Management Style: Some Similarities and Differences Between Japanese and Canadian Managers in Canada." In *Advances in International Comparative Management*, vol. 4, 183–220. Greenwich, CT: JAI Press.

Punnett, B.J., E. Dick-Forde, and J. Robinson. 2006. "Culture and Management in the English-Speaking Caribbean." *Journal of Eastern Caribbean Studies*, June.

Sinha, J.B.P. 1984. "A Model of Effective Leadership Styles in India." *International Studies of Management and Organization* 14(3): 86–98.

———. 1994. "Cultural Embeddedness and the Developmental Role of Industrial Organizations in India." In *Handbook of Industrial and Organizational Psychology*, vol. 4, 727–764. Palo Alto, CA: Consulting Psychologists Press.

Smith, B. 2002. "Worldview and Culture: Leadership in Sub-Saharan Africa." *New England Journal of Public Policy* 19(1): 243.

Vroom, V.H., and P.H. Yetton. 1973. *Leadership and Decision Making*. Pittsburgh, PA: University of Pittsburgh Press.

Walumbwa, F.O., Orwa, B., Wang, P. and J.J. Lawler. 2005. "Transformational leadership, organizational commitment, and job satisfaction: A comparative study of Kenyan and U.S. financial firms." *Human Resource Development Quarterly* 16(2): 235–256.

9

Cross-National Dimensions of Communication and Negotiation

Introduction

It is essentially impossible for any person to feel and understand completely what another person feels and understands. This is due to the fact that the only way we can share our feelings, thoughts, attitudes, beliefs, and emotions is through verbal and nonverbal language. The process by which language modes (verbal and nonverbal) are shared is what we call "communication." Imagine how communication is complicated when we add cross-national considerations, where people speak different languages, practice different religions, have different histories, and so on. In this chapter, we explore the difficulties of communication across nations and consider the barriers to effective cross-national communication. In addition, a major aspect of international management, which is fundamentally influenced by communication, is negotiations. In this chapter, we discuss the negotiation process and consider various aspects of negotiations and how these can differ from location to location.

In a book called *The Rituals of Dinner,* Margaret Visser discusses manners. She says that manners are as old as human society because the active sharing of food is what makes us different from other animals (1991, 1). This activity, she argues, gives rise to many basic human characteristics, such as kinship systems (in which people eat together), language (for discussing food and planning its acquisition and sharing), technology (how to ensure a supply), and morality (deciding what is a just portion). Manners, or appropriate behavior, guide what we do and how we interact with others. The book describes the dinner party ritual among the MinChia of Yunnan in China during the 1930s, where guests received a written list of all the other people invited several days before the dinner so that they could decide whether or not they wanted to attend (103). These rituals are important to society, and they need to be observed in communication and negotiation. Effective communication and negotiation are often about manners, that is, understanding the rituals and following them.

The *Economist* ("Getting the Message, at Last" 2007) reported the following: In 1864, a number of British politicians received telegrams late in the evening; they became concerned that war had broken out or the monarch had been taken ill, but the telegram said nothing of the kind. Rather, it was to advise that the Dental Practice of Messrs Gabriel would be open from 10 A.M. to 5 P.M. The politicians were infuriated at this early example of "spam." The *Economist* article goes on to note that when the telephone first appeared, no one was sure what to say when picking up the receiver. Alexander Graham Bell suggested "Ahoy, ahoy," but Thomas Edison's suggestion of "Hello" won, and this expression, which was rarely used before, has become the norm on the telephone and elsewhere. Currently we wonder what to do about mobile phones that ring, beep, and play music at inappropriate times and in inappropriate places. Apparently the outlines of mobile phone etiquette are starting to emerge, but regional variations are interesting—in parts of Scandinavia, it is expected that you text someone to ask if you can call them, and in Japan, making voice calls on trains is frowned upon. A new communication challenge is how to regulate the appropriate use of cell phones on airplanes, where reportedly their use is likely to be authorized in the near future. This is a tough question because airlines bring together strangers from many different backgrounds and cultures.

The Communication Flow

The communication flow is often discussed in terms of a sender and a receiver. The sender is seen as the originator of the message to be communicated, and the receiver is the one for whom the message is intended. This may be pictured simply as follows:

Step One: sender has an idea to communicate;
Step Two: sender encodes message and chooses the medium or media (more than one may be used) for sending the message;
Step Three: receiver receives message and decodes it;
Step Four: receiver ends up with an idea;
Step Five: receiver provides feedback by which sender judges the result of the communication.

If the receiver ends up with essentially the same idea as the sender, then we say that good communication has taken place. Unfortunately, there is a lot of potential "noise" in the communication system. Noise, in the communication context, is anything that gets in the way of effective communication. This may be actual noise or it may be interference related to differences in perceptions, expectations, backgrounds, and so on. There are lots of differences that affect communication even between senders and receivers who are relatively similar. Naturally, there are even more when the sender and receiver come from different national backgrounds. Exhibit 9.1 outlines the communication process. Within this general framework, six dimensions of communication can be considered.

Communication Is a Process

"Communication has no determinate beginning or end; rather, it is an ongoing exchange of messages between two or more people" (Haworth and Savage 1989, 234). We cannot assume that our communication relationships with the same people will remain the same: people change, the circumstances around the relationship change, topics of communication change, and so on.

Communication Includes Purposive and Expressive Messages

When people communicate, they exchange verbal and nonverbal messages with each other. One kind of message is a purposive message, that is, a message that communicates the direct intention of the sender of the message. A second kind of message is expressive. Expressive messages are sent unintentionally along with purposive messages. Expressive messages may be anger in one's voice along with the spoken words "That's okay, just don't let it happen again." The speaker, in this case, is saying that he/she forgives the other person verbally, but through the tone of the speaker's voice, the receiver of the message is not sure whether to believe the purposive message.

Communication Is Made Up of Multi-Unit Signals

Human communication travels through a variety of signals, not just words. Kinesic (gestures, facial expression, body position, body movement), proxemic (closeness), olfactory (smells), and other signals picked up by the five senses are "units" of human communication. These various units of communication do not occur one at a time in human communication; they occur simultaneously. For example, a receiver of in-person communication simultaneously hears words, sees body positions, observes nonverbal signals (such as hand gestures), observes the proximity of the sender, smells various odors, and so on. Similarly, communication by mail is accompanied by a variety of units, including the paper used, writing, style, and so on. If the combined package of these units is comfortable, understandable, and familiar to the receiver,

Exhibit 9.1 **The Communication Flow**

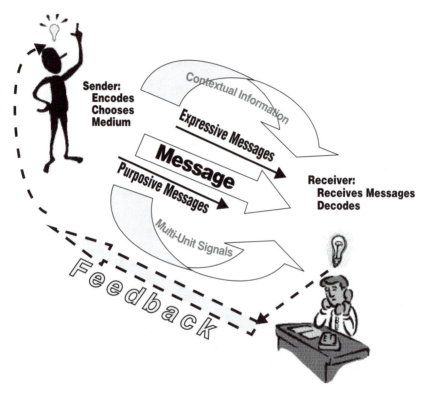

relatively clear communication takes place; however, if the units present an array of confusing communication messages to the receiver, misunderstanding will be more likely to occur.

Communication Depends on the Context for Its Meaning

Context refers to the environment in which an event or a communication occurs. Ease or difficulty of communication depends on the degree to which the communicator and the listener share a common background of knowledge and experience. This occurs when both individuals have a common history, or at least a shared understanding, of each other's lives, intentions, experiences, and so on. When the context is understood to a great degree between two communicators, much can be said even though little is actually spoken, because they can "read between the lines" of each other's verbal statements. Some societies are high-context ones where people do not really need to talk that much to communicate. Others, for example, Canada and the United States, are considered to be low-context societies because people rely substantially on verbal communication. In high-context societies, a nod, grunt, sigh, bow, or wave of the hand may communicate a lot of information.

Japan is considered a high-context country, and the term used there for such high-context communication is *hara-gei,* which translated into English is "belly-language." Traditionally, emotions in Japan were seen as residing in the stomach; thus, when people's emotions are naturally understood because of a shared knowledge of communication norms, there is little need for high levels of verbal communication to aid in communication. A visitor to Japan from a low-context culture will hear lots of grunting, nodding, short phrases, and silence and wonder how the Japanese communicate (Mendenhall, Punnett, and Ricks 1995, 536).

Communication Depends on the Competence of the Communicators

If a person is able to send and express messages clearly and receive and interpret messages correctly, then communication is enhanced. When a message is poorly expressed or incorrectly interpreted, misunderstandings occur. This can happen at different levels of the communication process. For example, if an expatriate cannot speak the host language very well, misunderstanding may occur due to the expatriate's inability to express basic sentences clearly. Even if the expatriate is quite fluent in the host country's language, misunderstandings may still occur because the host nationals may interpret the purposive message correctly, but also pick up an unintended, expressive message that is negative in nature. The expatriate's words may be perfectly understood, but the perfume she uses may be unpleasant to the host national; if this is the case, the message's importance may be distorted, the expatriate judged adversely, and so on. In parts of India, the gesture for strong agreement is a "head wobble"—a mix of up and down and side to side, which implies being unsure to English speakers. English speakers are confused when an Indian colleague says, "I think it's a great idea" while shaking his head to indicate that he is unsure. The communication would be fine between two people who understood the body language, but it can become miscommunication when one party does not understand the body language. It is also possible, if one develops a rapport with someone, to communicate quite well without speaking the other's language. If people share an understanding and appreciation of similar things, communication through sign language, gestures, and appropriate facial expressions may be possible.

Each of the above assumptions about human communication can apply within any national culture, but there are likely to be greater variations, and perhaps unique variations, from country to country. That is why living and working with people from diverse countries can be both challenging and interesting. It is almost as if to communicate with someone from a different national background one must first learn not only the language, but also the rules for how the language is used in differing contexts and situations.

Barriers to Cross-National Communication Competence

Consider two examples that illustrate cross-national communication difficulties (see Mendenhall, Punnett, and Ricks 1995, from Haworth and Savage 1989):

> An American expatriate in Seoul beckons to a Korean store clerk with the typical U.S. "come here" wave of the hand. The Korean store clerk is amazed and appalled and avoids the American. The American waits, sees that he is being avoided, and angrily walks out of the store. The Korean store clerk was offended that the American would use a gesture to call him that is used in Korea to call only dogs. The American was incensed that the clerk would ignore him and refuse to assist him.

> A male Chinese student studying in the United States earned money tutoring American students. A female student he tutored, thanks in part to his efforts, received a good grade on her test. She was so happy she embraced the Chinese student, praised and thanked him for his efforts, and was surprised at the subsequent look of amazement, consternation, and embarrassment on his face.

In order to communicate effectively with someone from a national background that is different from one's own, there are certain barriers that must be understood and surmounted. These are outlined below.

Ignorance of Rules of Communication

It has been estimated that approximately 65 percent of communication is nonverbal in nature—that is, when listening to someone talking to us, we pay attention to things like the tone of the speaker's voice, how physically close the speaker is, the body position of the speaker, and physical gestures the speaker is using. Each nation/culture has different rules regarding nonverbal communication. Consider the following cross-cultural differences in kinesics (Dodd 1977, 53–54):

When North Americans use hand gestures to "say good-bye," they typically place the palm of the right hand facing out, extend the fingers, and move the fingers up and down. In India, West Africa, and Central America such a gesture would be interpreted as beckoning someone to come toward you. In these countries the gesture is often used for beckoning taxicabs.

It is common in Indonesia to converse with someone while in their home by sitting on the floor and talking. As one sits down on the floor, great care must be taken not to point the soles of one's shoes or feet toward the host. Doing this is a grave offense, for the gesture indicates that the person is seen as being beneath you.

During the Cold War era, Soviet premier Nikita Khrushchev visited the United States. As he emerged from the airplane, the officials, news reporters, and other visitors greeted him cordially. In response, Khrushchev clasped his hands together and raised them above his head. To television viewers and observers in the United States, the gesture appeared like a boxer raising clasped hands signaling victory. However, Khrushchev intended the gesture to represent a clasping of hands in friendship.

Without knowledge of basic kinesics for the location in which one is operating, misunderstandings and bad feelings can be caused rather easily. Hall (1977), a noted anthropologist, summarizes the importance of kinesics by holding that it is one of the most basic of all modes of communication and is only partially readable across cultural boundaries. Further, "in new and unknown situations, in which one is likely to be most dependent on reading non-verbal cues, the chances of one's being correct decrease as cultural distance increases" (75). The only way this barrier can be overcome is to become familiar with the kinesics of a new location.

Spatial relationships in human communication are also important. This includes fixed features of space (e.g., architecture, buildings, room divisions), semi-fixed features of space (e.g., seating arrangements, office layouts), and dynamic space (use of personal space) when communicating.

Consider how fixed features of space influence organizational behavior. A large office in the United States communicates status and power. The smaller the office, the less status is connected with the occupant of the office. In contrast, in India, high government officials may share a room of perhaps 15 feet by 20 feet with six other lesser employees (Dodd 1977, 56). If a businessperson or government official from the United States visits India and is ushered into a typical Indian office to meet his/her host, the visitor may make incorrect judgments regarding the host's true position and power. Buildings themselves can embody a value, an emotion, a belief system. For Americans, visiting the Lincoln Memorial and the Vietnam War Memorial arouses emotions around the values of justice, freedom, sacrifice, and gratitude. A visit to the Sengakuji Shrine in Tokyo, the burial place of the ashes of the forty-seven samurai, arouses emotions in the Japanese that relate to the values of duty, sacrifice, obligation, and honor.

In many parts of Latin America, academia and politics traditionally were seen as separate entities. Politicians who were invited to speak at universities were not supposed to use the venue to support their own political agendas. Also, because many Latin American countries have histories of military dictatorships, the presence on campus of military personnel was seen as threatening to academic freedom and was almost always avoided. When Richard Nixon was vice president of the United States, he visited Latin America. At one stage of his visit, he desired to give a speech at a university. Unfortunately, he spoke on politically related topics and employed an interpreter from the local military who was in full-dress uniform. While Nixon hoped to improve the relationship between the United States and the host country, the setting, the kinesics of the military uniform of the interpreter, and the subject matter of the speech all combined to have the opposite effect from the one Nixon intended (Mendenhall, Punnett, and Ricks 1995).

Consider how semi-fixed features of space affect communication. The layout of office furniture and workspace directly influences how people communicate with each other. High-context locations, where people share communication norms to a larger degree than low-context ones, tend to have more open and less private workspaces. For example, in Japan, managers and subordinates work together in large open offices, with several people sharing the same workspace. If a Westerner were to walk into a Japanese office looking for a particular individual, he/she would be confronted with a large room wherein desks are linked together in long rows. Without understanding the meaning behind the layout, it would be difficult for the visitor to find the person he/she was looking for. Japanese cultural norms reinforce working groups and being part of a group. There are no partitions separating desks; everyone can overhear what everyone else is saying on the telephone or in work-related conversations. Compare this with the strong need for perceived privacy in North American companies. Large workspaces are partitioned and subdivided with movable "walls" in such a way that cubicles are formed. In each cubicle, a person has his/her own desk, often surrounded with personal items marking that territory as being the worker's private working space. North American cultural values of independence, individualism, and privacy dictate to a large degree how workspace is arranged, and this structure reinforces the norms associated with those values. Interestingly, in Japanese, there is no word that translates the value of "privacy" adequately; that value is simply not as strong in Japan as it is in North America.

Consider how personal space influences communication. Researchers have found that humans unconsciously structure and measure the space around their bodies. It is sort of an invisible measuring that allows us to feel comfortable with others. Hall (1977, 58) noted that "the flow and shift of distance between people as they interact with each other is part and parcel of the communication process. The normal conversational distance between strangers illustrates the importance of the dynamics of space interaction. If a person gets too close, the reaction is instantaneous and automatic—the other person backs up. I have observed an American backing up the entire length of a long corridor while a Latin American whom he considered pushy tried to catch up with him." This illustration shows that different peoples have different measurements of personal space. For North Americans, there is a radius of eighteen inches around them that they view as being "intimate space." People who are allowed to enter that space are people one knows and trusts and feels comfortable with. Latin Americans and people from the nations of the Middle East have a much smaller "intimate space." In some of these countries, "being close enough to breathe on another person during a conversation is deemed appropriate. In fact, the breath is like one's spirit and life itself, so sharing your breath in close conversation is like sharing your spirit." When interacting with a North American who is consistently backing up in order to retain a comfortable sense of his or her personal space, the individual might soon consider the North American to be cold, aloof, or not interested in the topic of conversation; conversely, the North American may indeed be interested in the topic of conversation, but might view the other person as being pushy, backward, uneducated, uncivilized, or even dangerous.

Perceptual Biases

Cognitive researchers have found that in order to store information, make sense out of what we perceive in the world around us, and simplify the world around us, humans develop mental categories. For example, out of a reported 7,500,000 colors in the world, there are about 4,000 English words to represent all of these colors. Of the 4,000 words, only 8 (the primary, secondary, and tertiary colors) are commonly used—a ratio of one word per 937,000 colors (Oddou and Mendenhall 1984, 79). There are four important reasons why humans have developed this capacity for information categorization.

First, it allows us to reduce the complexity of the environment. There is no way that humans could remember 7,500,000 different words for colors; we would undergo information overload. Second, it helps us to identify objects and behaviors in the environment, and English speakers have chosen over the process of time to rely on the basic colors of the spectrum or variants of them (e.g., "light" and "dark" green) to identify the color of objects. Third, categorization reduces the need for constant learning and reclassifying; thus simplifying colors down to the basic colors and their general variants enables English speakers to classify the color of something quickly without having to undergo long mental processing episodes. Fourth, classifying provides quick information and knowledge of appropriate and inappropriate actions to take in any situation; for example, a yellow light at a traffic signal means "slow down to stop," and the driver does not have to think about the shade of the color, and so on, before taking the appropriate action.

The mental categories by which a person sorts out and responds to the world reflect the environment into which that individual was born; thus, people from different places learn to attach meaning and expect certain responses in various situations according to experience and socialization. In other words, our categories are to a large degree taught to us by others (e.g., parents, teachers, peers). The research indicates that people from different cultures process and categorize information differently; it is almost as if people's "software" is different based upon the environment in which they were raised. The case of the Inuit of northern Canada, mentioned previously, has often been cited in this context because of their different words to describe types of snow. Survival in their environment demands a more specific knowledge of snow and its forms than in the typical Canadian environment, where snow is seen on a continuum of wet to dry. A conversation about snow between an Inuit Canadian and a Canadian from Toronto might well be confusing to both parties.

It seems that categorizing what we see in the world around us into more simple, workable frameworks allows us to live life more efficiently and effectively; however, the danger is that since we oversimplify the true reality of the world around us, we might have the tendency to actually misperceive it and make mistakes in our mental processing. Regarding the possible effect that communication categories have on one's ability to interact effectively with people from other environments, Szalay (1981) observed, "the more we consider our views and experiences [i.e., our categories of the world] to be absolute and universal, the less prepared we are to deal with people who have different backgrounds, experiences, culture, and therefore different views [categories] of the universe" (138). Triandis (1964) noted that as we utilize the categories in our minds to make sense out of the world around us, we experience positive and negative experiences associated with those categories. Thus, attached to those categories are emotions. For example, an Indonesian may know that a Westerner is unaware that it is an insult to show the soles of the feet, but the Indonesian will still feel revulsion, shame, or other negative emotions if this occurs.

Our mental categorizations assist us in the world by allowing us to make sense out of, and predict what will happen in, our environment. When we take our categories into a new location, those categories may not be in congruence with those of the host nationals, and this can result in misperceptions on both sides.

Faulty Attributions

When we judge the motives behind people's behavior, we attribute reasons to their actions. This is called making attributions. For example, if while driving down the freeway, a car races up to you from behind, passes you, and then cuts you off with a dangerous turn, speeds up, and begins to weave in and out of traffic while exceeding the speed limit, a number of things may go through your mind. You may think that the driver is an idiot who has no regard for the rights of others or that the driver is drunk; but it may be that the driver has a pregnant wife in the backseat who is close to delivering, and he is speeding to the hospital. If that were the case, you would have made a faulty attribution based on the behavior that you observed.

Similarly, if an expatriate observes behavior in a business context that is strange to him or her, the expatriate might make attributions about why that behavior occurred. In the case of the American expatriate who waved the Korean store clerk over, both parties made inaccurate and faulty attributions about the motives behind the observed behaviors, based on different beliefs. The American, when the clerk refused to wait on him, may have thought that the Korean was rude or hated Americans, while the Korean may have thought the American's hand gesture was a sign of arrogance, prejudice, or rudeness.

Once a behavior is observed, in milliseconds our brain goes through a kind of "library index card" retrieval until it finds the category that makes sense out of the behavior we observed. Once a category is accessed, emotions that are linked with that category are triggered and these are in turn linked to evaluations of what we observe. In the case of the Korean store clerk, evaluations of the American's hand gesture would be along the lines of bad, immoral, dirty, condescending, and so on. This takes place in milliseconds and virtually automatically, so it is essentially unconscious.

Researchers have found that people make two general kinds of attributions about the behaviors they observe: internal and external. Internal attributions are made when the behavior is viewed as caused by the other individual's internal characteristics, personality, and so on. This was the kind of attribution both the American and the Korean made about each other. Each viewed the other's behavior as connected to the character or the personality of the other person. External attributions are made when the behavior is viewed as caused by external factors or conditions. If the Korean had been aware that culture influences hand gestures, he might have made external attributions—for example, assuming that the American was merely using a different cultural gesture—and thus avoided the misunderstanding. Culture can be seen as an external factor that influences people's behavior. If the American had thought it likely that the Korean wanted to serve him, he might also have concluded that he (the American) was doing something inappropriate.

Based on our attributions, we select a behavioral response. In the case of the American, it was to storm out of the store. In the case of the Korean clerk, it was to avoid the American. Based upon one's personality traits, one chooses a response. We usually respond the way we would in our familiar environment at home. As the example illustrates, this may be the wrong response in an unfamiliar environment. A key aspect to improving communications cross-nationally is the need to check one's perceptions and put one's attributions on "hold." You should not automatically assume that your evaluation of a situation has been correct. Often it is helpful to ask someone from the other culture how they would interpret a particular situation.

Stereotypes

Another barrier to effective communication is stereotyping. Stereotyping refers to categorizing a group of people based upon some feature that they hold in common, such as nationality, race, or religion. Research studies show that individuals tend to favor those from their own group in nearly every respect and disfavor a different group, attributing more positive characteristics to their own group and more negative ones to the other (Oddou and Menden-hall 1984, 86). Furthermore, such research has firmly established that the favoring of one's own group can be attributed to the perceived existence of an out-group, regardless of any actual differences among people that would merit division. Once one feels part of an in-group, others who are not part of that group are considered the out-group, categorized on a variety of issues (intelligence, industriousness, education level, language accent, and so on) in negative terms.

Stereotyping is a major barrier to cross-cultural communication. In the American/Korean example, the lack of communication is even more likely if each party has a stereotype of the other; for example, if the Korean thinks that Americans arc all loud and rude, he would be even more likely to take offense at the gesture, and if the American thinks all Koreans dislike foreign-ers, he would be even more likely to assume he was being ignored. If a group is stereotyped as dishonest (as the gypsies often have been), it is difficult for the holder of this stereotype to trust anything that someone of that group does or says. Yet stereotyping is also a helpful means of classifying groups of people. When we say that Americans are competitive, or West Indians are laid back, we are using stereotypes and attributing general characteristics to a group based on nationality. Stereotyping allows us to make decisions about a group, and where our stereotype is based on a realistic assessment of the group, this is helpful. When I visit a new country, it is helpful, at least initially, if I can deal with the people as a group. After I have spent time in the new country, I will find many variations from the stereotype, but to begin with, the stereotype can be useful. We all hold stereotypes of various kinds, and if we are to be effective with communications, especially in cross-national situations, we need to be conscious of these stereotypes. We need to make a deliberate effort to overcome negative stereotypes, and to recognize that other, non-negative stereotypes will not apply to all the people in a given group.

The discussion up to now has given an overview of the communication process and illustrated some of the many barriers to effective communication. Communicating well with people from varied backgrounds is a major challenge for international managers. The international traveler cannot take communication for granted as she might at home; instead communication has to be a carefully thought-out process. Particularly in new situations, one needs to pay close attention to all aspects of the communication process, to check one's perceptions and attributions, and to be sensitive to the feedback one receives. A major communication hurdle that international managers face is that of negotiation. The balance of this chapter will examine issues associated with cross-national negotiation.

Negotiations in International Contexts

Fisher and Ury (1991) begin their well-known book *Getting to Yes* with the statement "like it or not, you are a negotiator" (p. xvii), and go on to comment that everyone negotiates something every day. This is true whether you are at home or running a large multinational or transnational organization. Negotiating is complex anywhere, but it is one of the most important arenas of cross-cultural communication for international managers. Negotiations take place between investors and governments, potential business partners, buyers and sellers, employers and employees; in other words, negotiations permeate the international business world. Business will not take place unless negotiations are successful, yet, if the parties come to the negotiating table without understanding the barriers to, and complexities of, cross-cultural communication, there is a high probability that negotiations will not be successful. In this part of the chapter, we will look at the negotiation process and how it can differ from one location to another. It is important that negotiators try to understand the negotiation process from the point of view of the other party because this allows them to be more skillful and improves the likelihood that they will be able to conclude the negotiations and reach a deal that is beneficial for their organization.

The Negotiation Process

The negotiation process has been described in terms of four stages (Adler 1991). The stages are relationship building, exchange of task-related information, persuasion, and making concessions and agreements. These stages occur in all negotiations. However, groups of people differ in terms of the value placed on each stage of the negotiation and the time spent on each one. In the following discussion, the Japanese and the Americans are used to illustrate how two groups may approach the same stage from very different perspectives.

Relationship Building

The first stage of negotiations involves the building of interpersonal relationships between the negotiating parties. Some groups consider developing a good relationship as the key to working together. These groups devote a lot of time and effort at the beginning to relationship building in the belief that once you develop a relationship and trust the other group, you should be able to negotiate a mutually acceptable agreement. Others see developing a relationship as essentially a waste of time until you know that you will be working together. These groups devote little initial time or effort to relationship building. For these groups, developing a relationship is more likely to come after a mutually acceptable agreement has been reached.

Japanese negotiators view relationship building as a very important part of the negotiation process and spend considerable time building relationships with those with whom they are negotiating. Essentially, the Japanese want to do business with you only if they believe they can have a good relationship, therefore they do not want to go forward with the negotiations until this relationship is established. Conversely, Americans see building relationships as less important and spend much less time on this phase than do their Japanese counterparts. Americans believe that if you can work out a good business deal you should work together, and that there will be time for socializing and relationship building once parties have reached an agreement. In addition, Americans rely on the legal system to enforce any agreement reached, and they do not see a need to like their business associates in order to structure a successful arrangement. For the Japanese, it is important to spend a lot of time after the official meetings out on the town, eating and drinking with their counterparts; in this way, formal barriers are broken down between the parties and a sense of trust slowly develops. During the first meetings when Americans may want to get down to business, the Japanese will likely talk in vague generalities, for in their minds, the preliminary sessions are simply there in order to assist in building relationships. The "power breakfast" and the "power lunch," that is, making deals over meals, are promoted in the United States, and Americans are eager to cut through small talk and get down to business. This contrast with the Japanese, who want to know their counterparts before they will trust them enough to do business with them, can lead to frustration and failure.

Exchange of Information

The second phase of negotiations involves information exchange. This includes stating one's "situation and needs and . . . understanding the opponent's situation and needs" (Adler 1991, 197). It is difficult enough to understand the other party's situation, interests, and needs in a negotiation situation at home, but understanding these issues when the other party is from another country and culture adds substantially to the complexity of this phase. People from different countries view problems, reality, and business operations in very different ways. For example, the government in a developing country is likely to have very different objectives and expectations from the management of an international company. A potential partner from a centrally planned communist country will have a different view of production and marketing than the manager from a free-market country. Employees in Islamic countries will expect different employment conditions from those in predominantly Christian countries. All of the national factors discussed in this book come into play in determining what is negotiated and how. It takes real work and a sustained, sincere effort to both articulate one's own situation clearly and understand that of the other party in a cross-national negotiation.

The Japanese rate this as an important stage in the negotiation process and spend a fair amount of time on exchanging information. Americans rate it as being of moderate importance and spend relatively little time on this phase. Americans provide information in what they see as a straightforward manner, focusing on substantive issues of immediate concern, such as quality, price, delivery, and "telling it like it is." The Japanese are more interested in a holistic picture and want to see how the current issues will fit into their wider, longer-term, overall relationships. The type of information, and its specificity, may differ between the two groups, making it difficult for each to evaluate the information provided by the other side.

Persuasion

Persuasion involves influencing the other party to adopt one's viewpoint, position, or beliefs. Persuasion can take many forms. We can persuade by appealing to logic and rationality, providing facts and figures that prove our point. We can persuade by appealing to emotions, explaining why the two parties need each other. We can persuade by explaining why a deal contributes to the greater good of the country, humanity, the world, and so on. We can use different tactics to persuade. We can exaggerate the situation, we can walk out of the negotiations, we can threaten, we can be compliant, we can compliment, we can promise. These approaches to persuasion work to a lesser or greater degree depending on the circumstances. An important component of the circumstances in international negotiations is the national environment.

Americans like to "cut to the chase" and quickly begin to persuade the other party to agree with their offer, bid, contract, and so on. Americans view this as the most important part of the negotiation process and spend a substantial amount of time on persuasion. The Japanese also rate this as being important and spend a fair amount of time on it as well; however, for the Japanese, persuasion should only take place after mutual trust has been established. Americans feel that persuasion can take place quickly, with appeals to logic and rationality suppressing the need for warm interpersonal relationships. The Japanese often feel that Americans are pushy and aggressive in their persuasive tactics, and the Americans often feel that the Japanese are slow to make decisions and guarded in their willingness to share information. These differences in approach to persuasion can seriously affect the outcomes of any negotiations. The Japanese have been known to decide not to work with an American group because they do not feel they can work out a harmonious relationship with people who are seen as overly aggressive. Similarly, Americans have been known to walk out of a potential deal because they get frustrated with the apparent lack of progress.

Concessions and Agreement

Concessions are the "give and take" that allow two parties to reach agreement. In most, if not all, negotiations, each party has to give up some things in order to obtain others that are particularly important, or a party has to modify its position on one issue in order to get the other side to modify its position, and so on. While all negotiations probably include concessions, these can be given at different times, they can be of different sizes, and they can take different forms. Some groups expect large concessions to be made, so their initial negotiating position tends to be extreme (e.g., if price is being negotiated, these groups might ask for $100 when they hope to get $30, giving lots of room for concessions), while others expect only small concessions (they might start at $50, hoping for $40). Some groups make concessions throughout the negotiating process; others make them all at once when they expect the negotiations to be concluded. Some make many small concessions, others a few large ones. Some people believe you should start with small concessions and then increase the size of concessions; others the reverse—start with large and get smaller and smaller. The variations are almost endless, and clearly the impact on the final agreement is critical. Imagine person A, who starts close to his expected ending point, negotiating with person B, who takes an extreme position. It is likely they will never reach agreement, because person A is willing to go from $50 to $40, but person B expects him to go to $20 based on his initial position.

Agreements also take a variety of forms. Some groups expect to reach small, incremental agreements; others wait to agree on all points at the same time. Agreements may be verbal or written; they may be legal and formal or informal. Agreements may be binding and essentially unchangeable, or they may be considered the starting point for further negotiations. Some groups see the outcome of negotiations as a binding, final agreement. Others see the outcome as setting the stage for further discussions as the situation changes and relationships develop. It may be that low-context cultures rely more on binding contracts. Negotiators need to be clear about what kind of agreement they must have because of corporate and national requirements and in order to make their absolute needs clear to their counterparts. Within that framework, it is a good idea to be flexible in terms of the form of agreement.

The Japanese value the concession phase less than Americans do, though they spend about the same amount of time on this as Americans. Adler (1991) notes that "Americans negotiate sequentially: they discuss and attempt to agree on one issue at a time. Throughout the bargaining process, Americans make many small concessions, which they expect their opponents to reciprocate; then they finalize the list of concessions into an overall agreement" (199–200). The Japanese do not tend to spend a lot of time and energy on making small concessions that reciprocate their opponent's concessions. They tend to like to view the entire process holistically, trying to understand each side's views and needs, build trust, and make concessions, if any, only at the very end of the negotiations as a form of "wrapping up" the negotiations.

The Americans and the Japanese have been used here to illustrate the four phases of the negotiation process because a substantial amount of research has been devoted to these two countries. While the American and Japanese negotiating styles are different, they are also similar in some ways; and other contrasts may be even more striking. For example, studies that include Latin American countries with the United States and Japan found that the Latin American negotiators spent less time in silence than either of the others, interrupted others more, and gazed directly at them for longer periods. On these criteria, at least, the Americans and Japanese were somewhat similar when compared to their Latin counterparts.

The four phases of negotiation highlight the issues that arise because of different national approaches to negotiations. Understanding these differences is an important first step for the international negotiator. An important second step is to learn the specific negotiation norms of the group with whom you are negotiating. For example:

- Some groups seek to win at negotiations, others look for win–win solutions.
- Some groups select negotiators on the basis of specialized expertise, others on the basis of academic qualifications, still others on the basis of trust, seniority, status, and so on.
- Some groups send a large number of negotiators, others a small number; some expect to spend a long time negotiating, others a short time.
- Some groups rely on logic, others on emotion, still others on past precedent.

We cannot begin to discuss all of the issues associated with negotiations here. What we can stress is that a good negotiator tries to think the entire process through from beginning to end. For example, if you are traveling from the United Kingdom to the People's Republic of China, you know you will be jet-lagged when you arrive, so you should not schedule the start of negotiations too soon after arrival. If you are going to Saudi Arabia, you may find yourself sitting cross-legged on the floor with a counterpart, so you should practice this beforehand. It is quite possible that your negotiating counterparts will take your customs into account as well, but you can win points and negotiations by being ready for theirs and taking theirs into account whether you are the host or the visitor.

Horst (2007) described the many attributes that can be linked to successful negotiators as follows. Good negotiators plan their negotiations carefully and do the research necessary to understand those with whom they will be negotiating. This is particularly important cross-culturally, where cultural differences can be expected to affect the negotiations. In this context, effective negotiators establish goals and know the outcomes they hope to achieve, but they also have the capacity to be flexible on the specifics of their goals and the methods they will use to achieve these goals. They are able to make trade-offs in order to get their "must haves." Good negotiators are sensitive to cues from their counterparts that can give important information. This is especially critical in cross-cultural situations because cues can have different meanings and be interpreted differently because of the cultural context. The negotiator's "inventiveness" or ability to develop creative solutions is also relevant because this can allow the parties to reach mutually acceptable agreements. Patience is another attribute of the successful negotiator, who will continue trying to find solutions and to turn an adversarial relationship into a collaborative one. In sum, effective negotiators want to reach agreement.

Horst (2007) summarized cultural differences in negotiating styles as:

Goals—contract versus relationship
Attitudes—win/lose versus win/win
Personal Styles—informal versus formal
Communications—direct versus indirect
Time Sensitivity—high versus low
Emotionalism—high versus low
Agreement Form—specific versus general
Agreement Building—bottom up versus top down
Team Organization—one leader versus consensus

In cross-cultural negotiations, it is important to understand your own cultural style and preferences as well as those of the other party(ies) and how they relate to each other.

In the following section, we look at some specific countries and describe what seems to be typical in these countries.

Negotiating Norms in Selected Countries

It is impossible to cover the negotiating norms around the world in this chapter, but three countries will be highlighted in order to convey the importance of doing one's "cross-national homework" before going abroad to negotiate. These countries are Brazil, the People's Republic of China, and Russia—three very different negotiating environments. It is important to note that there are no hard and fast rules regarding negotiations, and that the following are only meant as examples. "Expect the unexpected" is probably the best motto for the international negotiator.

Brazil

A variety of researchers have done work on the negotiating approach used by Brazilians, and their findings point toward clear preferences of Brazilian managers. The results indicate that though Brazilian managers do use persuasive tactics, a more dominant tendency is to use a "receptive" style of influence that involves "linking" and "seducing" approaches.

Linking involves the desire to understand the frame of reference of the other party and is manifested by encouraging the participation of others, searching for points of agreement, listening, and empathetic behaviors. Seducing describes an influence approach that has at its heart the desire to win the opponent over to one's side by ingratiating oneself with the other party. It is manifested by sharing information, admitting mistakes, motivating others, praising them, and raising their spirits through gracious behavior.

If we compare the verbal and nonverbal negotiating behavior of Brazilians, Japanese, and Americans, we find that Brazilians talk more, touch more, and look directly at the other party more than do Japanese and Americans. These probably reflect active linking and seducing activities.

Amado and Brasil (1991) concluded from the studies of Brazilian negotiating behavior that "everything seems to happen in such a way that Brazilian managers somehow try to fix things up in order to avoid direct confrontation, which is experienced as dangerous, thus [the tendency of] establishing personal relationships and giving signs of an open mind and empathy" (41). Graham and Herberger (1983) noted that while Americans value persuasion in the negotiation process, Brazilians do not; they state that "Brazilians cannot depend on a legal system to iron out conflicts, so they depend on personal relationships" (163). This situation fosters linking and seducing behaviors that are aimed at forming tapestries of trust, obligation, and friendship between negotiating parties. After reviewing the research literature, Amado and Brasil (1991) concluded that Brazilian negotiators are open-minded, cooperative, and receptive (linking and seducing), while their tendency to direct persuasion and exertion of assertive pressure is relatively weak.

The People's Republic of China

The People's Republic of China (PRC) offers one billion potential consumers for products and services, and thus is very attractive to companies from elsewhere. Nevertheless, firms seeking to invest in the PRC need to recognize that most people in the PRC have little disposable income and only a small fraction of the population is currently likely to be consumers of Western products or services. In addition, infrastructure (such as roads) is limited. The manager negotiating in the PRC needs to investigate carefully to understand the reality of the situation rather than taking published reports at face value. An important part of the PRC environment is the communist system, which pervades the business system. Many businesspersons in the PRC are members of the Communist Party, and their decisions are made in the context of the Party's objectives. The Communist Party's objectives are not necessarily coincident with what free-market businesspeople would consider good business decisions.

To be successful in the PRC it is also critical to understand the cultural nego-tiating environment. Chinese negotiators, at the beginning stages of negotiations, prefer to seek out agreement on generalities from the other party and try to avoid dealing with specific details, leaving these for later meetings. This may be due to the Chinese belief that interpersonal conflict is inappropriate and should be avoided. This approach of agreeing on general principles allows the Chinese to develop a mental framework of the negotiation process. For the Chinese, these general declarations are important as they establish a framework and provide limits should the foreign negotiators want to go beyond appropriate boundaries. Pye (1982) noted that foreign negotiators give up an advantage when they agree too quickly to "general principles" because the Chinese can "quickly turn an agree-ment on principles into an agreement on goals and then insist that all discussion on concrete arrangements must foster those agreed upon goals" (42).

Graham and Herberger (1983) found that American negotiators tend to approach negotiations sequentially, that is, they "separate the issues and settle them one at a time . . . in an American negotiation the final agreement is a sum of the several concessions made on individual issues" (164). In the PRC, concessions are not made sequentially throughout the course of the negotiation—they come at the end. According to Yang (1986), "Chinese people, especially adults, tend to display a cognitive style of seeing things . . . in wholes rather than in parts while Westerners tend to do the reverse" (147). Yang also noted that the Chinese "will try to synthesize the constituent parts into a whole so that all parts blend into a harmonious relationship at this higher level of perceptual organization" (148). The result of this cognitive style is that the Chinese will not concede things that they have not integrated into their perception of what the final settlement should look like; thus, once the perception of the final settlement is in place in their minds, then and only then can concessions be made.

Conformity is highly regarded in Chinese society, and the Chinese consider harmonious interpersonal relationships to be of great importance in life and in business. Kirkbride and Tang (1990) noted that "this conformity . . . leads individuals to consider the relationship between themselves and the other party as one of the crucial factors in any conflict or negotiation situation. In order to preserve harmonious interpersonal relationships, the Chinese will avoid confronting the other party in negotiations at all costs" (7). If Western negotiators engage in confrontation, their Chinese counterparts experience deep levels of personal shame to have been treated in such a manner. What's more, behavior that may not seem to be overly aggressive, argumentative, or pushy to Westerners is likely to be viewed as such by Chinese. Negotiating a contract in the PRC requires an in-depth knowledge of both negotiation norms and cultural protocol on the part of the expatriate negotiator.

Russia

Many dramatic changes have occurred in the countries that formerly comprised the Union of Soviet Socialist Republics (USSR) during the years since the collapse of communism. These changes will no doubt be reflected in the negotiating style of the Russians today. The following discussion should be thought of in this context, as it is largely based on historical information. Historically, Russian negotiators have been quite secretive about themselves, their motives, and the goals they hold for their negotiations. Many feel this is due to the fact that they had lived in a society that was isolated from the international business community and thus were reluctant to reveal either their ignorance of common capitalist business practices or simply because of a general distrust of foreigners.

Russian negotiating behavior has been variously characterized by Western businesspeople as rigid, stubborn, inflexible, confrontational, and competitive. Some scholars note that Americans and Russians are influenced by two different systems. Within Western ethical systems, it is viewed as a positive thing to seek out compromises in order to resolve conflicts and come to agreement. However, Russians come from an ethical background in which it is positive for individuals to create new conflicts with adversaries and to exacerbate existing ones. The very word "deal" itself has negative associations in the Russian language because anyone seeking compromises is considered cowardly, weak, and unworthy (Rajan and Graham 1991).

Reinforcing this view is the statement of Alexander Arefiev, CEO of INFORCOM (a management development firm): "My biggest problem is convincing my [Russian] clients to take a cooperative approach with Westerners" (Rajan and Graham 1991, 48). It is the nature of Russian negotiators, according to Arefiev, to be adversarial and confrontational in business negotiations. Research by Graham and his associates supports this view. In a fifteen-country study, they found that Russian managers did not focus on cooperative or creative solutions that would enable both parties to profit from the negotiations. Russians scored close to the bottom compared to the other fourteen countries that were studied.

Interestingly, the Russian word for "profit," has a negative connotation as well. It connotes exploitation, and the sense is that profits are always at the expense of another human being. In English it can have that connotation as well, but it can also imply monetary success that is due to hard work and that can improve one's quality of life.

The Russian negotiating style appears, from the Western standpoint, to be very adversarial; however, historically, the Russians have been extremely reliable in honoring all contractual arrangements. John Minneman, Chase

Manhattan's vice-president/representative in Moscow, stated that his Russian banking counterparts were "sophisticated and tough, but they never lie and always pay on time." Another international businessperson concurs: "Although [they] drive a very hard bargain in contract negotiations, they will faithfully abide by its provisions, and expect the other party to do the same. They have an excellent record in honoring their financial commitments" (Rajan and Graham 1991, 50). Thus, while Westerners may not like the way Russians bargain, once a contract is in force, for many Western businesspeople the ramifications of doing business in Russia are positive in nature. Russia has gone through many changes in the past decade and continues to change and modernize. These changes are likely to have a substantial impact on the negotiating style that one will encounter in Russia.

These brief negotiating profiles are intended to give the reader a flavor of how negotiating styles and conditions can differ from place to place. There are many other variations that may be found, and there are books devoted entirely to international negotiations and negotiations in particular locations. Along with this information, the good negotiator constantly remains sensitive to the dynamics of a particular situation and reacts to these.

Summary and Conclusions

Communication is an essential part of management. In any management situation it can cause difficulties or provide solutions, thus effective communication is a key challenge for managers. Good communication is especially difficult in international management because of the differences that are likely to exist between parties in the communication process. Differences such as language, political beliefs, cultural values, attitudes toward work and the like all influence how we communicate and what we understand. This chapter has explored the basis of human communication as well as some barriers to good communication. A substantial portion of the chapter was devoted to negotiations. Negotiations are ongoing in international management, and communication is key to their success or lack thereof. We looked at the process of negotiation and considered the factors that influence success in international negotiations. The chapter also included a brief description of negotiations in three different countries to give a flavor of how different groups view the process. These and other country descriptions are not meant to be definitive. The international manager will find that there is much to be discovered and learned through experience in any country.

When communicating or negotiating across nations, preparation is critical. It must include an in-depth study of communication norms, negotiation norms, and the general national environment. Time and patience are critical to effective communication and are an integral aspect of successful international negotiations. Mistakes will be made that will hurt the personal and business relationships of both parties if managers do not make the effort to understand both the communication and the negotiation processes.

The picture of the businessperson getting on a plane with several books to read en route to a foreign country comes to mind as the wrong approach. The effective manager tries to think and understand the process beforehand, including the details. For example, Who will meet you? Where will you stay? What will the negotiation setup be like? It is easy to take these things for granted and then to be surprised. Imagine that your counterparts have said they will meet you and make arrangements for accommodation and you have agreed. You need to know what, specifically, this means, or you may be surprised. If you are surprised, you will not start the negotiations at your best. Preparation is key to effective negotiations.

The world is a constantly changing place, and both communication and negotiation styles will change, so the international manager will not always find the situation as described here or elsewhere. The national descriptions here are intended to indicate how communications and negotiations may differ. Most importantly, businesspeople around the world are becoming sensitive to national and cultural differences, so the Westerner who bows in the Far East may well find a hand held out for a handshake.

References

Adler, N.J. 1991. *International Dimensions of Organizational Behavior.* 2nd ed. Boston: PWS-Kent Publishing.

Amado, G., and H.V. Brasil. 1991. "Organizational Behaviors and Cultural Context: The Brazilian 'Jeitinho.'" *International Studies of Management and Organization* 21(3): 38–61.

Dodd, C. 1977. *Perspectives on Cross-Cultural Communication.* Dubuque, IA: Kendall Hunt.

Fisher, R., and W. Ury. 1991. *Getting to Yes—Negotiating Agreement Without Giving In.* New York: Penguin Books.

"Getting the Message, at Last." 2007. *Economist* (December 15): 18.

Graham, J.L., and R.A. Herberger. 1983. "Negotiators Abroad—Don't Shoot from the Hip." *Harvard Business Review* (July–August): 160–168.

Hall, E.T. 1977. *Beyond Culture.* New York: Anchor.

Haworth, D.A., and G.T. Savage. 1989. "A Channel-Ratio Model of Intercultural Communication: The Trains Won't Sell, Fix Them Please." *Journal of Business Communication* 26(3): 231–254.

Horst, P.R., Jr. 2007. *Cross-Cultural Negotiations.* http://www.au.af.mil/au/awc/awcgate/awc/horst_crosscultural_negot.pdf (accessed March 22, 2012).

Kirkbride, P.S., and F.Y. Tang. 1990. "Negotiation: Lessons from Behind the Bamboo Curtain." *Journal of General Management* 16(1): 1–13.

Mendenhall, M., B.J. Punnett, and D. Ricks. 1995. *Global Management.* Oxford: Blackwell.

Oddou, G., and M. Mendenhall. 1984. "Person Perception in Cross-Cultural Settings: A Review of Cross-Cultural and Related Cognitive Literature." *International Journal of Intercultural Relations* 8(1): 77–96.

Pye, L. 1982. *Chinese Commercial Negotiating Style.* New York: Oelgeschlager Gunn and Hain.

Rajan, M.N., and J.L. Graham. 1991. "Nobody's Grandfather Was a Merchant: Understanding the Soviet Commercial Negotiating Process and Style." *California Management Review* (Spring): 40–57.

Szalay, L. 1981. "Intercultural Communication: A Process Model." *International Journal of Intercultural Relations* 5: 133–146.

Triandis, H. 1964. "Cultural Influences upon Cognitive Processes." In *Advances in Experimental and Social Psychology,* ed. L. Berkowitz, 486–495. New York: Academic Press.

Visser, M. 1991. *The Rituals of Dinner: The Origins, Evolution, Eccentricities, and Meaning of Table Manners.* New York: Grove Weidenfeld.

Yang, K.S. 1986. "Chinese Personality and Its Change." In *The Psychology of the Chinese People,* ed. M.H. Bond, 106–170. Hong Kong: Oxford University Press.

10

Human Resource Choices in a Cross-National Context

Introduction

Human resource (staffing) choices are complicated in an international company because more human resource options are available and because each choice has different benefits and costs. Further, human resource choices have to be made in the context of the many cross-national differences that we have explored in this book: culture, politics, history, geography, economics, demographics, language, and religion. This means that issues associated with recruitment, selection, training, compensation, promotion, retirement, and so on take on added dimensions when we consider international firms. The human resource manager in such a firm is faced with a multiplicity of issues when making decisions.

This chapter looks at the various groups of employees that an international firm can consider for different posts. It examines the benefits and costs associated with each group. The chapter outlines approaches for effective recruitment, selection, and training in the international context. Chapter 11, which follows, deals with a specific aspect of human resource management (HRM)—the management of expatriates.

Groups of Employees in International Firms

In order to identify the main groups of employees among which an international firm can choose for staffing, consider the following example:

A Japanese firm, JapanCo, with headquarters in Japan, has a wholly owned manufacturing subsidiary in the United States (Ja-USA), a sales office in Canada (Ja-Can), and a joint venture with a Mexican company (Ja-Mex) for Mexican production of its products. JapanCo has to staff its operations in Japan, the United States, Canada, and Mexico, and it has employees available from all these locations who can be used in its staffing. At least theoretically, it also has access to persons anywhere else in the world. For simplicity, we can divide current and potential employees into three groups:

- Parent Country Nationals (PCNs). These are persons from the parent country and usually persons who are employed with the parent firm in the parent country. In our example, PCNs would be Japanese nationals, usually employed with JapanCo.
- Host Country Nationals (HCNs). These are persons from one of the host countries, working in the host country operations. In our example, American nationals working in Ja-USA, Canadian nationals working in Ja-Can, or Mexican nationals working in Ja-Mex are HCNs.
- Third Country Nationals (TCNs). These are neither PCNs nor HCNs. They are usually from one of the countries where operations are located, but they are not working in their country of origin. In our example, they are American nationals working in Ja-Can or Ja-Mex, Canadian nationals working in Ja-USA or Ja-Mex, or Mexican nationals working in Ja-USA or Ja-Can.

These three categories cover many employees, although in reality things may not be this straightforward. For example, some people carry more than one citizenship and do not fit neatly into one category or another (Is an American Israeli working in Israel a PCN or an HCN?). Others carry one citizenship, but most of their education was in another country (Is a Chinese citizen educated in the United States and working in China a PCN or an HCN?). Still others have substantial experience in a given country or region (Is a Canadian who has worked throughout the Caribbean really a TCN if she takes a job with a Japanese firm's subsidiary in the Caribbean?). These subtle variations are important, and international firms may seek employees because of their special mix of nationality and experience. Initially, however, we will deal only with the three groups identified as the main international employee groups. The following section will consider each group in terms of the benefits and drawbacks broadly associated with it.

It is also the case that companies are becoming increasingly global and thus less identified with one parent company or country. Joint ventures, mergers, acquisitions, and other forms of transnational alliances mean that it is often not clear who the parent is and where it is located. As an example, in the 1990s, Barclays Bank (UK parent) and the Canadian Imperial Bank of Canada (Canada parent)—called the heritage banks—formed the First Caribbean International Bank. The new bank was a regional entity with its own headquarters in Barbados and staffed with people from many countries in the region as well as from the UK, Canada, and elsewhere. In this regional situation, the PCN, HCN, and TCN terminology does not really work. Nevertheless, the categories are helpful in understanding the benefits and drawbacks of various groups of employees, as discussed in the next section.

Employee Groups: Benefits and Drawbacks

Each of the three major employee groups identified provides benefits to a firm in cross-national staffing, but there are also drawbacks associated with each group. These benefits and drawbacks might be described as generic benefits and drawbacks; that is, they apply generally to the specified group, but they do not necessarily apply to any particular individual within the group. For example, PCNs generally cost the firm more than HCNs, but a specific PCN candidate evaluated against a specific HCN candidate may not be more costly. The following discussion considers the generic benefits and drawbacks for each group.

Parent Country Nationals (PCNs)

Parent country nationals, when looked at by headquarters, often seem like a good choice for an assignment abroad, because they are well-known individuals. Usually they are employees who have worked with the parent company for some time and have reached a stage of their career where they are being considered for an overseas assignment. The following section briefly describes the main reasons given by parent company chief executives and international human resource managers for selecting PCNs.

Benefits of PCNs

- PCNs are seen as providing a superior level of control in a subsidiary. Because they are well known at headquarters, PCNs are expected to act with the parent company's interests as their foremost concern. Particularly in new subsidiaries, executives may feel that they can lose control if they use HCNs or TCNs.
- PCNs are believed to have superior education, know-how, and expertise. In some locations, it may be difficult to find HCNs with appropriate levels of education, know-how, or expertise to fulfill a particular function.
- PCNs are familiar with the parent company and the parent company's way of doing things. They already understand the parent company culture and will readily comply with parent company policies and procedures. Moreover, they will be able to spread the culture to the subsidiary and train subsidiary personnel in appropriate policies and procedures.

- PCNs provide an easy communication channel between parent and subsidiary. They literally speak the same language (e.g., Japanese). It is comforting to know that when you call a subsidiary in a foreign country, you will get someone you can speak to. PCNs also speak the same language in a figurative sense—they understand the nuances of what is said or not said, the implications of the use of different media for certain communications, and so on. Also, they usually have well-developed personal relationships with head office colleagues.
- PCNs provide a foreign image and sometimes such an image is desirable. In some locations, foreign managers may be admired and thought of as "better" managers than their local counterparts. This may be a local stereotype, or it may be that local managers lack managerial education and experience. Whatever the reality, a PCN can be a good choice in such a situation.
- In certain situations, PCNs may be used to avoid local ethnic or racial tensions. In countries where two or more groups are antagonistic toward each other, any local manager selection will likely be unpopular with some group. In this case, using PCNs in sensitive positions can avoid local conflict and stress.

Many international companies have policies that stipulate, or imply, that to reach a top management position at the parent company, managers must have substantial international experience. International assignments give parent company managers increased responsibility and usually an opportunity to function at a higher level (albeit in a smaller subsidiary). Companies choose PCNs for the benefits outlined previously; they also choose them in order to give promising managers a chance to prove themselves internationally and advance within the company as a whole. There are, of course, drawbacks to selecting PCNs.

Drawbacks of PCNs

The choice of a PCN can seem like a good one for a number of reasons, as outlined previously. Yet the benefits need to be weighed against the drawbacks outlined below; they also need to be considered relative to the benefits of the other groups, which will be discussed in the following sections.

- It is costly to send PCNs to foreign locations (this will be discussed in more detail in chapter 11). Costs often include an array of items, such as international travel, housing, local transportation, and club memberships. Costs are even higher when the PCN has a spouse and family, because their needs must be taken care of as well.

- A substantial number of PCNs are reported as "failures" in their foreign assignments. For a variety of reasons (again, discussed in more detail in chapter 11), some PCNs are not able to adjust well to foreign environments and either return early or do a poor job in the subsidiary. The cost of failure is high for the parent company, as a PCN who returns early or does a poor job is likely to have a negative effect on overall company performance and a host of relationships—with the government, suppliers, customers, creditors, colleagues, unions, employees, and so on.
- PCNs may experience difficulty communicating in the local subsidiary environment. Unlike communication with the parent, they may speak a different language, both literally and figuratively, than the locals. Misunderstandings are likely to occur because of differences in accents and dialects, even when the PCN can speak the local language. In some cases, PCNs have to rely on translators or interpreters, which makes communication slow and awkward.
- PCNs project a foreign image, which is negative in some locations. The use of PCNs may imply that the company believes no locals are good enough for the assignment, and this can antagonize other managers as well as workers. Locals may be proud of their levels of education, know-how, and expertise, and be offended if a PCN is selected over an HCN. Specific PCNs also have a negative image in certain locations— for example, the British are not always liked in some former colonies, Americans have a reputation for being arrogant in some places, and the Japanese are believed to be ethnocentric by some other cultures.

These drawbacks to using PCNs need to be carefully considered when selecting personnel for international posts. If PCNs are used in foreign locations, it is critical that they have the appropriate local knowledge and sensitivity in order to function effectively in a particular location.

Host Country Nationals (HCNs)

To some extent, the examination of HCNs is the mirror image of that of PCNs. The drawbacks associated with PCNs are the benefits to using HCNs, and the benefits for PCNs become the drawbacks for HCNs.

Benefits of HCNs

Many companies prefer HCNs because of their familiarity with the local subsidiary environment. This can be a substantial advantage in many locations. The following discussion outlines these benefits:

- HCNs understand the local environment. They can move easily in this environment and interact with a variety of local constituencies in a normal and expected local manner. HCNs are usually a good choice when extensive local interactions are necessary.
- HCNs can communicate relatively easily and well with local groups, and can provide access to local groups—the government, creditors, suppliers, and so on. HCNs speak the local language, understand local customs, and have developed local networks of contacts.
- HCNs are culturally in tune with local customs. They can interact effectively with other local managers as well as with employees. HCNs' managerial style is likely to be consistent with local expectations.
- HCNs provide a local image for the subsidiary. This is important in many locations. Using HCNs suggests that the parent company trusts people from the host country and that they believe HCNs can do a good job. This can be good within the subsidiary and is also good for the company's image in the larger community.

In addition to these benefits, HCNs generally cost substantially less than PCNs in any particular position. The additional costs mentioned as a drawback for PCNs do not exist for HCNs. There may be some training costs for HCNs, but these are usually minor relative to the costs associated with PCNs and their families. Although this is generally true, interestingly, in some locations where skilled and experienced HCNs are in short supply and there is a high demand for these skilled and experienced HCNs, the reverse can occur, and they can actually be more expensive than PCNs.

Drawbacks of HCNs

Where local understanding is important, and where interactions with the local community are needed, the HCN provides clear benefits. There are drawbacks to using HCNs, however, and these need to be assessed.

- HCNs may know a lot about the local environment, but often they do not have the formal qualifications, required expertise, or adequate experience needed by the company for a particular position. Education and opportunities for experience differ from country to country, so it is often difficult to find the requirements expected in the parent company in the host country.
- HCNs may need a substantial amount of job-related training, and these costs can be relatively high. HCNs may need to spend time at the parent company in order to understand what is required in the subsidiary, to

become familiar with the parent company culture, and to learn the parent policies and procedures.

- HCNs can have difficulty communicating with people at headquarters. They may speak a different language and have different patterns of communication. HCNs who speak a language different from that spoken in the parent country have problems when they want to phone the parent or send an e-mail memo.

While HCNs provide certain clear benefits, the drawbacks to using HCNs have to be carefully considered. The appropriate choice depends on the situation. HCNs are best in some situations, but not necessarily in all.

Third Country Nationals (TCNs)

TCNs share some of the benefits of both PCNs and HCNs as well as some of the drawbacks. Like PCNs, they are foreigners in the host country; like HCNs, they may not be thoroughly at home with parent company culture; however, they usually provide valuable needed experience and expertise. The following summarizes the benefits and drawbacks.

Benefits of TCNs

Generally, companies select TCNs for their particular skills or experience. If JapanCo, described previously, needs a specialist in interactive networking systems to update its information technology in its Mexican subsidiary, Ja-Mex, expertise is critical for the job. The company might use a PCN or an HCN if one is available with the appropriate expertise. Nationality is relatively unimportant in this case, so if a person with the expertise can be found in the Canadian subsidiary or the U.S. subsidiary, the choice will be a TCN. The company may even go outside its stock of current employees and recruit from around the world to fill a specialist position. JapanCo, if it has no specialists in interactive networking systems currently available, can advertise in a magazine such as the *Economist,* which is read around the world. The best applicant for the post may be from India, where specialists in information technology are becoming plentiful and are often seeking positions outside India.

Although expertise is the primary criterion for selecting TCNs, many companies that consider themselves truly global adopt the approach that nationality, on its own, should not be the primary factor in human resource choices. Chief executives and human resource managers in these firms believe that the best person for the job should always be selected.

This approach should provide opportunities for employees throughout the global organization, and employees from any subsidiary should be able to reach the top at home, in another subsidiary, or in the parent company. Such an approach would mean that in JapanCo, you might well find a Mexican as chief executive in Japan, an American as chief executive in Canada, and a Canadian in Mexico. In reality this mix is unusual, although it is becoming somewhat more difficult to clearly identify companies as "American," "French," "British," "Indian," "Chinese," and so on, as the ownership of large firms becomes more international.

TCNs, like PCNs, are foreigners, so they also provide an international image for a subsidiary. The image projected by TCNs may in effect be global rather than simply international. PCNs are seen as representing the parent country whereas TCNs seem to represent the world in some sense. Some managers describe international firms as developing a small cadre of internationalists. These internationalists spend their careers in foreign locations and are as at home in Japan as they are in Mexico, Canada, or anywhere else.

Drawbacks of TCNs

TCNs might not be very familiar with either the parent culture or the host culture. This means they could need to adapt to two cultural sets at the same time. This can be stressful for the individuals and their families. A Japanese manager (PCN) moving to Canada has to learn about Canadian culture and business practices. A Canadian manager in Canada (HCN) working with a Japanese parent company has to adapt to Japanese approaches. A Mexican manager working with a Japanese parent company and moving to Canada (TCN) will need to learn about Canadian culture and business practices as well as adapt to Japanese approaches.

The need to deal with multiple cultures can make communication a challenge for TCNs. The Mexican just described is a native Spanish speaker. He/she will need to speak English to function effectively in a managerial role in Canada. He/she may also be required to communicate with Japanese managers on a regular basis. The communication needs and the requirement of dealing with multiple cultures means that the TCN may need substantial training in nontask issues.

TCNs can be costly for the same reasons as PCNs. The need to ensure cultural adaptation also means that failure rates could be high, although there is no empirical evidence of this. In fact, the anecdotal evidence is the reverse: the international cadre mentioned earlier is usually described as especially adaptable, and willing and able to function well in a variety of locations.

As discussed previously, TCNs project a global image for a firm. This can be negative as well as positive. When firms seek work permits because they cannot find a host country national to fill a post, it is usually assumed that they will fill the post with a parent national. Selecting a TCN instead can sometimes be misunderstood locally. Local employees expecting PCNs may be surprised by TCNs.

* * *

This brief discussion of the benefits and drawbacks of the three main groups of employees—PCNs, HCNs, TCNs—illustrates the challenges of making the right staffing choice for a particular job in a specific location. The choice has to be seen in the context of both the job and the location. The human resources manager needs to evaluate the importance of various factors, such as parent country/company knowledge, host country knowledge, and need for local interaction, in order to decide which group of employees is most likely to produce a suitable candidate for a particular position. Once a decision has been made to fill a position from a particular group of employees, understanding the general, or generic, benefits and drawbacks of that group allows the human resource manager to make appropriate decisions about the training that is needed for an individual or group of employees.

Most companies use some of each group of employees, but certain groups tend to be used more at certain levels in the organization. Lower-level employees and supervisors/first-level managers are usually HCNs because the skills needed at this level are usually available locally and the cost of bringing in expatriates at this level would often be prohibitive. Chinese companies have been the exception in some locations. The Chinese have argued successfully that their Chinese low-level personnel are more productive and less expensive than local workers in these locations, and they have sometimes received government agreement to bring in a Chinese workforce to complete a labor-intensive project. This is an unusual situation as it means the project does not create local employment, so each project would have to be presented to the government in the host country and the benefits of such an arrangement would have to be argued on a case-by-case basis.

Technical personnel and specialists are quite often PCNs or TCNs because the skills and expertise needed are specific to the position, and the company will select the person with these skills regardless of nationality. Middle-level management is often a mix of PCNs and HCNs, drawing on the local population as much as possible, but using some PCNs to train local managers and to ensure that parent company policies and procedures are followed. Top-level positions, chief executives, and highly sensitive positions such as chief financial officer are visible and play a critical role in a subsidiary—this means that the choice of personnel for these positions is especially important. Some companies are more comfortable with PCNs in these roles because their use increases the sense of control by headquarters. Other companies prefer HCNs in these positions because of the need to interact with the local constituencies (government, suppliers, customers, creditors, unions, and so on) and because this choice is often positive both politically and publicly.

Some companies tend to favor PCNs wherever permitted, others prefer HCNs, and some argue that nationality should not matter and that personnel at all levels should be chosen on the basis of their skills, expertise, and experience. A preference for PCNs is referred to as an *ethnocentric staffing* policy, reflecting the belief that the parent country and company ways are best (see the discussion of ethnocentrism in chapter 2). A preference for HCNs is considered a *polycentric staffing* approach, reflecting the fact that subsidiaries are staffed with local personnel, so that each subsidiary has its own makeup. A *geocentric staffing* approach means that nationality is not considered in staffing decisions, suggesting that personnel can come from anywhere in the world.

Some companies are essentially ethnocentric, polycentric, or geocentric because of fundamental beliefs at headquarters. That is, top management in some parent companies genuinely believes that PCNs are better choices, and therefore favors this group. In other companies, top management believes that HCNs are better because they understand local conditions. In still others, top management believes that global companies should be globally managed and that the true mark of a global company is its ability to benefit from the diversity of a global mix of its management, executives, and directors.

For most companies, the staffing approach reflects the needs of the company at a particular time. For example, if no HCNs are available with the qualifications to be chief executive, then a PCN will be used. If local know-how is of paramount importance in a particular location, an HCN will be used, even if this choice requires extensive company and/or product-related training. If PCNs have a negative image and qualified HCNs are not available, then a TCN might be considered the best choice.

Staffing policy tends to change over time as well. Early in the life of a subsidiary there are usually at least some PCNs in top or sensitive positions and some TCNs in technical positions. As the subsidiary matures, these people are often replaced with HCNs. Over time, as HCNs are trained and become familiar with parent company policies and procedures, the parent company develops trust in their ability and loyalty; as this happens, more HCNs replace PCNs and TCNs.

Many companies do not look at subsidiaries individually, but rather on a regional basis. For example, the Canadian Imperial Bank of Commerce operated its banks throughout the English-speaking Caribbean as one region. Global companies often divide the world into regions—say, North America, Latin America, the Caribbean, Western Europe, Eastern Europe, Southeast Asia, the Pacific Rim, the Middle East, West Africa, and so on. Companies that are structured into regions are likely to look at staffing on a regional basis rather than a host country basis. Within a particular region, say the English-speaking Caribbean, employees could be moved from country to country (e.g., Barbados to Jamaica) and essentially treated as though they were all host country nationals. In addition, PCNs are often assigned to a region rather than to a particular country in the region. This staffing approach can be called a *regiocentric* one.

Staffing and the International Product Life Cycle

One can also think of staffing policies as changing with the international product life cycle. The product life cycle is often described in the marketing literature. The concept of the product life cycle is, simply, that a process of birth, growth, maturity, decline, and eventually death applies to products, as it does to people. The life cycle varies from product to product; for example:

- Some products have a very short life cycle in some markets and die soon after birth (these products are never accepted by potential customers).
- Other products go through rapid growth, but decline quickly (these products are initially accepted well, but customers quickly find other, better products to meet their needs).
- Still other products have a long life; they reach maturity and remain viable for extended periods (these products continue to meet customers' needs over time).

International business specialists have related international strategies to the product life cycle and in turn to human resource choices. Products are typically "born" or developed to meet the needs of the domestic market, and during their early growth stages, the company focuses on making adaptations to ensure that a product is accepted in this market. A product may be exported if foreign customers seek it out, but there is little interest in foreign markets at this stage of the life cycle. As a product matures in its home market, growth rates slow and new markets are sought for the product. Foreign markets become the focus of interest at this stage, and these foreign markets go through their own growth. The focus now is on making adaptations to ensure that the product is accepted in a variety of differing foreign markets. Finally, as a product declines in its domestic market and matures in foreign markets, the focus is on costs. Adaptation is no longer needed, and instead standardization is sought for cost savings.

In terms of human resource choices, consider the following:

- During the early stages of the product life cycle, only PCNs are involved. PCNs will handle exports and will travel overseas to sell the product or oversee licensing and so on. Staffing will be essentially ethnocentric.
- During the middle of the product life cycle, when the focus changes to satisfying different foreign markets, HCNs will be important because their local know-how helps adapt the product to host country needs. Staffing will be essentially polycentric.
- In later stages, PCNs may be used for control purposes, HCNs will be used where they provide a cost advantage, and TCNs will provide specialized services. Staffing will be essentially geocentric.

This explanation is, of course, simplistic. International firms have many products and product lines, and these will likely be at different stages of the product life cycle in different markets, so that it is not possible to apply this idea to an entire company. Nevertheless, it can be helpful for a manager looking at a specific product or product line to relate human resource choices to the product focus at different stages of the life cycle.

Foreign Guest Workers

In addition to the groups discussed, throughout the world there are many "guest workers" who have left their country of birth to work in a country where higher pay and a better standard of living exist. These guest workers are different than TCN managers because they are brought in to work in jobs that members of the local populace choose not to hold: garbage collection, maid service, repetitive factory work, manual labor, and so forth. How guest workers come to find themselves working in foreign countries can be illustrated by the following example: A vice-president of an international construction firm was assigned the responsibility of staffing a major reconstruction project in Kuwait following Operation Desert Storm. In order to staff the project, he had to go to the Philippines and hire laborers because the labor market for construction workers in Kuwait was small, and because the Kuwaiti standard of living is so high that very few Kuwaitis need to work in manual labor jobs. The Filipino laborers would be making more money than they could in the Philippines but would be separated from their families for long periods of time and would not be accepted into the mainstream culture of Kuwait.

Guest workers are making up increasingly large portions of the labor force around the world, and they are almost always denied citizenship in the countries in which they work. They can be deported if an economic downturn occurs; their children cannot enter the apprentice systems or, often, the local universities; their career mobility is virtually nil; and their quality of life is always much lower than that of the majority of the citizens of the country in which they work, even though they contribute significantly to the national income and are the foundation upon which many industries' profits rest. Whether they are illegal aliens or legal short-term residents, the life of foreign guest workers tends to be one of uncertainty, unequal treatment compared to the country's citizens, and poor upward mobility. They usually live in isolated "ghettos," and because they may hold different religious beliefs, eat different foods, wear different clothes, and hold other cultural preferences that differ from those of the local citizens, conflict between them and HCNs inevitably occurs. Some governments are rethinking their policies toward the use of guest workers because of these concerns.

During the civil unrest in the Middle East in countries such as Tunisia, Egypt, and Libya in 2011 and 2012, foreign guest workers constituted one group that faced substantial hardship. In many cases, their employers held their passports, and they had difficulty retrieving these documents. Because these workers were usually from the very poor countries, their home countries were not always able to assist them in coming home. Employees from richer countries such as Canada, France, the United States, and so on were usually evacuated on special flights arranged by their home country. The same was not true for the foreign guest workers from poorer countries. They often had to walk to the borders or find whatever transportation they could in order to return home with a few possessions.

The issue of illegal migrants, and illegals working in the host countries, has been important both in Europe and the United States. The European Union experienced waves of illegal immigration, largely from Africa, during the first decade of the twenty-first century, and the United States experienced the same thing with migrants largely from Cuba, Haiti, and Mexico, but also from Central America and the Caribbean. Attitudes toward illegal migrants vary widely. At one extreme, some believe that they provide valuable services that better-off citizens of the European countries or the United States are not willing to provide, and that they contribute positively to the economy. At the other extreme, some believe that they take jobs from citizens and are a burden on the economy, because they use services provided through citizens' taxes. The first argument leads to calls to legitimize the status of illegal migrants and to make it easier for them to immigrate legally. The second leads to calls to deport all illegals and make it harder for them to cross borders. In 2008, the

United States built walls at the Mexican border to deter illegal immigrants. Europe has instituted a policy in Africa to publicize the dangers of trying to get to Europe from Africa, and has tried to improve the legal migration option. Which, if either, of these approaches will prove successful remains to be seen. It is noteworthy that illegal immigrants appear willing to accept the dangers associated with crossing into the United States by boat or desert, and similarly African illegal immigrants accept that many do not survive the journey to Europe. This determination, even in the face of grave danger, means that it is difficult to deter these migrants.

Although we think of the illegal immigration issue as largely associated with migrants from poorer developing countries going to rich developed ones (for example, Mexicans going to the United States), in reality many developing countries have illegal immigrants as well. People in the very poor countries of the world migrate to developing countries that are better off, especially if they are close by and if entry is relatively easy. This is the case, for example, in Africa, where a country like South Africa is home to a large number of guest workers from very poor or conflict-ridden African countries. Similarly, in the Caribbean, better-off islands have guest workers from worse-off countries. The arguments are the same in these countries, and foreign guest workers are often looked upon negatively and treated badly.

Foreign guest workers, both legal and illegal, play an important role in their home economies. These workers work abroad, save a substantial portion of their wages, and send money home to their families. This money sent home is known as "remittances," and in many countries, remittances account for a substantial part of the economy. The need to transfer money home has opened up new opportunities for a company such as Western Union, with a large part of its business in money transfers from the United States, its clientele is almost entirely made up of foreign guest workers and other members of the diaspora sending money home.

Organizational Structure and International HRM Choices

The previous discussion implicitly assumes a certain organizational structure: there is a parent company headquartered in a particular country with subsidiaries that it controls in a variety of other countries. This, of course, is only one possible structure internationally. International firms do business in a variety of other ways: they are involved in licensing, franchising, contracts, joint ventures, strategic alliances, mergers, and so on. These structural choices have a critical influence on human resource choices, as the following examples illustrate:

- A licensing agreement relies on a company in a foreign location to produce the parent company's product or service. The licensor (company for whom the product is being produced) is usually concerned with factors such as quality and capacity in the foreign location, and uses its own personnel (PCNs) to train employees and monitor activities at the licensee (company producing the product), but these assignments are usually short-term.

- A franchising arrangement involves the franchisor selling the rights to operate a franchise to a franchisee (for example, McDonald's, an American franchisor, sells rights to operate McDonald's restaurants to franchisees in countries around the world). Franchises are usually owned and run by locals (HCNs). The owners and employees often go to the franchisor's headquarters for short-term training courses (McDonald's United States has intensive courses to ensure that all McDonald's restaurants around the world meet the same standards). Managers from headquarters also visit franchisees to provide training and ensure that standards are maintained. Because of the particular ownership structure, neither of these groups can be classified using the PCN/HCN/TCN terminology.

- A contracting arrangement involves an agreement to provide particular services for a specified period (for example, an engineering firm is contracted to oversee the construction of a bridge, or a management consulting firm is contracted to carry out a survey of employee attitudes). International contracts are usually used where local expertise is not available, and, consequently, this means that foreign personnel from a foreign company are hired to complete a contract. In large projects, personnel may come from several different companies and countries (for example, in a World Bank–funded government restructuring contract in Jamaica, there were people from Australia, Canada, the United Kingdom, and the United States all working on the project in Jamaica at the same time). These people are expatriates, but they cannot be considered PCNs because there is no parent company in this business structure. Although contracts use foreigners because the expertise is not available locally, there is often a requirement for contractors to use local counterparts to effect a transfer of skills and expertise, and to improve the local skills base. This is the case with many management consultancy projects that are funded by the international financial institutions and aid organizations.

- A joint venture involves ownership of a company by two or more parent companies. For example, a Canadian company may form a joint venture with a French company to operate a company in France, in Canada, or in a third country, say Taiwan. Again, the distinctions between PCNs, HCNs, and TCNs are not as neat as described earlier. In this example, if operations are in France, a French employee is both a PCN and an HCN; if operations are in Taiwan, both Canadian and French employees are PCNs, and so on.

• Strategic alliances are arrangements in which two or more firms mutually agree to work together on a particular project of strategic importance to them. For example, the Body Shop, a UK-based franchisor with franchises around the world, might form a strategic alliance with Greenpeace, a worldwide environmental activism organization, to publicize information on endangered species. In this case, there is no parent or host country, and personnel working together on the project would not be classified in this way.

• International mergers involve two companies from different countries becoming one. For example, the Daimler-Benz company of Germany and the Chrysler company of the United States became Daimler-Chrysler some years ago. In a true merger, there is no dominant partner, thus there is no sense of one entity being the parent and the other, the host. (In the Daimler-Chrysler case, the German partner was often described as being dominant—and some have noted the Daimler name ahead of Chrysler as an indication of this. The Germans in the United States at Daimler-Chrysler were usually thought of as PCNs.) The Daimler-Chrysler merger disintegrated in 2007 after an apparently stormy and unproductive "marriage."

International structures that do not involve a parent company in a host country are becoming more and more common. For example, Barclays Bank (United Kingdom based) and the Canadian Imperial Bank of Canada (Canada based) merged their operations in the Caribbean early this century to create the First Caribbean International Bank, with a regional mandate. In this organization, categorizing employees using the traditional categories does not work well. Although this makes the PCN, HCN, TCN terminology less useful, the concepts discussed using this terminology are still helpful. For example, the issues that PCNs face working in a host country apply to expatriates in many situations. The benefits of HCNs apply generally for local employees in any country, and the same reasons for choosing TCNs apply even where there is no parent or host.

Each situation requires its own analysis. Appropriate selection and training depend on the business structure and the ownership arrangements, as well as the product or service, the location where business is done, and an array of other considerations.

Selection and Training of International Managers

The selection process for international managers basically involves identifying the important characteristics for a particular position, identifying a pool of potential candidates, evaluating the candidates in terms of the characteristics deemed important, short-listing the best candidates, reviewing and interviewing the short-listed candidates, and, finally, selecting the best candidate. The process is never this simple in reality, particularly for an international firm. As the foregoing discussion illustrated, there are both benefits and drawbacks to each of the groups of employees from which one can select. The same is true for any individual—one candidate may have excellent job-related skills and speak several languages but have no experience working with people from different cultural backgrounds; another may have moderate job-related skills and speak only her/his native language but have substantial experience working in multicultural situations. Evaluating these two candidates against each other is complex.

Training is designed to ensure that the selected candidate can perform well. Training can focus around job-related factors or around non-job-related ones, such as an individual's abilities to relate to others (relational) and deal with differences encountered in different locations (cross-cultural adaptation).

The following discussion suggests two structured approaches to the selection and training processes that are helpful to managers making human resource choices in international firms. After this general discussion, we point out some of the particular issues to be considered when selecting and training PCNs, HCNs, or TCNs.

Tung (1981) proposed a selection model that has become well known in the literature. The model relates job characteristics to selection strategies. The model asks a variety of questions about the position and uses the answers to identify the appropriate selection/training. The following is a simplification of this model:

1. Is an HCN available? If so, the position should be filled by HCN and training should focus on improving technical and managerial skills. If not, ask:
2. What is the degree of interaction required with the host community? If low, focus on job-related training. If high, ask:
3. How similar are cultures? If low similarity, focus on cross-cultural training, and include the family. If high, emphasize job-related training (adapted from Tung 1981).

This is a simple but useful model. It can provide a good guide in the selection process. There are, however, some extensions to the model that should be considered:

- The model assumes that HCNs should be selected if they are available and have the requisite skills. This may be true in many cases, but, as our earlier discussion illustrated, there may be times when non-HCNs are preferred.
- If HCNs are used, the model suggests a focus on technical and managerial

skills. This focus is appropriate but overlooks the need for the HCN to deal with colleagues in other subsidiaries and counterparts in the parent country. An overlooked aspect of training in much of the literature is the need to train HCNs in cross-cultural skills so that they can deal effectively with their foreign counterparts.

- If a non-HCN is selected, the model focuses on training the candidate and family for the foreign experience. This is, of course, critical, but the employees in the host country are ignored, and it may be equally important to ensure that they receive some training in cross-cultural issues so that they will accept foreign assignees.

An alternative approach suggested by Punnett and Ricks (1989) involves the following steps:

- Begin the selection process by asking what the legal limitations are; it may not be possible to use a PCN or TCN in some situations. If the company is limited to using an HCN regardless of skills and other factors, then the company must deal with this reality.
- If there are no legal restrictions, identify the needed job-related expertise and experience and develop a pool of candidates with the appropriate expertise and experience from throughout the company, including PCNs, HCNs, and TCNs.
- Identify non-job-related characteristics, including preference for using a particular group of employees and relational, cross-cultural abilities.
- Eliminate from the pool candidates who do not have the non-job-related characteristics.
- Remaining candidates should have both job and non-job characteristics and should meet legal requirements. These candidates can be evaluated relative to each other and training tailored to suit the candidate selected (adapted from Punnett and Ricks 1989).

These models are not meant to provide blueprints for selection and training, but to give general guidelines on the process and illustrate different approaches. The key seems to be that in selection, both job-related and relational/cross-cultural abilities are important. That is, the candidate must be able to do the job, but this is usually not enough in an international situation. The candidate must also be able to relate to others effectively and to adjust to new cultures. The literature has stressed this from an expatriate perspective, but it is also important when selecting among HCNs.

Human resource choices in an international firm inevitably result in cultural interactions. A firm that uses a wholly polycentric staffing policy in which HCNs are used everywhere overcomes this, but only to a certain extent. Polycentric subsidiaries do not operate in a vacuum. PCNs may visit these subsidiaries to introduce new products, new policies, and new procedures; to ensure that the subsidiaries are well managed and to evaluate performance; to audit operations and finances; and to train and develop managers and employees.

Similarly, HCNs visit the parent country to learn about new products, policies, and procedures; to report on subsidiary performance, operations, and finances; and to attend training and development sessions. Personnel from different subsidiaries also interact for a variety of reasons. Cross-cultural interactions are, thus, a normal part of an international firm's activities. Anyone whose position entails interactions with counterparts from different countries and cultures should have the following characteristics:

- an ability to get along well with people;
- an awareness of cultural differences;
- open-mindedness and a tolerance for foreigners; and
- adaptability and an ability to adjust quickly to new conditions (adapted from Ricks 1983, 59).

Once a candidate has been selected, training needs to be tailored to deal with the candidate's deficiencies, whether job-related or relational and cross-cultural. Although any individual candidate will have to be evaluated on the basis of a variety of factors, the following outlines the general training needs of the three groups of employees we have been discussing.

PCNs

PCNs particularly need to learn about the host country and how business is done there. The PCN needs to understand specifics of the job that differ from the job at home, including reporting relationships, time frames, and the subsidiary's relationship to the rest of the organization. The PCN also needs to be familiar with the country's host economic, legal, political, and labor environments. Sometimes the most important aspect of PCN training is the cultural environment and management practices in the host country because these affect every aspect of day-to-day operations and interactions.

HCNs

HCNs particularly need to understand the parent company and what it requires of them. The HCN needs to be familiar with the specifics of parent company policies and procedures, understand the reason for these, and be able and willing to comply with them. The HCN also needs to be able to communicate effectively with counterparts at the parent company. If an HCN appointment is to be successful in terms of the overall organization, the HCN needs to receive training to facilitate subsidiary–parent interactions.

TCNs

TCNs play an interesting role as "in-betweens." Often, as described, they are specialists and, therefore, being comfortable with the local environment in terms of their particular specialty is vital. TCNs also need to understand the host environment more generally, as well as the parent environment and the interaction between host and parent. Many TCNs, as described, have substantial international experience, and this can mean that in-depth, rigorous cross-cultural training can be minimized for that particular group.

The Training Process

The training process has most often been addressed from the perspective of a PCN and family being sent on an expatriate assignment (the following chapter deals explicitly with these expatriate issues). In this section, concepts of training rigor and matching the rigor of training to the needs of the candidate are introduced. These concepts are often discussed in terms of expatriates, but they are as applicable to the HCN or TCN as to the PCN.

Cross-cultural training methods have been described as varying from passive with low rigor to participative with high rigor (Black and Mendenhall 1990). Low-rigor and passive training methods focus on factual issues and include books, lectures, and area briefings. Moderate-rigor and somewhat active methods are described as analytical and include films, classroom discussion, and sensitivity training. High-rigor and fully participative methods seek to really involve the candidate in cross-cultural experiences; they are described as experiential and include role-playing, simulations, and field trips.

International and cross-cultural training can be relatively expensive. The greater the participation and rigor, the more expensive the training. International firms clearly want to optimize training expenses. Tailoring training to the needs of the candidates allows the company to use training resources to best effect. This approach means that expensive, participative, rigorous training is used only for those candidates who need this and will benefit from it.

Using Tung's (1981) model (presented earlier), it seems that as cultural differences increase, and as the need for cultural interactions increases, greater participation and rigor become more critical.

In the past, companies tended to provide in-house training for their employees. In the last decade, as many staff functions have been outsourced, international and cross-cultural training has often been undertaken by firms that specialize in this type of training. This seems to be the trend today. International firms should take advantage of the specialized training expertise of these training firms, but this choice also means that the specific needs related to the company could be overlooked. An ideal choice may be both in-company training dealing with company-specific issues paired with outsourced training incorporating in-depth knowledge of particular locations.

Compensation and Benefits

Compensation and benefits decisions in international firms are extremely complex, and this discussion barely outlines the issues that have to be addressed. Consider the various groups that have been discussed previously.

PCNs

PCNs who accept a foreign assignment generally expect to at least maintain the standard of living to which they are accustomed; this includes benefits and pensions. PCNs also expect to be able to live as their local counterparts do in the foreign location, even if this is in effect a higher standard of living than at home, and they usually expect to maintain the accustomed level of pay, benefits, and so on that they received at home. Many companies deal with PCN compensation on this basis; that is, salary and benefits at least equal to that at home, with premiums to allow a living standard equivalent to that at home or to local counterparts, if appropriate. From the outside, it seems that PCNs get the best of both worlds. This, in fact, is a point of contention when PCN salaries and benefits put them well above their local counterparts. International firms need PCNs and therefore want to compensate them in ways that are fair from the PCN point of view, but they do need to consider the host view as well.

In addition to regular compensation and housing/living allowances, PCNs expect additional benefits such as schooling for their children, regular trips home, access to recreational clubs, and so on. Some assignments are seen as unattractive. In these cases, PCNs may require additional incentives, referred to as hardship pay. Altogether, the package for PCNs can be substantial.

HCNs

HCNs are usually paid on the basis of local salaries and benefits. Some international companies pay at the high end of local scales, so that jobs with these companies are often seen as desirable and prestigious locally. At the same time, some HCNs can feel disadvantaged when they know that PCNs, TCNs, or HCNs in other subsidiaries are being compensated on a higher basis. This provides a new challenge for the international firm—firms are blamed for inflating local prices if they pay above local norms, but they are accused of discrimination if local compensation levels are lower than the parent or other subsidiaries. There is no easy solution to this dilemma, but the firm must seek to be fair in its compensation policies in all locations and must be able to explain the basis on which it decides on compensation.

TCNs

TCNs are a particularly difficult blend from a compensation perspective. Should they be paid like PCNs? Should they be paid the equivalent of HCNs? Or should their compensation be equivalent to what they would receive in their home country? The answer is probably a mix; compensation should reflect host country norms, but be adjusted to account for home country expectations and incorporate some of the extra benefits usually afforded to PCNs. This approach sounds reasonable, but has not necessarily been implemented in reality. Some companies seek to attract candidates for international assignments from countries like India for the very reason that they are relatively inexpensive. This may be effective in the short term, but often leads to these candidates' feeling disillusioned, with consequences of decreased motivation and performance. Companies need to realize that these employees are expatriates and put into place the needed administrative structures to ensure that the employees succeed.

In compensation decisions, the issue is one of equity as well as the ability to demonstrate equity. This is especially difficult for international firms because of the different expectations and standards of living encountered around the world. In some locations, it is normal to have a maid, a nanny, and a chauffeur, but the cost of these may be relatively low. In that case, should additional allowances be granted to hire these people, or should the expense come out of one's salary? Many human resource managers indicate that these trade-offs are made on a case-by-case basis. There is some advantage to tailoring the compensation package to the individual's needs, but this is also likely to result in charges of inequity. Compensation and benefits remain a major concern for international companies, with no clear evidence regarding best practices. A Mercer survey in 2008 reported that 26 percent of companies surveyed had no overarching policies for providing expatriate employee benefits, although 86 percent felt that benefits were a priority for achieving international success (Mercer 2008).

Promotion, Career Development, Retirement

Selection, training, and compensation issues form the basis for an international assignment. Yet the firm also has to pay attention to what happens to these employees over time. Issues of promotion, career development, and retirement are all part of the human resource decision process. As always, these decisions are made complex by their international nature. Consider the following situations:

- A Canadian employee spends most of her career in Africa. Where will she want to retire? How will her pension funds be invested and paid out?
- A West Indian from Trinidad works for a U.S. company and serves around the world, from the United Kingdom to the United Arab Emirates and Malaysia. Where are his retirement funds kept? Where are they paid out? How are taxes paid on them?
- A university professor who is an Australian national spends part of her teaching career in Canada, then moves to the United States for several years, followed by a stint teaching in Brazil. She wants to retire in Brazil with her Brazilian husband. She has accumulated retirement funds in Canada, the United States, and Brazil. How does she deal with these separate funds?
- An American spends all his working life in the Middle East, but his pension is vested in the United States. Can he retire in the Middle East? Must he pay U.S. taxes on his retirement income?

Tax laws further complicate these issues. Some countries tax individuals on the basis of citizenship, some on the basis of residency, and some on the basis of the location of the work carried out. Tax treaties are in place for many countries and are designed to help avoid double taxation. These tax issus are complex for the average individual to understand. Some issues need to be worked out by corporate lawyers, but they also need to be considered and discussed by human resource managers and employees. The previous examples illustrate the complexities that are a necessary part of international careers. These examples focused on retirement. Similar issues are inherent in promotion and career development questions:

- How do within-country promotions compare to promotions at headquarters or to headquarters?
- Are expatriate assignments really good for your career?
- How should you evaluate a home country promotion relative to an expatriate posting?

International staffing decisions, like any decision affecting careers and incomes, are among the most sensitive for human resource managers and employees alike. Mistakes, lack of transparency, and perceived inequities can prove costly both in terms of individual motivation and performance, and employee well-being, as well as to the company in terms of overall effectiveness. International companies need to consider this wide array of issues in their human resource choices.

Summary and Conclusions

This chapter provided an overview of the issues that human resource managers need to consider when making cross-national human resource choices. The issues are many and varied, and the choices have serious implications for employees and the company. The importance of making good choices cannot be overemphasized.

Different employee groups were discussed in this chapter to illustrate the benefits and costs associated with different choices. This discussion led to consideration of appropriate selection and training to maximize the benefits and minimize the costs associated with staffing choices. In addition, the chapter briefly examined compensation and career development issues, although these complex issues could not be dealt with in detail here. Overall, the chapter sought to identify ways in which human resource allocation can be optimized in an international firm, considering the multiple facets of people, location, product/service, structure, and longevity.

References

Black, J.S., and M. Mendenhall. 1990. "Cross-Cultural Training Effectiveness: A Review and a Theoretical Framework for Future Research." *Academy of Management Review* 15(1): 113–136.

Mercer. 2008. "Expatriate Employee Numbers Double as Companies See Increased Value in Expatriate Assignments." Press release, October 27. http://www.mercer.com/press-releases/1326180 (accessed March 24, 2012).

Punnett, B.J., and D. Ricks. 1989. *International Business*. London: International Thompson Press.

Ricks, D. 1983. *Big Business Blunders*. Columbus, OH: Grid.

Tung, R. 1981. "Selection and Training of Personnel for Overseas Assignments." *Columbia Journal of World Business* 16(1): 68–78.

11

Managing the Expatriate Experience

Introduction

A favorite cartoon of mine depicts a young man in front of his boss's desk. The boss says something to the effect of "You want to go far with the company; we have decided to open an office in Tibet." Another portrays Santa Claus announcing to his elves that he has decided to relocate to Taiwan. Dilbert has a great series on a subsidiary in the fictitious "Elbonia," and the experiences of expatriates sent there.

These cartoons illustrate the reality of the business world today. Cartoonists would not choose these subjects unless the audience could empathize with people in these situations. International business means that people have to travel to, and often live in, places that are foreign to them. These expatriates (people living outside their home country) may be parent country nationals (PCNs) in short-term or long-term positions with foreign subsidiaries, joint ventures, sales offices, and so on; they may be people from subsidiaries, joint ventures, licensees, and so on, who are with the parent organization; or they may be people hired for their special skills who are not PCNs but third country nationals.

The Mercer report on expatriate employees (Mercer 2008) reported that the number of expatriate employees had almost doubled over the previous three years. This is the largest report of its kind and covers almost 250 multinational companies and nearly 100,000 expatriates. Mercer sees this as a normal part of globalization and expects these trends to continue—one principal commented that companies bring in their own experts to lead projects on a short-term basis because they believe this will ensure they successfully launch new ventures abroad and gain a competitive advantage. Forty-seven percent of responding companies reported an increase in traditional expatriate assignments, and 38 percent reported an increase in "global nomads," or employees who move continuously from one international assignment to another. Clearly, managing expatriates is important for these firms.

Just Landed (2011), predicted that in 2010, more than 200 million people would be living abroad. While this 200 million consists of many groups other than the expatriates discussed in this chapter, the figure gives an idea of the degree to which people move around the world at the beginning of the twenty-first century. In this chapter we will be looking at a particular subset of this 200 million—those sent on an international assignment by their companies.

Expatriates present special issues for firms, and substantial attention needs to be paid to their management if the firm is to use them effectively. This chapter will explore the special issues associated with expatriates (or expats as they are often called), including effective approaches for their selection, training, motivation, retention, and repatriation.

Special Issues Associated with Expatriates

Expatriates, by definition, are operating (at work and at home) outside of their home country. This means that they are expected to function in an unfamiliar environment; for example, the culture, religion, language, politics, geography, and history of their work country may all be different from those of their home country. The expatriate thus faces a substantial degree of adjustment if he/she is to perform effectively in the new environment.

The expatriate usually has a family whose needs have to be considered as well. The decision about the expatriate assignment thus cannot be made on the basis of the employee alone—the firm has to consider how the expatriate's family will be affected by the international assignment. This may involve decisions about the spouse and children accompanying the expatriate. It can also involve decisions regarding visits home to see parents and relatives, who may be elderly. The author interviewed one expatriate who described moving from his home in Africa to the United Kingdom and then Canada; once settled in Canada, he brought his parents from Africa to Canada, where they settled nicely. His company then asked him to go to Barbados, in the Caribbean; it was a good career and financial move, and he decided to accept. Once in the Caribbean, he was faced with the question of what to do about his parents. Another expatriate described moving to the new location and finally selling his house in the parent country; he called his daughter at university to tell her the good news, and, to his dismay, she responded, "You haven't sold our house, you have sold my home!" These examples illustrate the complex issues that expatriates face.

Decisions may relate to extended-family members, siblings, in-laws, and so on, who encounter difficulties that require the expatriate's attention during the assignment. These sorts of issues are not considered in at-home appointments; in the home country setting, employees' family lives are expected to be separate from their work lives. In fact, in some locations, it is against employment laws to ask about, or use, a person's family situation in employment decisions. The same should not be true in an international assignment, because the family is required to make major adjustments and the employee cannot deal with personal matters as readily from abroad.

The varying religious, political, and cultural environments in different countries around the world may require expatriates to be selected and trained with these environments in mind. Consider Saudi Arabia, where women cannot drive or stay in a hotel unless accompanied by a male relative, and must enter rooms through doors reserved for women: one needs to ask if a woman expatriate can function effectively under these conditions, and if she can, what training and support she will need. Similarly, can a firm send a Jewish employee to an Arab country, or an Islamic one to Israel? These questions will be examined in more detail in chapter 12, and they are mentioned here to illustrate the complex issues faced in international assignment decisions.

Expatriate Adjustment

The literature suggests that a fairly large number of expatriates experience problems during their international assignments, and estimates of failures (i.e., expatriates who return home early or do a poor job) have ranged from 15 percent to as high as 40 percent. According to Bird and Dunbar (1991), an additional 30 to 50 percent of American expatriates stay in their international assignments, but are regarded as either marginally effective or ineffective by their organization. According to evidence accumulated over the past twenty years, roughly only one in three managers sent overseas gets the job done the way headquarters wanted it done.

Clearly, this evidence means that a substantial proportion of expatriates do not adjust effectively, and this is costly to firms. Direct costs to the firm include the expatriate's salary and benefits (which may be higher than at home) as well as relocation costs, schooling for children, club memberships, housing, and visits home. Sometimes there are signing bonuses or hardship allowances for less desirable locations. Indirect costs of failure include lost business and worsened relationships with suppliers, creditors, employees, customers, government, and other host groups. In addition, an expatriate who fails may suffer health problems and be less effective on returning home than previously.

If the characteristics that help expatriates adjust effectively can be identified, then companies can select people based on the degree to which they possess these characteristics, and training can be designed to ensure that expatriates develop and use the needed characteristics. The expatriate adjustment begins when the expatriate leaves the familiar social, cultural, and work environments to enter a new and different set of environments. Expatriates find themselves in a new world literally overnight. They have to get used to the fact that the host nationals think, behave, and believe differently from themselves and from people at home. It is not easy to adjust to, or even tolerate, new behaviors. For example, the author found it impossible to slurp soup in Japan even though she knew it was the proper way to show enjoyment, and she never accepted the Chinese staring and pointing at her (somehow, her mother's voice was always there saying, "Don't slurp your soup" and "Don't point or stare"). Yet, these are a normal part of life in Japan and China. In Bangladesh, she made the mistake of asking where one could buy a bathing suit (the hotel did have a swimming pool) and quickly realized by the male clerk's reaction that this was a most improper suggestion.

The expatriate does not know all of the social rules and norms that dictate what is and is not acceptable behavior at work and in society, thus, he/she experiences psychological uncertainty and anxiety. People tend to become anxious when faced with situations in which they feel uncertain and do not know how they should behave or how others are likely to behave toward them. This anxiety is often described as culture shock. To illustrate this, the author uses a cartoon of a person trying to buy a map from someone with a sign that says, "MAPS"; the person with the sign says, "Get lost." The response of the map seller is, of course, uninterpretable to the person who already feels lost. This is how one feels in an unfamiliar culture—the "answers," or events around you, often don't make sense from your home perspective.

When we interact with others in our own culture, we respond to behavioral cues that let us know what we should do next. For example, in North America, we sense intuitively when it is appropriate to shake hands and when it is not. In a class at New York University, my classmates (largely American) were discussing bowing and other unfamiliar forms of greetings. Our Asian classmates had difficulty describing how one knew when and how much to bow; they said they just knew. When asked how and when one shook hands in North America, the Americans had the same difficulty; they just knew and could not describe the rules. From the Asian perspective, according to my Asian classmates, shaking hands in North America appeared random.

In a new culture, a host national may do something that he/she perceives as being a cue, while the expatriate, not knowing the rules of social behavior, will not respond appropriately, leaving the host national to conclude that the expatriate is crazy, rude, backward, or stupid. Similarly, the expatriate finds that host nationals do not respond to cues "appropriately" (from her/his perspective) and thinks that the host nationals are crazy, rude, backward, or stupid. It is not surprising, therefore, that people experience culture shock in foreign assignments.

The Cycle of Culture Shock and Cross-Cultural Adjustment

The cycle of culture shock is usually described as consisting of four stages: honeymoon, culture shock, adjustment, and mastery.

The Honeymoon

In this first stage, the expatriate is fascinated by the host culture and excited by the opportunity to be in the new country. Often, the expatriate and his/her family are living in a hotel. Everything is new and exciting, and the host nationals seem exotic and interesting. The company is providing support for the expatriate and family, such as help with shopping, getting the children enrolled in school, transportation, and so on. This stage is often also called the tourist stage, because, in essence, the expatriate and family are living rather like tourists and enjoying the new experiences as tourists would. This stage usually lasts from a few weeks to as much as two months.

Culture Shock

After a period of time, company support lessens and the expatriate and family are left to fend for themselves. Suddenly, what seemed exotic and exciting becomes frustrating and confusing. The expatriate and family have to figure out how and where to shop, travel, communicate with doctors and dentists, find entertainment, make friends, and so on. This often proves difficult. For example, North Americans are accustomed to their meat being neatly packaged and stored in a refrigerator at the store. The Chinese and many other nationalities believe meat should be as fresh as possible. Thus, if you go to a Chinese market to purchase chicken, you are likely to be offered a live chicken so that you can kill it at home when you are ready to cook it. When expatriates and their families encounter these cultural challenges, they become dissatisfied and struggle to adjust. This stage may last for several months and can be particularly difficult for the spouse and family. The manager has a familiar, or relatively familiar, job and support at the workplace. The spouse and family have more difficult daily tasks to accomplish and thus may encounter more of the challenges. Some people never adjust, and can actually suffer severe depression and psychological trauma. These people are the ones who end up being described as failures.

Adjustment

Adjustment occurs as the expatriate begins to learn the norms and "ways of getting things done" in the new culture and job. This is a gradual adaptation and occurs generally from about the ninth month on. Of course, these time frames vary substantially from individual to individual depending on their adaptability, previous foreign experience, and so on. Adapting to a new culture requires effort on the part of expatriates—it does not occur naturally. Knowing that culture shock is likely to occur, and that one needs to work to overcome it, is helpful in achieving adjustment. If one does not expect it, the effects can be quite devastating.

Mastery

Eventually, over time, the successful expatriate will begin to function effectively in, and enjoy the nuances of, the host culture and its institutions, norms, traditions, and activities. Expatriates may not agree with or embrace all they learn about the host culture, but at this stage of adjustment they are able to understand why aspects of the host culture, even those they find unattractive, exist, and also to see that aspects of their own culture are unattractive to others. Not everyone reaches real mastery in a new culture, but successful expatriates achieve a level of comfort that allows them to be productive.

Where companies select expatriates and their families carefully, provide needed training, and offer support in the foreign location, the degree and length of culture shock is likely to be reduced. As noted previously, expatriate failure is costly for companies; therefore, investment in selection, training, and support to minimize culture shock and increase the likelihood of success is worthwhile.

Determinants of Expatriate Adjustment

Research has suggested that there are a variety of identifiable characteristics that contribute to expatriate adjustment. The following outlines the most important of these.

Self-Efficacy

Self-efficacy refers to confidence in one's abilities. Because expatriates have to deal with unexpected cross-cultural challenges, a sense of self-efficacy, or a belief in one's own ability to deal with these challenges, is important to effective adjustment.

Stress Management

Because expatriates often have to deal with frustration, conflicts, social alienation, pressure to conform, loneliness, and differences in housing, climate, cuisine, all of which are stressful, management of stress is critical to the productive functioning of the expatriate. Different people and different cultural groups may manage stress differently, but all expatriates need to have an ongoing stress reduction program that works for them. Activities that have generally been found to be helpful in managing stress include meditation, religious worship, writing in a diary, physical activity, and hobbies of various kinds.

Substitution Ability

Because familiar activities are often unavailable in the foreign location, successful expatriates find alternative activities as substitutes (Brein and David 1985). This involves "replacing activities that bring pleasure and happiness in the home culture with similar—yet different—activities that exist in the host culture" (Mendenhall and Oddou 1985, 40). For example, the author's husband really enjoys hockey and football (American or Canadian) in Canada, but could not watch the games when they moved to Jamaica and Barbados. He has adapted well and is now a cricket fan.

Relational Abilities

Because expatriates need to interact with host country nationals, the ability to develop relationships is very important. The majority of expatriates meet host nationals on a daily basis and in a variety of settings; for example, work, grocery shopping, public transportation, church, and the neighborhood. Expatriates have to decide whether these interactions will be purely superficial, or if they will try to develop relationships. Those who actively try to develop relationships seem to be more effective and productive. Two skills emerge in this context: finding mentors and a willingness to communicate with host nationals.

Finding Mentors. Expatriates who develop close relationships with host nationals generally are better adjusted and more productive in their international assignments than expatriates who do not try to develop such friendships (Mendenhall and Oddou 1985). Establishing friendships with host nationals means that the culturally experienced person guides the neophyte through the intricacies and complexity of the new organization or culture, protecting him/her against mistakes and helping him/her to develop appropriate behaviors (42). If an expatriate develops and nurtures a relationship with a host national, then the expatriate can go to the host national with questions whenever the expatriate is confused. Developing such relationships takes time, and the payoff for the expatriate for investing time and energy in developing friendships with host nationals may not show up for a year or more. Torbiorn (1982) found that satisfaction with living overseas was different for expatriates based upon who their friends were. Expatriates who limited their friendships to other expatriates were more satisfied during the first year than were expatriates who sought out host nationals as friends. However, this changed at the one-year point of the overseas assignment. From then on, expatriates who had friendships with host nationals experienced higher levels of satisfaction and adjustment than did expatriates who limited their friendships to fellow expatriates.

Willingness to Communicate. Communication is essential to success in an expatriate position. People often assume that being fluent in a foreign language is necessary in order to be a successful expatriate; however, that is not always the case. While complete fluency is a desired goal, it is not a precondition to international adjustment. Researchers have found that, in developing relationships with host nationals, it is not so much the level of fluency that is important, but rather that the expatriate shows that he/she is learning the language in order to get to know and become more familiar and intimate with the host nationals and their culture. Fluency becomes a powerful tool when it is used by expatriates to create and foster relationships with host nationals.

Perceptual Abilities

Because expatriates are dealing with an unfamiliar environment, their perceptual abilities are especially relevant. The expatriate's ability to understand why host nationals behave and think the way they do, and to make correct inferences as to the motives behind these behaviors, means that they can relate effectively to the host nationals. If expatriates understand the motives of host nationals, they are able to reduce to a large degree the psychological uncertainty of cross-cultural experiences. Knowing the reasons or motives for host nationals' behavior allows the expatriate to feel comfortable in the presence of the host nationals. The more understanding an expatriate has about the way people think and the reasons why they do what they do, the more likely the expatriate will be able to predict how people are likely to behave in the future. Being able to predict how people will treat you reduces psychological uncertainty. Unfortunately, this "understanding of what goes on in other people's minds" is not a skill that comes naturally to a lot of people. Research shows that people from different cultures usually misinterpret each other's behavior due to the way they have been socialized about how they should perceive and evaluate the behavior of others. Most important is the ability not to be judgmental when faced with confusing situations. This means not labeling people as being "backward," "stupid," or "unsophisticated" when they do or say things that would be viewed as such at home. The ability to put your natural evaluations of people "on hold" until you can collect more information about why they did what they did is a critical skill for international adjustment.

In addition to the personal characteristics described, there are environmental factors that influence the expatriate's ability to adapt to a foreign location. The most important of these are outlined in the following discussion.

Culture Novelty

The wider the differences in values, norms, religious beliefs, sex roles, and so on of the host country compared to those of the home country, the more novel or new the culture will be for the expatriate. The greater the novelty in the host culture, the more difficult it will be for the expatriate to adjust to that culture. Many experts who have reviewed studies on international adjustment have found this to be a consistent and important aspect of international adjustment (Stening 1979). Interestingly, some people feel that going to a culture very similar to one's own also poses special challenges. For example, Americans relocating to Canada often assume that things will be just like they are at home; to their surprise, the subtle differences are very real and also require substantial adjustment.

Family-Spouse Adjustment

The expatriate may have excellent cross-cultural skills and be doing very well on the job, but research shows that if that expatriate's spouse and/ or family members are having trouble adjusting, then the expatriate will have problems that could lead to a premature departure from the overseas assignment. This is an important issue, since approximately 85 percent of American expatriates are married (Black 1988). In a 1989 study, Black and Stephens found a relationship between expatriate adjustment and the adjustment of expat spouses for a large group of American expatriates in several different countries, findings that are consistent with those of other researchers. Important issues may be:

- the spouse's initial view (positive or negative) of the assignment;
- the spouse's willingness to engage in self-initiated cross-cultural training;
- the social support network available to the spouse;
- the standard of living conditions in the host country;
- the spouse's involvement in the international assignment from early in the selection process; and
- the degree of culture novelty.

If the spouse views the assignment positively and initiates cross-cultural training, if a support network is available, and if the spouse is involved early in the selection process, then the spouse is more likely to adapt successfully. If the culture is relatively similar to the home culture, then adapting is likely to be relatively easy.

In addition to personal characteristics, it is important to consider aspects of the job and work environment in the expatriate's adjustment.

The Job in an International Assignment

It is clear that to be successful in an international assignment, the expatriate must perform at acceptable levels at the job. There are a number of job aspects that seem to be important:

Role clarity relates to how clear the new job's tasks, demands, and roles are for the expatriate. Does the expatriate have a clear idea about what is expected on the job, or is the expatriate basically uninformed about his/her duties? High role clarity reduces the amount of uncertainty associated with the work situation, and this helps the expatriate adjust to the new workplace.

Role discretion relates to the degree to which the workplace is flexible in its rules, expectations, procedures, and policies. In a situation where the workplace is flexible, the expatriate can influence what his/her role will be in the office rather than having to adapt and conform to rigid work restrictions. The greater the degree of role discretion, the higher the level of adjustment the expatriate will experience toward his/her job.

Role novelty relates to how different the new job's duties, tasks, and responsibilities are from the previous job the expatriate had back home. The greater the degree of role novelty, the greater the difficulty the expatriate will have in adjusting to the new job.

Role conflict relates to conflicting signals from people at work as to the expatriate's role, duties, and performance standards. These conflicts add to the expatriate's stress levels and make adaptation more difficult.

Adjustment to the Organizational Culture

All organizations have cultures, or sets of rules, norms, expectations, sanctions, and operating procedures, both written and unwritten, that influence how employees get the work done. When an expatriate takes on a new assignment in a foreign country, he/she will likely have to learn a new organizational culture. Adjusting to the new organizational culture is necessary to perform the job well. Organizational culture novelty is similar to culture novelty and role novelty; if the expatriate job is high in organizational culture novelty, the expatriate will have a difficult time adjusting to the new work situation and will in turn have a more difficult time adjusting to the culture in general.

It is clear that companies should put a lot of thought into foreign assignments and give careful consideration to the issues discussed in this chapter before deciding which manager should be sent to the foreign office. While the research shows that to be successful in international assignments, one must possess a variety of individual, interpersonal, and organizational skills, often the main criterion actually used to assess whether a candidate should go overseas or not is technical performance. Companies should be encouraged to take a broader view of the selection criteria for expatriates and their families.

Cross-Cultural Training

Cross-cultural training programs are designed to educate the trainee in the key cultural norms, values, behaviors, beliefs, and other important aspects of the country to which he/she is assigned. The assumption is that if an expatriate is taught about these things, he/she will then be able to transfer that knowledge when overseas in terms of making sense out of why the host nationals are doing what they are doing and in terms of adjusting his/her own behavior to fit the requirements of the host culture's social system. Another assumption is that if expatriates are able to transfer the knowledge gained in cross-cultural training programs into new cognitive and physical behaviors, then they will be more satisfied with their overseas assignments, more productive in their jobs, and better able to interact with host nationals. Long-standing research supports the value of cross-cultural training:

> [I]t is important to note that those studies that included rigorous research designs (e.g., control groups, longitudinal designs, independent measures) . . . found support for a positive relationship between cross-cultural training and the following variables: cross-cultural skill development, cross-cultural adjustment, and performance in a cross-cultural setting. Thus, the empirical literature gives guarded support to the proposition that cross-cultural training has a positive impact on cross-cultural effectiveness. (Black and Mendenhall 1990, 119–120)

Approaches to Cross-Cultural Training

The following approaches are taken from Landis and Brislin's (1983) categorization of training methods.

Information or Fact-Oriented Training

The most common approach to cross-cultural training in the business world is to present expatriate candidates with briefing lectures about the country they will be assigned to. In addition to lectures, videotapes, reading materials, and pamphlets, panels of returned expatriates or host nationals can be used to relay information about the country's culture.

Attribution Training

This training approach aims at helping trainees understand why host nationals behave the way they do. The goal is to learn the values, norms, and perceptual maps by which the host nationals evaluate behavior in their country so that the expatriate can get a better idea of how the host nationals think, evaluate the behavior of others, and respond to various cross-cultural scenarios. Once this is understood, the trainees are encouraged to adapt their behavior to the norms of the host country.

Cultural Awareness Training

The focus of this training approach is to teach trainees about the values, attitudes, and behaviors that are common in their own culture; this has the effect of making the trainees more aware of how their own behavior is culturally determined. Once this occurs, it is assumed that the trainees can better understand how culture affects the behavior of host nationals.

Cognitive–Behavior Modification Training

The goal of this training approach is to help trainees link what they find to be rewarding and punishing in their own culture and then to learn about the reward/punishment norms in the country they are assigned to. By comparing similarities and differences in reward and punishment structures between the two countries, the trainees are assisted in constructing their own personal strategy to obtain rewards—and avoid negative experiences—in the host culture.

Experiential Learning Training

The purpose of this training approach is to expose the trainees to the real nature of life in the host country via field trips, visits to the host country, complex role-plays, and cross-cultural simulations. It gives the trainees the opportunity to practice the skills they have learned from the other types of training approaches. By practicing cross-cultural skills in hypothetical situations, the trainees can get a sense of what living and working overseas might really be like instead of extrapolating what it might be like from information gained in the other training approaches.

Within each of these training approaches, a variety of specific training techniques can be used by cross-cultural trainers. Some of these methods have been mentioned already, but others have not. The common types of training techniques are:

- area briefings,
- lectures,
- books and reading materials,
- films,
- classroom language training,
- case studies,
- culture assimilators,
- sensitivity training,
- interactive language training,
- role-plays,
- field trips, and
- simulations.

Most of these will be familiar, but a few may be new and will now be addressed.

A culture assimilator is simply a questionnaire that requires the trainee to respond to a number of cross-cultural scenarios. After reading about a hypothetical cross-cultural scenario, the trainee is required to choose from between five and seven behavioral responses. The key is to choose the behavioral response you would most likely choose if you were in that situation "right now," and not the one that you think might be the most cultur ally appropriate response. Then, based upon his/her choice, the trainee is given instructions to go to a certain page in the booklet. On this page, the trainee's behavioral choice is evaluated as to its cultural appropriateness, and the trainee is given feedback about what would likely occur later if that behavioral response were chosen. In other words, the trainee learns the consequences of that action.

Sensitivity training is designed to assist the trainee in coming to a greater awareness of his/her values, assumptions, behavioral tendencies, interpersonal strengths and weaknesses, how he/she is perceived by other people, and his/her prejudices and biases. This type of training often uses a trainer who is expert at drawing out of people information that they would not normally disclose to others. This type of training cannot be done in an afternoon—it requires significant amounts of time away from work in order to be successful.

Simulations are highly complex role-plays that attempt to replicate the reality of a cross-cultural situation and thus give the trainee a sense of what it will feel like to be in a new environment. Well-done simulations are very effective, but they are usually expensive and thus not used often.

Some of these training approaches could be described as more "rigorous" than others; that is, some approaches require the trainee to participate directly in the learning experience (e.g., simulations) while others simply require the trainee to passively absorb information with little mental and emotional effort on his/her part (e.g., listening to an area briefing). More rigorous approaches, which require the trainee to exert significant cognitive, behavioral, and emotional effort, are more effective than less rigorous approaches (Black and Mendenhall 1989). However, it takes significant amounts of time and money to conduct rigorous training programs effectively, and most companies cannot afford to take a manager off the job for two months of off-site training.

An important question for any company is "How rigorous does our training need to be?" Three aspects of the job seem to be important in answering this question.

Job Novelty

Job novelty is the degree to which the new job is different from the previous job. The newer, or more "novel," the tasks of the new job are, the more assistance the expatriate will need in order to be effective overseas. Expatriate assignments usually offer the manager higher levels of decision-making power, job autonomy, strategy design and implementation, and general responsibility. An expatriate assignment that rates high in job novelty will be a challenging one for the expatriate; thus, such managers need to be prepared in the cross-cultural managerial skills necessary for success in their foreign position.

Degree of Interaction with Host Nationals

If a manager will be required to manage a host-national workforce and interact with host-national customers, suppliers, government officials, and industry leaders, then he/she needs to have an in-depth understanding of how the host culture operates.

Culture Novelty

Unique and unfamiliar cultures are more difficult to adjust to than cultures that are low in novelty; also, the more novel the culture the more difficult it will be for the expatriate to absorb the information given in training programs. Thus, if an expatriate is assigned to a country that is high in culture novelty, that expatriate will need more rigorous training.

Appropriate Training

Tung's (1988) framework, which included a selection rationale for cross-cultural training methods based on rigor, is helpful in selecting appropriate training methods for expatriates. She concluded that there were two main dimensions that should be used in selecting cross-cultural training methods: (1) the degree of interaction required in the host culture; and (2) the similarity between the expatriate's home culture and the host culture (or what other researchers have since come to call "culture novelty"). Tung proposed that if the degree of interaction with host nationals was low and culture novelty was low, then the content of the training should focus on task- and job-related issues. The rigor needed for this training would be moderate to low. Conversely, if there was a high degree of level of interaction with the host nationals and culture novelty was also high, then she proposed that the content of the training should focus mainly on cultural issues and cross-cultural skill development in addition to task-related training. The level of rigor for this training would range from high to moderate.

Mendenhall and Oddou's (1985) framework built on Tung's. It provides a grouping of specific training methods by level of rigor and proposes a relationship between degree of interaction, culture novelty, and training rigor with the needed duration of time for the training program. Black and Mendenhall's (1989) model is based on social learning theory (Bandura 1977). Black and Mendenhall linked and integrated culture novelty, job novelty, and training rigor, arguing that the greater the culture novelty, required degree of interaction with host nationals, and job novelty, the greater the need for rigorous cross-cultural training. However, they noted that adjusting to the host culture and interacting with host nationals were more difficult than adjusting to the overseas job.

Cross-cultural training helps expatriates adjust to the new culture and to the foreign assignment. Those who do not receive such training are not as effective overseas as those that do, all other things being equal. If managers and their families are being sent overseas to do a job, it does not make sense from a profit–loss standpoint to skimp on cross-cultural training for expatriates. However, as with anything else in the business world, if top management does not believe it is important, it will not occur.

Many companies, even those that do substantial training, assume that short-term assignments are different from longer-term ones. Many expatriates, however, go on short-term assignments that are crucial to their companies' future well-being. Sending people on important short-term assignments with no training increases the risk of failure, as it does in longer-term assignments. If a person is going on a short-term assignment and the degrees of interaction and culture novelty are high, then that person does need predeparture training—at least at the moderate level of rigor.

Today, an array of companies provide training for foreign assignments. A search of the Internet will identify many of these. Businesses, of course, have to be careful in selecting among these to ensure that the training will meet their particular needs.

Dual-Career Couples

In this chapter, the expatriate and the spouse have been mentioned throughout. International firms are finding, more and more, that their married employees are part of a dual-career couple. Dual-career couples are those in which both partners work and both spouses see their work as not simply providing financial remuneration—they see it as representing an important occupation that they wish to pursue for personal achievement and advancement. In addition, a growing number of women are being offered, and are accepting, expatriate assignments. These trends imply that international firms in the twenty-first century need to pay attention to dual-career couples directly. In spite of their apparent importance, however, many companies have not yet addressed the issues related to dual-career couples and international assignments. A Mercer survey shows that female expatriates are less likely than their male counterparts to have a partner prior to going on assignment. Three-quarters of companies said the majority of their male assignees had partners before going on assignment, but only a quarter said that the same was true for their female expatriates. In addition, studies suggest that partners of successful women have high-powered careers; thus, when a woman is offered an international assignment, her partner may be less willing to make career concessions to accompany her (Amble 2006). Yet the survey makes clear that two-thirds of companies provide no incentives or support to help partners settle in the host location, and where support is available, it is usually given only when specifically requested.

In the past, when the role of the spouse in the success or failure of the expatriate was acknowledged by firms, it was usually assumed that the spouse would be a nonworking wife, and that if she had a career, she was willing to forgo immediate career advancement in favor of the foreign assignment and her husband's career advancement. The situation changes when one considers female expatriates and their spouses, most of whom, in the current social system, will have their own careers. The situation is more complex when the husband must make the decision whether or not to accompany his wife, because the current social system makes it difficult for many men to adjust to the role of secondary breadwinner or homemaker. The secondary and homemaker roles are still more socially acceptable for women, and women, even those with careers, may make the transition to the secondary position more easily than men. Society generally judges men by their career advancement more so than it does women; thus, undertaking a negative or even neutral career move can be especially troublesome for many men. Also, because the majority of expatriate managers are still male, the nonworking expatriate spouse group is largely female; a nonworking husband could thus find himself the lone husband in a group of wives. Finally, the traditional volunteer activities that females have been encouraged to undertake may not be available or appropriate for males in some countries; thus, husbands may be barred from the productive activities available to wives.

Finding work for a professional spouse can be a challenge. Work permit restrictions of some host societies make it difficult if not impossible for the spouse to work; for example, countries such as the United States, Australia, and Switzerland seldom grant work permits to a spouse unless he or she has expertise and skills that are in short supply. In other countries, while there are no work permit restrictions, there may be a bias against women working in predominantly male occupations or vice versa, or it may be socially unacceptable for the husband to be the "homemaker." Even if the spouse can work, career advancement is less likely in a foreign environment. For example, professional requirements and designations can vary from country to country; thus, one spouse usually has to make career sacrifices.

As discussed earlier, research on expatriate transfers has identified the family, and particularly the spouse, as being critical to the expatriate's success overseas. Spouses who are well prepared for the foreign environment and receive support while overseas generally adjust well, and this increases the likelihood of successful transfers. The adjustment is often more difficult for spouses because they lack the focus and support provided by work. Spouses accustomed to working and having a career might be particularly frustrated if they cannot work or if they encounter difficulties finding work. These difficulties are likely to add to the already stressful transfer situation and could increase the possibility of failure. Add to this the additional emotional stress that may be engendered when the male is the spouse in this position, and it is not surprising that some couples have concerns about foreign assignments.

There are a number of alternative approaches that firms can adopt to offer active assistance to dual-career couples facing international transfers. These deal specifically with assistance to the spouse. Some time ago, Aluminum Co. of Canada, according to the *Toronto Globe and Mail* (Gibb-Clark 1991), reached an agreement with Immigration Canada to waive the requirement that employers first try to find a Canadian to fill a job that a noncitizen spouse would like—on condition that the country from which the manager and spouse is coming to Canada agrees to make a reciprocal arrangement. The following points illustrate other proactive approaches that companies can initiate to help alleviate the concerns of dual-career couples moving internationally:

- Provide more time for the move so that the spouse can investigate job opportunities, and provide a pre-move trip to make initial contacts.
- Develop career-oriented employment networks; for example, public sector organizations can coordinate with other public and private sector organizations to publicize employment opportunities.
- Provide letters of introduction, office space, telephone and secretarial support, and other similar services for spouses seeking foreign employment.
- Provide the services of an international job search firm.
- Consider opportunities for job sharing when both spouses are in the same field, and give the spouse preference for available jobs within the organization overseas.
- Provide realistic pre-departure information on foreign job opportunities and help in obtaining requisite visas, permits, etc.
- Consider the re-entry problem; spouses again have to seek employment and need the same support as when going overseas; in addition, recognize that employees who meet and marry spouses overseas and return home with them will need similar, likely additional, assistance.
- Address questions of unemployment, benefits, pensions, and so forth as they relate to the accompanying spouse.
- Provide, or help identify and apply for, research funds for which spouses could apply; this would provide funding to do research in a career area while overseas; it would allow a spouse to further his or her career without undertaking paid employment—for example, an accountant could study the system in a foreign location (say, Japan) and later use this for career advancement.
- Establish education funds to provide the opportunity to further a current career or change careers.

- Provide help, in terms of networking, focused on professional employment opportunities rather than (as currently perceived) lower-level employment. Executive search services could be provided.
- Provide more recognition for the work that the spouse does to assist the employee (e.g., hosting social functions).

Career-oriented women are likely to be married to career-oriented men and vice versa. Male spouses who have accompanied their wives on foreign assignments have some specific concerns. In interviews, a male spouse group consisting of a cross-section of careers, including a landscape architect, a sculptor, a banker, an advocate for the handicapped, a foreign-service officer, and a lawyer, made the following comments:

- Spouses have to be flexible and have to fend for themselves in terms of finding appropriate employment; if they can't find appropriate employment, then the transfer won't be successful.
- Organizations have to realize that most spouses have careers and are not interested in just any job; it needs to be something that contributes to a sense of self-worth and future career opportunities.
- The lifestyle of a well-paid corporate family and a wife's advancement are positive aspects of accepting a trailing male spouse role, but the specifics of the situation can be negative, including being the only male spouse, being streamed into traditional spouse activities, and being ignored.
- Spouses want activities that can benefit their careers and provide interest while in a foreign location.

In general, this male spouse group expressed a sense of being overlooked. Yet they felt they were important to the success of the assignment. They wanted organizations to recognize that there were many things that could alleviate their situation. These were spouses who had been willing to go overseas and were willing to talk about the experience. One could conjecture that spouses with less transportable careers, and who were less willing to go, may have found the experience more difficult. Overall, the research on dual-career couples internationally suggests that the number of such couples is increasing and that this trend is likely to continue. Firms that pay attention to the concerns of these couples may find it to their benefit in terms of attracting, retaining, and motivating these employees.

The spouses of expatriates need different support systems at different stages of the expatriate process. Before going on an assignment they need support in terms of understanding the reality of the foreign location so that their expectations will be appropriate. If they would like to be productively employed, they need to know what opportunities will be available and how they can identify opportunities that are appropriate for their situation. Once on-site in the foreign country they need support in dealing with the practical realities of setting up a household in a new location. Day-to-day events can be quite different in a new place: where and how to bank, shop, eat, get mail, access the Internet, find schools, and so on can be daunting if one does not have help. Expatriates who have been on-site for a period of time can be very helpful at this stage, and in many countries a group of expatriate spouses takes on the role of showing the new spouse and family "the ropes." This can assist in avoiding the more negative dimensions of culture shock. As spouses adapt and become part of the community, having productive activities becomes most relevant and they may need support in identifying and finding such activities, whether paid or provided on a volunteer basis. In the later stages of the expatriate assignment, the spouse has to prepare her/himself and the family to return home, and different support systems are necessary for this step. The expatriate spouse now has to dismantle the household, and this may be painful if the couple has come to enjoy the location. In addition, they have to start the process of reestablishing themselves back home in terms of both home and family and resuming their careers.

The spouse's adjustment is apparently critical to the expatriate employee's success. It is appropriate, therefore, for international companies to put into place systems to help ensure this adjustment. The suggested support needs provide a framework for companies to design systems to meet these needs.

Summary and Conclusions

Expatriates are a normal aspect of doing business internationally, but these individuals face particular challenges because they are required to live and work in an unfamiliar environment. Adjusting to this new environment is often difficult, and expatriates suffer from culture shock. This can result in costly failures for international firms. To reduce the likelihood of culture shock and failure, firms can design careful selection and training programs for expatriates and their families. There are a variety of characteristics that need to be taken into account in the selection process, and there are numerous training methods available. The international firm assesses these to determine the most cost-effective approaches. A special group of expatriates that is growing is dual-career couples. These couples face special issues, and firms can do more to address them.

References

Amble, B. 2006. "Big Rise in Number of Female Expats." *Management-Issues,* October 12. http://www.management-issues.com/2006/10/12/research/big-rise-in-number-of-female-expats.asp (accessed March 12, 2012).

Bandura, A. 1977. *Social Learning Theory.* Englewood Cliffs, NJ: Prentice Hall.

Bird, A., and R. Dunbar. 1991. "Getting the Job Done Over There: Improving Expatriate Productivity." *National Productivity Review* (Spring): 145–155.

Black, J.S. 1988. "Work Role Transitions: A Study of American Expatriate Managers in Japan." *Journal of International Business Studies* 19: 277–294.

Black, J.S., and M. Mendenhall. 1989. "A Practical But Theory-based Framework for Selecting Cross-Cultural Training Programs." *Human Resource Management* 28(4): 511–539.

———. 1990. "Cross-Cultural Training Effectiveness: A Review and a Theoretical Framework for Future Research." *Academy of Management Review* 15(1): 113–136.

Black, J.S., and G.K. Stephens. 1989. "The Influence of the Spouse on American Expatriate Adjustment in Overseas Assignments." *Journal of Management* 15: 529–544.

Brein, M., and K.H. David. 1985. *Improving Cross-Cultural Training and Measurement of Cross-Cultural Learning.* Vol. 1. Denver: Center for Research and Education.

Gibb-Clark, M. 1991. "Career Move May Include Spouse's Job." *Globe and Mail,* April 15, B4.

Just Landed. 2011. "Expatriates: An Overview of the Expatriate Market." http://www.justlanded.com/english/Common/Footer/Expatriates (accessed March 20, 2012).

Landis, D., and R.W. Brislin. 1983. *Handbook of Intercultural Training.* Vol. 1. Elmsford, NY: Pergamon Press.

Mendenhall, M., and G. Oddou. 1985. "The Dimensions of Expatriate Acculturation." *Academy of Management Review* 10: 39–47.

Mercer. 2008. "Expatriate Employee Numbers Double as Companies See Increased Value in Expatriate Assignments." Press release, October 27. http://www.mercer.com/press-releases/1326180 (accessed March 24, 2012).

Stening, B.W. 1979. "Problems in Cross-Cultural Contact: A Literature Review." *International Journal of Intercultural Relations* 3: 269–313.

Torbiorn, I. 1982. *Living Abroad: Personal Adjustment and Personnel Policy in the Overseas Setting.* New York: John Wiley.

Tung, R.L. 1988. *The New Expatriates: Managing Human Resources Abroad.* Cambridge: Ballinger.

12

Special Issues in International Human Resource Management

Introduction

This chapter focuses on two special topics: human resource issues associated with gender, and ethics in international management decisions. The issues that relate to gender are paralleled by those that arise because of race, religion, disability, sexual preference, and other such personal characteristics. In many countries, it is illegal to make human resource choices on the basis of these characteristics. In other countries, however, these characteristics are especially important and may be *the* basis for making human resource decisions. Although the focus here will be gender, similar issues arise if there are racial problems or religious discord, or any other form of nonacceptance or discrimination on the basis of personal characteristics. Decisions associated with gender, race, religion, and so on often involve ethical considerations, as do many other international decisions. This chapter briefly considers the question of ethics in international management decisions.

These issues associated with race, religion, and so forth have not received much attention, either from practicing managers or from academic researchers, because people are uncomfortable addressing them. They are particularly important current issues, however, given the "Arab Spring" in the Middle East, and in light of the terrorist attacks that the world has experienced in recent decades. These events, among others, have brought to light the major religious and racial divides that continue around the world. They have also made people more aware of the dangers they may face traveling to different parts of the world. In the following sections, we look at the role of women in the world of business, how this differs in different parts of the world, and how this impacts on international firms. We conclude this section with a brief discussion of other characteristics that may affect human resource choices. The chapter then considers some ethical issues.

The Role of Women in Business Around the World

The role of women in society varies from country to country and even from region to region within a country, and it varies over time. Some examples:

- Women may be excluded from the general workforce and expected to work only in the home.
- Women may be excluded from management jobs but accepted in lower-level jobs.
- Certain work may be considered acceptable for women and not men, other work the reverse.
- Women may be expected to work before they marry but not following marriage.
- Women and men may work at the same jobs, but women are compensated at a lower rate.

Research on the role of women in various parts of the world suggests that the variations may be deeply rooted in early agricultural practices. There is some evidence that in places where the hoe was used, women are still considered an intergral part of the working world. In places where the plow was used, women are generally not expected to work. If the role of women is still determined by these centuries-old differences in agricultural practices, no wonder it is difficult to change a culture's view of the rightful place and activities for women. Nevertheless, the role of women seems gradually to be changing, and women are more readily accepted in the workplace today than they were even fifty years ago.

Women account for about 40 percent of the total global workforce, but 58 percent of all unpaid work, 44 percent of wage employment, and 50 percent of informal employment (ILO 2009). This situation is reflected in statistics from a variety of countries around the world. Catalyst compares the proportion of women "legislators, senior officials, and managers" in a variety of countries and finds the following proportions for selected countries: Peru 27.6 percent, Argentina 23.2 percent, Croatia 20.8 percent, Czech Republic 28.7 percent, Egypt 10.8 percent, Ethiopia 15.7 percent, China 16.8 percent, and Vietnam 22.2 percent. Globally, the number of women in senior management in large corporations is very low. Catalyst (2009) reports that in the 1,000 largest companies, only twenty-four women hold chief executive officer positions.

The World Economic Forum's Global Gender Gap Index (Hausmann, Tyson, and Zahidi, 2009) compares 134 countries on the equality of women, with scores potentially ranging from 0 to 100. The best countries score in the low 80s (Iceland, Finland, Norway, and Sweden are the highest scorers at 82.8, 82.5, 82.3, 81.8, respectively), showing that there is room for improvement even in countries that perform well. Interestingly, two Caribbean countries Trinidad and Tobago (#19) and Barbados (#21), are the leaders in the Western hemisphere, outperforming both Canada (#25) and the United States (#31). Two African countries, South Africa (#6) and Lesotho (#10), made the Top 10 list; the Philippines (#9) lost ground for the first time in four years but remains the leading Asian country in the rankings; at the bottom part of the rankings, India (#114), Bahrain (#116), Ethiopia (#122), Morocco (#124), Egypt (#126), and Saudi Arabia (#130) all made improvements relative to their rankings in 2008, while at the bottom of the rankings, Iran (#128), Turkey (#129), Pakistan (#132), and Yemen (#134) displayed an absolute decline relative to their performance in 2008. Overall, more than two-thirds of the countries covered in the report posted gains in overall index scores, indicating that the world in general has made progress toward equality between men and women. Unfortunately, at the other end of the scale, there are still news reports of women being stoned to death in a variety of countries, reminding us of the huge gaps that persistently exist.

One coauthor of the gender gap report, Saadia Zahidi, commented that countries that do not fully capitalize on what is half of their human resources run the risk of undermining their competitive potential, observing, "We hope to highlight the economic incentive behind empowering women, in addition to promoting equality as a basic human right" (Tonkin 2009). These statistics all speak to the unequal positions of men and women in the world of work. This situation inevitably affects the way organizations are managed, the kinds of decisions that are made in organizations, the strategies that are employed, and the human interactions—in effect, all aspects of organizations that ultimately result in the organizational culture and climate.

Much of the literature has focused on the challenges that women face in entering the workforce generally, and particularly the professions, as well as the difficulties they face in advancing to higher levels within organizations or professions. It seems clear that women continue to face stereotyping, biases in performance appraisal, promotion, and salary, and difficult work-life trade-offs.

Women, however, have succeeded in all kinds of positions and at all levels, around the world, as illustrated by a series of interviews on BBC News with women in jobs traditionally associated with men ("Women's Work" 2005). The women interviewed by the BBC included Marin Alsop, the first woman to head a major U.S. orchestra; Sandra Edokpayi, Nigeria's first female mechanic; Holly Bennett, one of Europe's only female explosives engineers, and

Tahany Al-Gebaly, Egypt's first woman Supreme Court judge. These success stories illustrate what women can achieve; at the same time, however, the very fact that these women are described as unusual indicates the challenges that women confront in traditionally male preserves.

Some illustrations of the role of women in selected countries give a sense of the barriers that women can face in different parts of the world:

- In Saudi Arabia, women are not permitted to drive, to travel on an airplane alone, or to stay in a hotel without a male family member.
- In Japan, women seldom work after marriage.
- In the United States, women have attained a certain degree of equality in the business environment but are seldom found in top management positions.
- In Ireland, the constitution has been interpreted to mean that a woman should join the workforce only if her husband is not able to look after the family economically.
- In St. Vincent, a West Indian island country, the minimum wage for women has been lower than that for men, regardless of the work performed.
- In Canada, the great majority of nurses and secretaries are women while the majority of firefighters, construction workers, and foresters are men.
- In the People's Republic of China, women hold many of the same positions as men but they are required to retire at an earlier age.

Ramachandran (1992) gave the following example of the role of women in parts of India: In Rajasthan, when a social work organization wanted to establish a hospital for women, there was a great deal of hostility and resistance. The village men could not understand why so much fuss should be made over women; they insisted that what they really needed was a hospital for their farm animals.

In contrast to this negative portrayal, Punnett et al. (2006) have illustrated the success that women can achieve professionally, both at home and overseas. The book *Successful Professional Women of the Americas: From Polar Winds to Tropical Breezes* reports on a study of successful professional women in nine countries in the Americas (Argentina, Brazil, Canada, Chile, Mexico, the United States, and three West Indian island countries—Barbados, Jamaica, and St. Vincent and the Grenadines), outlining the characteristics and support mechanisms that allow women to achieve professional success, in spite of the challenges that they face.

International managers, whether they are men or women, cannot avoid dealing with the question of the role of women in business. They must often decide whether to employ women, when to employ them, which ones to employ, where to employ them; then they must decide how to manage the women employed. In addition, international managers need to recognize that men and women may view roles differently, and differential treatment can be interpreted in a variety of ways. Differential treatment of women can be considered protection or discrimination; it can be readily accepted or contested; it may be regulated by law or culturally accepted; differential treatment may be conscious or unconscious.

Understanding and working with the role of women in a new country is complicated by the biases that managers bring from home. As discussed in terms of culture and ethnocentrism, people often find it difficult to accept the fact that values contradicting those held in their home society can be anything but wrong. This is often particularly true of issues associated with gender roles and the place of women in society. The role of women is generally well known in the home culture, and a manager's reactions to this role are defined at an early age. When faced with contradictory views of gender roles, many people are especially disquieted and find these differences hard to accept. For example, managers who strongly believe in equality and whose training has emphasized nondiscrimination may find it very difficult to accept and adjust to a situation where women are generally treated as inferior in the business world. Women managers may find it particularly challenging to deal with this situation.

International managers need to pay particular attention to understanding the role of women in society and business in each country where they do business. They also need to assess consciously their reactions to this role. Managers in a country where women's role in business is unfamiliar can react in a number of different ways. Foreign managers can accept the new and unfamiliar role and adjust to the host country's view of the role of women, or they can try to influence people in the host country to change the role. Alternatively, foreign managers may seek out colleagues and employees who see the role of women in a way that is similar to that at home because they will be more comfortable interacting with such people. In most cases, some acceptance and adjustment will be necessary, but input that may help change the role is possible, as is seeking out colleagues and employees whose views on the role of women are not typical of the host country.

Some Examples of Women's Role in Business

Following are some general descriptions of the role of women in business in selected countries or regions. These are intended to give students only a feel for some of the differences that may be encountered. A detailed examination is not practical here, and it is important to recognize that the situation in any country or region will change over time.

Managers moving from the more developed countries to the developing may be particularly struck by differences in the status of women. The United Nations Center on Transnational Corporations reported that international firms employ about 2 million women in the developing countries (UNCTNC 1988—although this report is twenty years old, little appears to have changed). This represents a very small proportion of the total labor force in these countries and only about 3 percent of the worldwide employment by international firms. The typical role of women in these countries can be seen in a number of comments from the report:

- In some countries, women are employed, frequently with the whole family, in plantations owned by transnational corporations (TNCs) which often date from colonial times and grow such crops as tea and rubber. Their position in the plantation labor force is inferior to that of men.
- In the service sector, a small proportion of the total employment of women by TNCs is in white-collar occupations in banks and commercial establishments. However, most women employed in services hold low-level jobs as maids, cleaners, waitresses, and salesgirls in hotels, offices, and retail establishments.
- TNCs in export processing zones (EPZs) have become significant employers of women, who work as low-paid, unskilled, or semi-skilled workers. Wages tend to be low, and they are often below those earned by men. Therefore, the practices of TNCs largely reflect prevailing local circumstances. Firms often favor employing women in EPZs because they are seen as more efficient and stable than men and, at the same time, their wages are lower than those for men and it is easier to hire and lay off women. It is important to recognize that many of these women would otherwise be unemployed, and that they likely prefer to be employed in these jobs than not at all. The inferior role to that of men is also likely accepted by most of the women. This illustrates the dilemma faced by many international managers. The balance between providing employment and exploiting female workers is not always clear cut.

The role of women in business in the Arab world is often difficult for Westerners to understand and accept. Women are described as equal, but with different responsibilities. Once married, for example, women in Saudi Arabia go out only to visit close friends and relatives or to shop, and then they must be accompanied by a male relative. Women make up only about 10 percent of the workforce in Saudi Arabia, not because they are prohibited from working or from certain occupations, but because they are not permitted to work with men. The sexes must be kept segregated. Consequently, most organizations prefer not to employ women. Women who do work are in education, medicine, or social work, where contacts with males can be avoided. The situation is not very different in other countries in the region, even those with less stringent rules governing women's conduct. In Bahrain, for example, women are well educated and given equal opportunity, but affluence and social beliefs have discouraged them from seeking employment. This is changing somewhat with the emergence of a middle class and women interested in entering the professions.

Countries of the Far East vary in their acceptance of women in business:

- In Hong Kong, women are found relatively frequently at all levels of organizations and they are accepted as effective businesspeople. Nevertheless, they are found most often in secretarial positions and males are not found in traditionally female jobs.
- In Malaysia, women have "equal opportunity," but in reality they are sheltered and business is considered the preserve of males.
- In Singapore, increasing numbers of women are entering the workforce, with 80 percent of those between the ages of twenty and twenty-four working. Professional women are more likely to advance in firms linked with the government, but generally their role is subordinate to that of men.
- In South Korea, it is rare for women to be in positions of authority, and their prospects for advancement are slim, as many companies have a policy of employing women only until they are thirty or marry.
- In Thailand, women are seen as "the hind legs of the elephant," powerful but following, and are generally working in subordinate positions. This is tempered by educational and social background, which allows some women to hold top positions both in government and private industry.

The situation in the People's Republic of China is somewhat mixed. Virtually all women work, but women in upper-level positions are rare. Traditionally, women were not expected to partake in business activities, but the Communist Party promoted the idea that "women hold up half of heaven" and implemented educational programs that have led to a substantial increase in the numbers of women at work and in scientific professions and government. Women, however, are required to retire at an earlier age than men for "physical reasons," and their advancement and lifetime earnings are consequently diminished.

Japanese organizations have traditionally seen women as serving in lower-paid, lower-level positions, and even graduates of top universities were hired for clerical positions. More Japanese women have been and are entering the workforce, however, and in 1986, Japan passed a law prohibiting discrimination on the basis of sex. Anti-discrimination legislation is better enforced in the public sector than the private, and women are more likely to be treated equally in government and public offices. While the situation for working women may be improving in Japan, the traditional role of the woman remaining at home after marriage is still accepted by most Japanese.

In the countries of the European Union (EU), the situation also varies from country to country. For example, in Denmark, women in the public sector receive their full wage for thirty-two weeks of maternity leave; fathers are entitled to two weeks and may take the last ten weeks of the thirty-two in place of the mother. In comparison, in Greece, maternity leave is fifteen weeks and in Spain, sixteen.

Most EU countries have promoted equal opportunities for women, and there have been significant developments in legislation, anti-discrimination procedures, and changing attitudes toward women in the workforce. Specific programs have been aimed at:

- facilitating access to the labor market through education and training;
- improving the quality of women's employment through reevaluation of their contribution, career development, and social protection;
- reconciling work and family through childcare, family services, and housework sharing; and
- improving the status of women through their involvement in all levels of the corporate and governmental decision-making processes and their portrayal in the media.

In spite of, or sometimes because of, some of these efforts, women in the EU remain predominantly in lower-level, lower-paid positions. A particular result of efforts to allow women to combine work and family noted by Barry and Kelleher (1991) was increased flexibility in the workplace. While demanded by the women themselves, it has had the negative effect of putting certain women outside of the traditional employer–employee contract and often outside of labor legislation protection.

Even where women have relatively good opportunities to work and enter the professions, they face challenges associated with career advancement; these challenges have been described as "glass walls," "glass ceilings," and "glass cliffs" (International Labour Office 2004). Glass walls are unseen barriers that stop women from moving into certain male preserves, glass ceilings stop them from moving up in organizations, and glass cliffs are pitfalls awaiting those who do move into these male preserves or higher echelons. Nevertheless, there are women who are successful in many professions. Here is what some of them in the Punnett et al. (2006) study said about their careers:

- I am a successful person because I am passionate about 90 percent of what I do (Chile).
- When you love something very much, you will obtain (what you desire). I love art so much (Chile).
- I'm happy with what I have achieved in this business (Argentina).
- I am very satisfied with what I have achieved in my work (St. Vincent and the Grenadines).
- I feel that being successful allows me to give back to my society, and this gives me a great deal of satisfaction (Jamaica).
- I think that, fortunately, I have been very lucky . . . and perhaps one of the indicators . . . is that I have a very stable family . . . my children are full, productive persons, of whom I am very proud (Mexico).
- Yes, you see my husband got sick, and my children were at an age that they still needed much help; that's why I say I have been successful, because, being a woman I was able to get my whole family ahead (Mexico).
- Yes, of course; God has given me much more than what I would have thought I deserved (Mexico).

In this study, the researchers found that successful professional women across the Americas were self-confident and had a high need for achievement. They talked about the support they received from their husbands and families playing a major role in their success. Importantly, they were satisfied with their careers, families, and lives. Thus, professional success for women does not mean giving up other satisfying aspects of one's life, although the work-life balances are clearly challenges for women.

The Meaning of Equality

International managers need to understand the reasons for varying male and female roles, as well as contrasting interpretations of equality. As with other cross-cultural variations, understanding helps managers adjust to unusual practices.

Most cultures differentiate between the appropriate roles for men and women. This can probably be attributed to women being the child bearers and consequently the child rearers in most societies. Women have traditionally stayed in the home and carried out activities associated with the home or activities that could be combined with homemaking. Men, in contrast, have performed those activities that occurred away from home. This meant that men were seen as more important in the business world.

These traditions have persisted even when it is no longer necessary for women to remain at home. The result has been that women who work outside the home often work in subordinate positions. In addition, the traditional role of women as caregivers and supporters persists. Women work more often in a supportive capacity, such as secretarial positions, and caregiving professions, such as nursing, than do their male counterparts.

These traditions are deeply ingrained. Consider, for example, Hofstede's cultural model discussed previously. One dimension of this model described traditional masculine and feminine values. Masculine values encompassed competition, assertiveness, achievement, and material possessions, while feminine values included nurturing, concern for others, and concern with the quality of life. Many people see the masculine values as contributing to success in the business world, while the feminine values contribute to success in a supportive and caring role. Changing these traditional views is not easy, but changes are occurring around the world.

Achieving equality in the workforce in Canada and the United States has focused on demonstrating the equal abilities of men and women. Legislation and social pressure have encouraged organizations to treat men and women largely in the same manner, suggesting that they should be given equal opportunities, training, and compensation for equivalent jobs. An alternative approach is to look at the unique contributions that men and women can make in the workforce. This approach focuses on the differences between men and women and assumes that they will be most effective in different roles, but that these roles are equally important.

The distinction between these interpretations of equality is that in the first, equality implies standardized, thus equitable, treatment for men and women, while in the second, it implies equitable valuation of different contributions. Those who believe in the first argue that focusing on differences tends to support the traditional view of women. Those who believe in the second argue that ignoring differences does not make the best use of the varying abilities and interests of men and women.

This distinction needs to be recognized because managers who believe in equality for women do not all mean the same thing. A European manager who believes in equality for women may feel that female employees are different from male employees and thus better at certain jobs—this manager may be surprised when working in the United States to find that U.S. employees reject this idea as discriminatory.

Women as Managers in Different Countries

International managers often need to focus on the role of women as managers as well as their more general role in business. In most parts of the world, women make up a relatively small percentage of management;

however, this seems to be changing. There are a number of reasons for this change, including an increasing number of women in the workforce generally, better educational opportunities for women, government regulations mandating equal treatment of women, and changing social and cultural values.

The issue of women as managers is faced in foreign countries when hiring or promoting local women to management levels. It is necessary in those situations to assess the legal and cultural factors that may militate against hiring women managers. As discussed earlier, legal provisions in some countries, such as Saudi Arabia, may make it onerous for local women to function effectively as managers. In other countries, such as Japan, local customs can make it equally onerous for different reasons. It is important to recognize these restrictions and make decisions within this framework. The international manager in such cases needs to be aware of the potential difficulties for the women as well as others in the organization and outside. If women agree to accept management positions under such circumstances, special provisions may have to be made to enable them to function productively.

The Role of Women as Managers in Selected Locations

The following brief discussion considers the role of women as managers in selected locations around the world.

Canada and the United States

The situation is better for women managers in Canada and the United States than in many other locations. Nevertheless, women are more likely to serve in jobs that are subordinate to men's: they are usually the secretaries rather than the bosses, the nurses rather than the doctors, the teachers rather than the principals, the assistants rather than the politicians. Legislation in both countries prohibits discrimination on the basis of sex, and this has encouraged women to seek management positions and organizations to fill these positions with women. At lower and middle management levels, women are quite well represented; at top levels, however, there are still relatively few women. The lack of women in top management has been attributed to several factors, including past discrimination, ongoing discrimination, a lack of interest on the part of some women, and a shortage of women with appropriate education and training. Whatever the causes, it seems likely that the situation is changing and that there will be increasing pressure on organizations to admit women to top management ranks.

Western Europe

Women are not as well represented in management ranks in Europe as they are in Canada and the United States. The situation varies from country to country, and each country has its own regulations and socially accepted views. Integration of the EC and standardization of regulations is likely to result in a more uniform role for women managers throughout the community, although social dissimilarities will likely continue to influence this role in individual countries. The European Community's Foundation for the Improvement of Living and Working Conditions has recently emphasized the need to take positive action for equality in the workplace, and this will likely have a positive impact on women's participation in management throughout the community.

Africa

Women's roles in Africa differ dramatically from place to place and may depend in many places on the particular ethnic group to which the women belong. In a number of cases the role of women is clearly secondary and inferior to that of men, as the following illustrate:

- Parkin (1978, 168) described one African group as defining women's status as "the producers of men's children" and "confined to domestic activities" while men were the "political leaders and wage earners."
- An executive who had worked in Africa described one location where female employees sat on the floor facing the wall when speaking with their male superiors.
- Ferraro (1990) described Kenya as one of the most Westernized and progressive African countries but said that the role and status of women remained characterized by traditional distinctions of inferiority. She described African men as having "considerable difficulty seeing women as anything other than wives, mothers, and food producers" (144).

In the author's current research, African respondents quite often described "effective leaders" as being male.

Japan

The Japanese social system has encouraged Japanese women to work full-time only until marriage; following marriage, they may work part-time when needed by the firm. This system has resulted in virtually no Japanese women currently in management positions. There is some evidence of a growing desire on the part of

Japanese women to participate more fully in Japanese business, but this movement is in its early stages and it is not possible to say what its impact will be.

The People's Republic of China

Top positions in China are almost entirely filled by men. The government has supported equal opportunity for women, however, and women have been encouraged to become entrepreneurs and managers. Nevertheless, there are relatively few women in business school programs, and women largely accept their secondary role in business.

The Middle East

The role of women in the Arab countries of the Middle East, as described previously, largely precludes their being managers. Even in situations where women run their own businesses, they generally employ a man as a "front," according to the *Economist* (1988). The situation in Israel is somewhat different from other Middle Eastern countries. Women in Israel are well educated and have been relatively well accepted as managers; nevertheless, only a small percentage of women in the Israeli workforce are in administrative and managerial positions. The picture in Israel is similar to that in most Western countries—management positions are dominated by men and clerical positions dominated by women.

Women as International Managers

The number of women undertaking international assignments in the early 1980s was relatively low, according to Adler (1984)—about 3 percent. This did not change dramatically throughout the 1980s, according to Kirk and Maddox (1988). By the 1990s, it had changed somewhat. By the early 2000s, women international managers accounted for about 15 percent of all international managers. This percentage remained constant over the next several years. According to Amble (2006) a survey of over 100 multinational companies with nearly 17,000 male and female international assignees by Mercer Human Resource Consulting found a startling increase in the number of women being sent to work in the Asia-Pacific, where companies say they have sixteen times more females on assignment this year than they did in 2001. More than half the multinationals surveyed (55 percent) by Mercer expected the number of female assignees to continue increasing steadily over the next five years, while a third believed the number would remain the same, and only 4 percent believed it would decline.

There are increasing numbers of female domestic managers, particularly in Canada, Europe, and the United States, and this means more of these women are candidates for foreign assignments. Many international firms want their top executives to have international experience in their background. This implies that if women are to reach the top, they need to accept expatriate assignments. In the past, some firms have been hesitant to ask women to go overseas because of the potential hardships associated with some locations. Women do not share this hesitancy, however. Among MBA students surveyed by Nancy Adler (1984), women were equally as willing as their male counterparts to accept international assignments and pursue international careers.

There is growing evidence that women make good expatriate managers. This suggests that firms will want to use more women in foreign locations. Particularly interesting is the evidence that women make good expatriate managers even in locations where local women would generally not be well accepted as managers. Many international organizations are concerned about assigning women to such countries as Japan in case they would not be accepted by male counterparts. A paper by Jelinek and Adler (1988) reported that this was not the case. They found that North American women managers in Japan were viewed as foreigners rather than as women and that their gender was not an impediment to competent management. Adler quoted one woman who worked successfully in Hong Kong as saying, "It doesn't make any difference if you are blue, green, purple, or a frog, if you have the best product at the best price, the Chinese will buy," and she concluded that in global business, pragmatism wins out over prejudice.

While the information currently available suggests that women make effective managers internationally, they clearly face difficulties. The previous reports of women's effectiveness are based on the small number of women who were offered, and accepted, international assignments. Given the general biases against female candidates, it is likely that these women were particularly good candidates. It is to be expected, therefore, that their performance would also be good.

It is only practical for firms, and for women seeking expatriate assignments, to investigate the reality of the foreign work environment for a woman manager. A realistic assessment of the environment means that the expatriate can be appropriately prepared and the firm can provide the needed support to allow for high performance. For example, if the woman cannot legally drive in a foreign country, she must be prepared to accept this limitation and the firm must provide a driver to give her needed mobility. If a woman will not be admitted to clubs where business is often conducted, she will need to develop alternative venues for making business contacts, and the firm should provide the necessary funding and contacts to accomplish this.

In spite of potential obstacles, the research generally suggests that foreign women can overcome local biases against women managers relatively easily. For example, Saudi men are uncomfortable working with women in general but treat foreign women with respect because of their assumed high status. In Saudi Arabia, where the man must precede the woman into a room, men will generally apologize to the foreign woman first. Successful women, however, generally do not openly contradict the values in the host country; for example, they dress conservatively and cover themselves where this is considered important.

The view that foreign women can be effective as managers where it would be difficult for local women is supported in a study reported by Dawson, Ladenburg, and Moran (1987). A majority of the women surveyed described themselves and their professional positions as outside the cultural norms in the foreign environment, but they were "challenged and happy with their lives overseas" (81). Rossman (1990) also illustrated the potential for women managers in a series of profiles of women internationally. Some excerpts from these are presented in Exhibit 12.1. The selected profiles show that virtually anywhere in the world it is possible for women to succeed. These profiles are more than twenty years old; given the positive changes relative to women in the workforce over this period, it is likely that even more positive profiles could be identified today.

Legislation in North America and a number of other places prohibits discrimination on the basis of certain personal characteristics, including gender. This applies to international assignments as well as those at home. Nevertheless, this legislation is tempered by requirements of particular jobs. For example, the Roman Catholic Church does not accept women for ordination as priests and is not required by this law to do so. Similarly, in foreign locations, there may be legislation governing the assignment of women to certain jobs, positions, or locations. In these circumstances the international firm has to abide by the foreign legislation. This creates a dilemma for the firm because it may be breaking the law at home, and possibly violating its own internal policies, in order to comply with the foreign legislation.

Situations such as these may need to be considered on a case-by-case basis in order to determine the most appropriate way of resolving the dilemma. In some situations, a female candidate may prefer not to accept a posting to such a location; in others, it may be possible to make special arrangements that provide a means to bypass the foreign requirements; in still others, a job title, duties, and so on might need to be modified. Perhaps a lesson can be taken from the Saudi women entrepreneurs who employ a man as a front. From the perspective of the firm, the important outcome is the effective use of women managers. From the woman's perspective, the important outcome is her ability to perform at an appropriate level.

Exhibit 12.1

Excerpts from *The International Businesswoman of the 1990s*

- Barbara Stewart has successfully conducted business in Saudi Arabia, Tunisia, Jordan, Iraq, and Egypt.
- Diane Simpson, president of a small New York–based management consulting firm, specializes in U.S.-Japanese business.
- Linda Pakh has negotiated loans in Budapest, Bucharest, Moscow, Prague, Warsaw, and East Berlin.
- Jane Altschuler successfully produced and directed a film shot in Nigeria—*Nigeria: The Unknown Giant.*
- Pat Winters, at 24, has made sales trips to the United Kingdom, Norway, France, Germany, and Italy.
- The author has worked as a marketing consultant in Latin America, Europe, and the Far East.

Source: Rossman (1990).

The actual experiences of women expatriates can vary widely. Some women find an international posting to be a successful and rewarding experience from both a career and a personal perspective; others find it unsuccessful, resulting in career setbacks and family breakups; still others have mixed experiences. Interviews with women executives suggest that there are a substantial number of women expatriates with careers (both women transfers and married women accompanying a spouse on an international transfer) and that their numbers will increase. Organizations that recognize this and pay attention to their concerns will likely benefit.

Other Personal Characteristics

In Jamaica, students agreed that discrimination on the basis of personal characteristics was improper. The author posed the following scenario:

> An American firm has selected a candidate to go to Jamaica to run the subsidiary there. He is an ideal candidate, with the right personal characteristics, substantial international experience, and good skills for the job. He is a homosexual and plans to take his long-term partner with him to Jamaica. They live openly as a homosexual couple and will do the same in Jamaica.

Students then agreed that certain personal characteristics did have to be considered. In essence the students said, "Jamaicans will kill him." They meant this literally. Homosexuality is illegal in Jamaica and most of the former British colonies in the Caribbean, and the people are generally homophobic.

In such an environment, it may not be appropriate for a homosexual and his partner to accept the assignment.

Similarly, if a Jewish candidate were the best person to send to a country with serious anti-Semitic views, such as Iran, the candidate and the company would have to consider the consequences before making a decision. Where serious racial or religious biases exist, these need to be taken into account. Sending a Jew to an anti-Semitic country, a Muslim to an anti-Muslim one, a Christian to an anti-Christian location, an Indian to an anti-Indian one, a Caucasian to an anti-white company, or a black person to an anti-black one, may be putting them in serious jeopardy. At best, they will be ineffective on the job because of discrimination. At worst, they may suffer physical harm. Where there are families involved, the situation is even more serious, as the families are likely to face discrimination in their everyday life, and possibly harassment or worse.

People with disabilities also pose a special challenge. In North America and Europe, it is often taken for granted that buildings will be accessible for those with disabilities and that these individuals will be treated as equal to others. The same is certainly not the case elsewhere. People with disabilities are regarded as crippled in many places, with pity as the best emotion they encounter. Even where this is not the case, in much of the world, little thought has been given to access for the disabled and it is extremely difficult for them to travel or get into and around buildings.

These issues must be taken into account in making decisions about who will work where. In the North American context, managers cannot and should not discriminate on the basis of disability, age, gender, race, religion, or sexual preference. Where the situation warrants consideration of these characteristics, it should be discussed with a potential candidate so that the company and the candidate can make an informed decision.

Ethics in International Management Decisions

At the beginning of the twenty-first century, the worldwide common concerns were ethics, social responsibility, corporate governance, and, in response to climate change, an interest in "green business." These concerns had come to the fore because of a variety of scandals in the business world and because of a growing recognition that humans had affected the environment to such a degree that human survival might be in question. In 2012, there was substantial concern about the growing disparity between the very rich and ordinary people around the world. The "Occupy Wall Street" movement that started in the United States spread around the world and was supported by a broad array of people, showing widespread dissatisfaction with the very rich getting richer.

Government bailouts of banks while executives still received high salaries and bonuses were almost universally disliked. These concerns all transcended national boundaries and were largely global in nature. They made it clear that ethics were a critical consideration in international management decisions.

At the same time, international managers face many ethical issues abroad that may not be obvious in their home country. At home, ethical rights and wrongs are at least somewhat clear, but in foreign countries, major questions can arise regarding what is right and what is wrong. For example, lobbying in the United States is considered a normal activity—companies and industries send representatives to "lobby" U.S. government representatives, asking these representatives to make decisions that will positively affect the company or industry and offering political support in return. In some countries outside the United States, this practice is considered unethical and equivalent to "buying" the government. In North America, it is normal to tip restaurant waiters and taxi drivers, but people from many other parts of the world are mystified by this practice because the waiters and taxi drivers are simply performing an expected service, simply doing their job. Similarly, in parts of Africa, Asia, and Latin America, tipping customs officials is considered normal, while North Americans see this as bribery because such payments are intended to get preferential treatment. This book has previously discussed the importance of understanding cultural preferences, but ethics go beyond this because they express fundamental beliefs about what is universally right and wrong. Ethical questions can arise because of issues associated with factors such as ethnicity, gender, race, or religion. Is it ethical to deny someone a job because of race, religion, or ethnicity if the discrimination is because of the difficulties the person would face in a foreign location?

Developing countries are believed to be generally more corrupt than developed countries. That is, there is more need for unreported payments and gifts in business dealings. These payments may be to civil servants, government officials, or other businesses. Transparency International's Corruption Index of 38 countries (as reported in the *Economist*, "Bribery and Business" 2002) lists the most corrupt 17 as developing countries; the least corrupt 17 are either developed or well on their way to being developed, such as Singapore, Hong Kong, Chile, Taiwan, and Hungary. There is some evidence that links corruption and development level quite closely. The UN's *World Development Report* (United Nations 2001) argues that corruption has large costs for development and that there is strong evidence that higher levels of corruption are associated with lower rates of growth and lower per capita incomes. The *Economist* ("Bribery and Business" 2002) illustrates the impact of corruption on foreign direct investment (FDI) by correlating FDI inflows with perceptions of corruption and finding a clear link; countries considered more corrupt receive much smaller amounts of FDI.

Some countries and companies have established rules intended to eliminate corruption. The United States Foreign Corrupt Practices Act makes illegal any payments by U.S. companies (other than small facilitation payments) to foreign officials or political candidates. The United Kingdom has enacted legislation extending its anti-bribery laws to cover British nationals and companies abroad. Many multinational companies have "no bribery" policies and codes of ethics that include statements about corrupt practices.

The situation faced by managers in foreign countries where bribery is commonplace is not always straightforward, however. For example:

- In India, a bribe may be expected to get your goods through customs or to be allowed to register at a hotel; managers may have little choice.
- In Nigeria, bribery may be largely taken for granted; managers may find themselves receiving gifts that they are unsure whether to accept.
- In the People's Republic of China, corruption is dealt with harshly, but gift giving among associates is expected; the difference between a gift and a bribe is not always clear.

A manager from a Canadian company with a subsidiary in Mexico illustrated the difficulty of dealing with corruption in the following story. The Canadian CEO of the Mexican subsidiary went to a party one night. Unfortunately, he stayed out too late and had rather too much to drink. On his way home, he was arrested and put in jail in Mexico City. The company had a strict "no bribe" clause in its code of ethics, and the Mexican police would not release the Canadian unless they received an appropriate sum of money. The solution was to hire a Mexican attorney to make the payment. The managers could claim they had not contravened the code; they had simply paid the attorney. The attorney was happy to receive a fee that also allowed him to pay the bribe to the police.

The foregoing story illustrates the ease with which rules can be contravened. While there are laws and codes of ethics, it remains relatively simple for companies to participate in corrupt activities. The *Economist* ("Bribery and Business" 2002) suggested that the incidence of bribery may have been growing and noted that in Uganda, the practice is estimated to increase companies' costs substantially.

By and large, the developed world seeks more policing of corruption and the developing world is more likely to be the locale for corruption. An issue like corruption is less clear cut than those previously discussed, however. One can argue that businesspeople from developed countries contribute to the existence of corruption as much as do their counterparts in the developing world. As noted, managers from developing countries often comment on the Western custom of tipping at hotels, restaurants, and other similar locales, and ask why this is not considered a bribe.

There are many other ethical issues that managers face as they do business and make decisions around the world. Consider the following two dilemmas:

• In some countries, child labor is normal. Children work to help support their families. Their parents may need to remain at home to look after other children and to manage livestock. Many children are proud of the work they do and their ability to help their families. Many people from more developed countries see child labor as morally reprehensible. *As a manager in an international firm, how do you handle the issue of employing children?*

• Developed countries may ban pesticides because of their potential damage to wildlife or potential for causing a variety of diseases. Some developing countries may wish to continue the use of these pesticides because they increase crop yields. The people of the country may be facing severe food shortages, and immediate survival is more important to them than their future or the environment. *As a manager in an international firm, how do you react to a request to provide a pesticide banned in North America to a developing country?*

It is not clear in the two situations described what is right and what is wrong. This is the essence of an ethical dilemma. There are good reasons to employ children where they would be worse off if you did not employ them. There are good reasons to provide pesticides where people would be worse off if you did not provide them. There are also good reasons to stop the practice of child labor and to avoid the use of dangerous pesticides. International managers face such dilemmas and need to weigh the pros and cons carefully. In the two examples given, some ethical answers might include:

• Employ the children but provide health care and education for them.
• Provide the pesticide for immediate use if it is the only effective one available, while investing profits to find a safe alternative.

Decisions that involve ethical dilemmas are difficult to make. There are no rules to apply in all situations. The best advice for an international manager is to think carefully about the implications of any ethical decision, and consider all of the stakeholders and how they will be affected. Make the decision then that leaves one with a clear conscience.

Universal Versus Culturally Contingent

Many ethical arguments revolve around whether ethics are universal or culturally contingent. Some scholars argue that what is good is good and what is bad is bad, no matter where you are in the world. Others believe that definitions of good and bad change from location to location, and even from one situation to another. For example, in the West, we generally believe that lying is wrong, yet in some situations, so as not to hurt someone, we may believe that lying is the ethical thing to do.

As managers, you may believe that ethics are universal or you may feel that a cultural contingency view is closer to reality. If you take the first view, you may find yourself at odds with other managers at times, but if you take the second view, you may find that you are sometimes put in the position of making a decision, or taking an action, that you feel is wrong.

The middle ground is to identify some actions, behaviors, and decisions that are always wrong—that is, cases of universal ethics—and others that are acceptable in some places but not in others. In the first group, I would include things like murder, rape, torture, sex with children, and so on. All of these are, to me, fundamentally and universally wrong. In the second group, I would include practices like tipping, small gifts, rules applying to relationships between men and women, family customs and relationships, and so on. These differ from place to place, and I am willing to accept the differences. For example, I would consider it wrong in my environment to segregate men and women socially, but I know that this is normal in other countries for religious reasons, and I would accept it even though I might find it strange.

Managers will need to decide on an individual basis what are universals and what are cultural contingencies, and act accordingly. What we can be sure of is that we will face many situations in foreign countries where what we think is ethical may be seen as unethical, and vice versa.

Climate Change: The New Ethical Issue

According to the *Economist* ("Special Report" 2007, 2), in the 1980s when the notion of global warming was first seriously addressed, businesses were reluctant to admit that human activity might be changing the climate, because this would mean that companies had to accept some responsibility. The United Nations set up the Intergovernmental Panel on Climate Change in 1989. In response, the big carbon emitters set up the Global Climate Coalition (GCC), and this body cast doubt on the science and campaigned against greenhouse-gas reductions. By the early 2000s, it was essentially universally accepted that global warming and climate change were a reality, and the GCC was disbanded in 2002.

Managers around the world now face the new challenges relating to the extent of their company's so-called "carbon footprint," or the extent to which they are contributing to carbon emissions. Few businesspeople today would disagree that climate change is happening and that it must be addressed.

Today's international managers are more likely to boast of their "greenness," and annual reports point to investments to offset emissions and the use of greener technologies, such as solar and wind power. There is clear moral and ethical pressure on businesses to find ways to address the issues of climate change. The impact of Hurricane Katrina in New Orleans, Al Gore's film, and other evidence of the negative effect of climate change on beloved species such as polar bears all combine to make this an ethical issue. At the same time, there are economic opportunities associated with developing new green technologies and products, and many companies are taking advantage of these opportunities.

A challenge for international managers in dealing with this issue is to find ways to address their operations in a variety of different countries. In some countries, there will be strict regulations regarding emissions and greater incentives to encourage greener operations; in others, regulations may not exist or might be loosely enforced, and there may be no incentives to change operations to less-polluting ones. Emissions, however, are not limited by national boundaries, and the carbon does not stay where it is produced. Carbon from a factory in China can affect Canada, Europe, and the United States, so the international manager operating in China has to recognize the global nature of her/his decisions. Of course, climate change provides opportunities as well as challenges, as we see with growing alternative energies and new approaches to addressing the world's energy needs.

Summary and Conclusions

This chapter began by looking at some of the issues associated with gender internationally. These issues can be extended to other special groups that international managers must consider. In general terms, it seems that women are participating in the workforce in increasing numbers in most countries around the world. The role of women varies considerably from place to place, however. International managers need to understand these variations and their implications for human resource policies and practices as well as for their management style. The role of race, religion, disability, sexual preference, and so on also vary dramatically around the world. Managers cannot assume that what is allowed, not allowed, expected, or not expected at home will travel around the world. These issues are sensitive ones, and it is their very sensitivity that makes them so important. These issues involve questions of ethics, and there are many other situations in international management that involve ethical considerations as well. This chapter also examined questions of ethics as a special issue in international management.

References

Adler, N.J. 1984. "Women Do Not Want International Careers, and Other Myths About International Management." *Organizational Dynamics* 13(2): 66–78.

Amble, B. 2006. "Big Rise in Number of Female Expats." *Management-Issues,* October 12. http://www.management-issues.com/2006/10/12/research/big-rise-in-number-of-female-expats.asp (accessed March 12, 2012).

Barry, U., and P. Kelleher. 1991. *Review of the Foundation's Work 1985–92 and Its Implications for Women.* Dublin: European Foundation for the Improvement of Living and Working Conditions.

"Bribery and Business." 2002. *Economist* (March 2–8): 63–65.

Catalyst. 2009. "Women CEOs of the Fortune 1000." www.catalyst.org (accessed November 4, 2009).

Davidson, M.J., and R.J. Burke, eds. 2004. *Women in Management Worldwide: Facts, Figures and Analysis.* Thousand Oaks, CA: Sage.

Dawson, G., E. Ladenburg, and R. Moran. 1987. "Women in International Management." In *Businesswoman: Present and Future*, ed. D. Clutterbuck and M. Devine, 76–90. London: Macmillan.

Economist. 1988. *Business Travellers' Guides: Arabian Peninsula on Business.* London: Economist.

Ferraro, G.P. 1990. *The Cultural Dimension of International Business.* Englewood Cliffs, NJ: Prentice Hall.

Hausmann, R., L.D. Tyson, and S. Zahidi. 2009. *The Global Gender Gap Report 2009.* Geneva: World Economic Forum. https://members.weforum.org/pdf/gendergap/report2009.pdf.

International Labour Office. 2004. *Breaking Through the Glass Ceiling: Women in Management: Update 2004.* Geneva.

International Labor Organization (ILO). 2009. "Global Employment Trends for Women." Report, March. Geneva. http://www.ilo.org/wcmsp5/groups/public/@dgreports/@dcomm/documents/publication/wcms_103456.pdf (accessed May 15, 2010).

Jelinek, M., and N.J. Adler. 1988. "Women: World-Class Managers for Global Competition." *Academy of Management Executive* 11(1): 11–20.

Kirk, W.Q., and R.C. Maddox. 1988. "International Management: The New Frontier for Women." *Personnel* 63(3): 46–49.

Parkin, D. 1978. *The Cultural Definition of Political Response: Lineal Destiny Among the Luo.* London: Academic Press.

Punnett, B.J., J. Duffy, S. Fox, A. Gregory, T. Lituchy, S.I. Monserrat, M.R. Olivas Lujan, and N.M. Fernandes dos Santos. 2006. *Successful Professional Women of the Americas: From Polar Winds to Tropical Breezes.* London: Edward Elgar.

Ramachandran, R. 1992. "The Silenced Majority: Sex Ratio and the Status of Women in India." *Canadian Women's Studies* 13(1): 60–66.

Rossman, M.L. 1990. *The International Businesswoman of the 1990s: A Guide to Success in the Global Marketplace.* New York: Praeger.

"Special Report." 2007. *Economist* (June 2): 2.

Tonkin, S. 2009. "Iceland Tops Forum's Global Gender Gap Report 2009." World Economic Forum, October 27. http://forumblog.org/2009/10/iceland-tops-forums-global-gender-gap-report-2009/.

United Nations. 2001. *World Development Report.* Oxford: Oxford University Press.

United Nations Center on Transnational Corporations (UNCTNC). 1988. *Transnational Corporations in World Development: Trends and Prospects.* New York: United Nations.

"Women's Work." 2005. BBC News, news.bbc.co.uk. Series of articles from August 1, 3, 4, 5, subtitled "Conductor of and Orchestra," "Nigerian Mechanic," "Explosives Engineer," and "Supreme Court Judge."

Index

A

Abo, T., 89
Absenteeism, employee, 158
Academy of International Business
    (AIB), 87–88
Achievement, 188
Activity orientation, 26
Adjustment, expatriates
    determinants of, 247–251
    family-spouse, 250–251
Adler, N. J., 48, 180, 209, 275–276
Affective autonomy, 46
Afghanistan, 58
Africa
    leadership in, 172, 186
    women's role in, 274
African Americans, 85
Age distribution, 138
Agreements, 208–211
Aluminum Co. of Canada, 259
Amado, G., 212
Amble, B., 275
American way, 85
Anti-Semitism, 279
Arab countries. *See* Middle East
Arab Spring, 18, 60, 112, 145, 263
Area briefings, 254
Arefiev, Alexander, 214
Argentina, 9–10
Arthur Andersen, 62
Asian Tigers, 9, 128
Association of Southeast Asian Nations
    (ASEAN), 98

Attitudes
    cultural values and, 24–25
    ethnocentrism and parochialism,
        57–58
Attribution training, 253
Attributions, faulty, 203–204
Autonomy, 188
Aycan, Z., 187

B

Baby boomers, 128
Baruch, Y., 6
Bata Shoe Company, 79
Behavior. *See also* Motivation
    cognitive-behavior modification
        training, 253
    geographic basis for, 84
    historical basis for, 84
    organizational behavior, 3, 5
Being-oriented society, 26, 28
Beliefs, societal, 20
Bhutan, 59
Bird, A., 244
Blake, R. R., 174
Blanchard, K., 174
Body language, 198–199
Brazil, negotiating norms in, 211–212
Brazil, H. V., 212
Bribes, 280–281
BRICS countries (Brazil, Russia, India,
    China, and South Africa), 6, 13,
    63, 128, 131
Brislin, R. W., 252

Bruton, G. D., 6
Buckley, P., 91
Buddhism, 118–120
Business
  as engine of growth, 64
  globalization of, 56
  government regulation of, 64–65
  positive views of, 64–65
  society and, 63–64
Business Environmental Risk
    Intelligence, 74
Business Fit International, 177
Business International, 74
Business risk. *See* Political risk
    assessment and management
Buy-local campaigns, 70

C

Canada, 61, 68–69, 82–83
  gender roles in, 273
Capitalism, 61
Carbon emissions, 284
Career development, 240
Caribbean island states, 101–102
  absenteeism, 158
  delegation and participation in, 165
  goals setting, 161
  Herzberg's *theory x/theory y*, 174
  leadership style in, 186
  uncertainty avoidance in, 188–189
Cartographers (mapmakers), 91–94
Castro, Fidel, 59
Catalyst, 264
Centrally planned economies, 61, 146
Charismatic leadership, 179–181
Chemical Bank, 73
Child labor, 282
China, 8, 11
  automobile industry in, 125
  central planning and free markets,
    61
  conformity in, 213
  negotiating style in, 212–213
  political environment, 146–147

China *(continued)*
  U.S. firms in, 57
  women's roles in, 269, 275
Christianity, 120–121
CIA (Central Intelligence Agency)
    Factbooks, 74
Climate change, 3, 283–284
Clinton, Hillary, 140
Co-lineal society, 27
Code of ethics, 281
Cognitive-behavior modification
    training, 253
Colonies, 60, 147
Common values, 16
Communication, 5
  competence of communicators,
    197–198
  context for, 196–197
  cross-national dimensions of, 193–194
  expatriates and, 249
  expressive and purposive messages,
    195
  flow, 194–196
  globalization and, 7
  multi-unit signals in, 195–196
  nonverbal, 198
  as process, 195
  translation, 113–114
  See also Cross-national
    communication
Company characteristics, political risk,
    75–76
Compensation policy, 238–240
Concessions and agreement, in
    negotiation process, 208–211
Confiscation of property, 69
Confucian dynamism (CD), 30–31,
    190
Consensus, 188
Conservatism, 46, 188
Constitutional monarchies, 59
Containing focus, 26
Context, for communication, 196–197
Contingency leadership, 174–175
Contracting arrangement, 232
Controlling focus, 26

Corporate reporting, transparency in, 62
Corruption, 147, 280
Country clusters, 34–35
  limitation of, 35
  role in international decisions, 36–38
Cross-border strategic alliances, 52
Cross-cultural training, 237, 252–257
  attribution training, 253
  cognitive-behavior modification training, 253
  common types of, 254
  cultural awareness training, 253
  experiential learning training, 253–254
  information or fact-oriented, 253
  Mendenhall and Oddou's framework, 256
  Tung model, 234–235, 256
Cross-national communication
  barriers to, 198
  faulty attributions, 203–204
  ignorance of communication rules, 198–201
  perceptual biases, 201–202
  personal space and, 200–201
  spatial relationships, 199–200
  stereotypes in, 204–205
Cross-national environment, 4–5
  communication and travel, 16
  convergence/divergence factors in, 14–17
Cross-national workforce, 5
Cuba, 59, 61, 70, 146
Cultural awareness training, 253
Cultural environment, 20
  convergence of, 56
  cross-national variations, 4
  importance of, 45
Cultural value models, 25–47
  alternative models, 46–47
  country clusters, 34–38
  Hofstede's value survey (VSM), 29–34
  Kluckhohn and Strodtbeck's model, 25–29

Cultural value models (continued)
  Smith and Peterson event management, 40–46
  world values surveys, 38–40
Cultural values, 5, 20, 23–25, 39
  attitudes and, 24–25
  international management and, 22–23, 52–53
  needs and, 24
  norms and, 25
  values and, 23–24
Culture, 5
  definition of, 22–23
  development and, 140–144
  history and geography, 81–84
  motivation and, 165–167
  national culture, 50–51
  negotiating styles, 211
  overlapping cultures, 51
  variation within, 48–49
Culture assimilator, 254
Culture, Leadership, and Organizations—The GLOBE Study of 62 Societies (House et al.), 180
Culture novelty, 250, 256
Culture shock, 246

D

Das, J., 6
David, K., 22, 107, 109
Dawson, G., 277
Decision trees, 176–177
Defensive political risk management, 76–77
  finances, 76
  management and logistics, 76–77
  marketing, 77
Democracy, 56, 144–145
Demography, 5
  age distribution, 138
  development and, 136–140
  gender roles, 139–140
  literacy and numeracy, 138–139

Demography *(continued)*
  population dispersion, 138
  population growth, 136–138
  world population estimates, 137
Deutscher, G., 106, 108
Developed countries, 129
  developing countries vs., 135
Developing countries, 126–127, 129
  characteristics of, 132
  defined, 128
  developed countries vs., 135
  Hofstede's model and, 140–141
  illness in, 127
  most/least livable countries, 133
  politics and, 145
  potential of, 127
  poverty in, 127, 134
Development
  cultural values and, 140–144
  definitions of, 128–131
  demography and, 136–140
  developed countries, 129
  developing countries, 129
  impact of level of, 134–136
  less developed countries (LDCs),
    129–130
  politics and, 144–147
  underdeveloped countries,
    129–130
  understanding issues of, 127–128
Dictatorships, 58–59
Doh, J., 89
Doing-oriented, 26
Dorfman, P., 175, 185
Dual-career couples, 257–261
Duffy, J., 266, 270
Dunbar, R., 244

E

Economic conditions, 20
Economic systems, 5
  freedom and income levels, 146
  history and geography, 89, 91
Economist Intelligence Units, 74

Egalitarian commitment vs.
    conservatism, 46–47
Electronic communication, 3
Embeddedness vs. autonomy, 46
Emerging countries, 130–131
Employee groups
  benefits and drawbacks of, 220–226
  foreign guest workers, 229–231
  in international firms, 218–220
  lower-level employees, 226
  staffing choice, 226
  supervisors/first-level managers, 226
  technical personnel/specialists, 226
Enright, M., 88
Enron, 62, 64
Environmental factors, 3, 5
Equality, 271–272
Equity theory, motivation and, 157–158
Esteem need, 152
Ethical issues, 5, 263
  bribery and corruption, 280–281
  child labor, 282
  climate change as, 283–284
  international management decisions,
    279–282
  pesticide use, 282
  universal vs. culturally contingent,
    283
Ethnocentric staffing approach, 227
Ethnocentrism, 57–58
European Union (EU), 10, 15, 63,
    98–99, 270
Exchange of information, 207
Expatriates, 4–5, 52, 242–243
  adjustments of, 244–224
  culture novelty, 250
  culture shock and, 246
  determinants of adjustment, 247–251
  dual-career couples, 257–261
  family-spouse adjustment, 250–251
  finding mentors, 248–249
  honeymoon period, 246
  interaction with host nationals, 255
  job novelty, 255
  mastery period, 247
  organizational culture and, 251–252

Expatriates *(continued)*
  perceptual abilities, 249–250
  relational abilities, 248
  self-efficacy, 246
  special issues of, 243–244
  stress management, 247–248
  substitution ability, 248
  willingness to communicate, 249
  See also Cross-cultural training;
    International assignment
Expectations theory, 162–164
Experiential learning training, 253–254
Expertise, 188
Export processing zones (EPZs),
  women's jobs in, 268
Expressive messages, 195
Expropriation of property, 69
Extrinsic motivation factors, 156

F

Family-spouse adjustment, 250–251
Faulty attributions, in communication,
  203–204
Feminine values, 30, 189–190
Fernandes dos Cantos, N. M., 266, 270
Ferraro, G. P., 274
Fertility rates, 138
Finances, political risk strategies, 76–77
Fisher, R., 205
Forced divestment (nationalization),
  70–71
Foreign business
  incentives and restrictions, 67–68
  as neocolonialism, 65
  view of, 65–66
  See also Globalization
Foreign direct investment (FDI), 13,
  280
  incentives and restrictions, 67–69
  negatives of, 67
  positives of, 66
Foreign guest workers, 53, 229
Foreign manager, view of home
  country, 68–69

Fox, S., 266, 270
Franchising arrangement, 232
Fraser Institute, 146
Free-market economy, 61, 63
Free trade, 7–8, 95
Free Trade of the Americas Agreement
  (FTAA), 99

G

G8 group, 6
G20 group, 128
Gates, Bill, 135
Gates Foundation, 64
Gender roles, 5, 139–140
General Agreement on Tariffs and
  Trade (GATT), 9
Geocentric staffing, 227
Geography, 5, 20
  behavior and, 84
  culture and, 83–84
  defined, 86
  values and behavior, 86–87
  world perspective and, 91–94
Getting to Yes (Fisher and Ury), 205
Gini index, 136
Glass ceilings, 260
Global Climate Coalition (CCC), 283
Global philosophy, 8
Global warming, 3, 64, 284
Globalization
  attitudes towards, 8–11
  developed vs. developing countries,
    10–11
  future of, 11–14
  meaning for managers, 7–8
  new economy based on, 9
  opportunities of, 7
  premises of, 7
  world beyond 2010, 17–19
GLOBE project, 179–181
Goal acceptance, 161
Goal setting
  in motivation, 161–162, 164
  to improve performance, 162

Government bailouts, 62
Government intervention, 62
Government regulation, 5, 20
  society and, 64–65
  unwelcome regulations, 71–72
  view of business, 64–65
Government relations, integrative
    political risk management, 78
Graham, J. L., 212–213
Grameen Bank of Bangladesh, 64, 140
Green developments, 63
Gregory, A., 266, 270
Gross domestic product (GDP), 126,
    132, 134
Guest workers, 53, 229–231

H

Hampden-Turner, C., 46, 167
Harmony, 26, 46
Herberger, R. A., 212–213
Hershey, P., 174
Herzberg, F., 156
Herzberg's *theory x/theory y*,
    173–174
Herzberg's two factor theory of
    motivation, 156
  intrinsic/extrinsic factors, 156
Hierarchy vs. egalitarianism, 46
High-context communication
    (*hara-gei*), 197
High-context locations, 200
Hilton Hotels, 57
Hinduism, 121–122
History, 5, 20
  behavior and, 84
  culture and, 83
  defined, 85
  understanding of, 85–94
Hofstede, G., 29, 140–141, 145, 154,
    161, 184, 186, 189
Hofstede's value survey model (VSM),
    29–34, 47, 272
  Confucian dynamism (CD), 30–31,
    190

Hofstede's value survey model (VSM)
    (continued)
  culture and leadership, 188–190
  individualism/collectivism, 29,
    140–141, 187–188
  in international management, 32–34
  limitations of, 31–32
  masculinity/femininity, 30, 189–190
  power distance, 30, 140–141, 187
  uncertainty avoidance, 30, 188–189
Horst, P. R., Jr., 210–211
Host country nationals (HCNs), 219,
    222–224, 232
  benefits of, 222–223
  compensation and benefits, 239
  drawbacks of, 223–224
  international managers, 236–237
  polycentric staffing, 227
  view of home country, 68–69
House, R. J., 180
Human nature, 26
Human relationships, 27
Human resource law, 21
Human resource management (HRM),
    3, 5
  organizational structure and,
    231–233
Human resource (staffing) choices, 37,
    218.
  foreign guest workers, 229–231
  international product life cycle,
    228–229
  See also Employee groups; Host
    country nationals (HCNs); Parent
    country nationals (PCNs); Third
    country nationals (TCNs)

I

Illegal workers, 230–231
Inca civilization, 81–82, 91
India, 155
  leadership research in, 184
Individualism, 29, 140, 187
Individualistic societies, 27

Industrializing economies, 130–131
Industry characteristics, political risk, 75–76
Information or fact-oriented training, 253
Infrastructure, 134
Instability, 74
Integrative political risk management, 77–78
  financial, 77
  government relations, 78
  management and operations, 78
Intellectual autonomy, 46
International assignment
  adjustment to organizational culture, 251–252
  job in, 251
  role clarity, 251
  role conflict, 251
  role discretion, 251
  role novelty, 251
  See also Cross-cultural training
International firms, groups of employees in, 218–220
International management
  corruption, 147
  country clusters in, 36–38
  cultural issues, 22–23
  current events, 102–103
  ethical issues in, 279–282
  forgotten locations, 6
  geography in, 81–83
  history and, 81–83
  Hofstede's value survey model (VSM), 32–34
  Kluckhohn and Strodtbeck model, 27–29
International managers
  compensation and benefits, 238–240
  country history and, 86
  cross-cultural training methods, 237
  cultural values and, 52–53
  environmental changes and, 3
  equality issues, 271–272
  history and geography, 94–102
  host country nationals (HCNs), 236–237, 239

International managers (continued)
  learning new languages, 113
  parent country nationals (PCNs), 236, 238
  personal characteristics of, 278–279
  Punnett and Ricks model, 235–236
  role of women in society, 267
  selection and training of, 233–241
  third country nationals (TCNs), 237, 239–240
  training process, 237–238
  Tung model, 234–235, 256
  women as, 275–278
International mergers, 233
International product life cycle, 228–229
International strategy, 100–101
International subsidiaries, 37
International trade, 95
Internet
  convergence/divergence, 17
  dependence on, 3
  development and, 135
  national regulations and, 56
Interpretation, 113–114
Intrinsic motivation factors, 156
Investment/investment flows, 95
Islam, 122–123

J

Jamaica, 83
Japan, 9
  communication in, 4
  concessions and agreement in, 209
  high-context communication (hara-gei), 197
  management practices, 66, 183–184
  negotiation process in, 206
  persuasion in, 208
  women's roles in, 269, 274–275
Jelinek, M., 276
Job descriptions, 178
Job novelty, 255
Joint ventures, 37, 232–233

Judaism, 123
Just Landed, 243

K

Kauffman-Doig, Federico, 81–82
Khadra, B., 185
Khrushchev, Nikita, 199
Kinesics signals, 198–199
Kirk, W. Q., 275
Kirkbride, P. A., 213
Kluckhohn, A., 25
Kluckhohn and Strodtbeck's value
    orientation model, 25–29
  activity orientation, 26
  basic human nature, 26
  human relationships, 27
  in international management, 27–29
  public/private space, 27
  relationship to nature, 26
  time orientation, 26
Kobrin, S., 88

L

Labor mobility, 21
Ladenburg, E., 277
Landis, D., 252
Language, 5, 20, 105–108
  history and geography, 89–90
  importance of, 107–108
  learning new languages, 113
  translation and interpretation,
    113–114
  See also Linguistic diversity
Latin America, 83, 200–201
  women in, 270–271
Lawler, J. J., 186
Leadership, 5
  charismatic leadership, 179–181
  defined, 170
  effective leadership, 170–171
  GLOBE project, 179–181
  individualism and collectivism,
    187–188

Leadership (continued)
  management vs., 171
  masculinity and femininity, 189–190
  path/goal clarification, 181–182
  power-distance societies, 187
  supports/substitutes for, 178–179
  transformational leadership, 179–181
  uncertainty avoidance, 187–188
  variation in, 182–186
Leadership style, 172–173
Leadership theories, 171–178
  contingency theories/leadership,
    174–175
  Herzberg's *theory x/theory y*, 173–174
  leadership style, 172–173
  participation, 176
  trait perspective, 171–172
  Vroom and Yetton decision tree,
    176–177
Least developed countries (LDC), 130
Lectures, 254
Less developed countries (LDCs), 129
Levitt, T., 14
Licensing agreement, 232
Linear societies, 27
Linguistic diversity, 109–113
  impact of heterogeneity, 109–110
  impact of homogeneity, 109
  linguistic change, 112–113
  linguistic hierarchies, 110–111
  national languages, 110
Linguistic hierarchies, 110–111
Linking and seducing approaches,
    211–212
Literacy rages, 138–139
Lituchy, T., 266, 270
Lobbying, 280

M

McClelland's motivation theory, 154
Maddox, R. C., 275
Madoff, Bernard, 17
*Management: A Developing Country
    Perspective* (Punnett), 97

Management, 5
  leadership vs., 171
  and logistics, defensive political risk
    strategies, 76–77
  by objectives (MBO), 33
  and operations, integrative political
    risk management, 78
  wealth and, 126
  See also International management
Managers
  globalization and, 7–8
  government intervention and, 62
  Japanese vs. American practices,
    183–184
  political assessment and, 57–58
  political systems and, 60
  strategies choices of, 78–79
  women as, 272–273
  See also International managers
"Mañana" syndrome, 83, 162
Mandela, Nelson, 172
Mangaliso, M. P., 186
Marketing, 37
  defensive political risk strategies, 77
Masculine values, 30, 189–190
Maslow's hierarchy of needs, 152–154,
    156
  cultural variations of, 153
  esteem level, 152
  physiological level, 152
  security level, 152
  self-actualization, 152
  social level, 152
Mastery, 26, 46
Mastery vs. harmony, 46
Mendenhall, M., 256
Mentors, 248–249
Mercer's *Benefits Surveys for
    Expatriates and Globally Mobile
    Employees*, 4, 240
Mexico, 6
Microsoft, 135
Middle East, 60, 146, 201, 230
  leadership in, 185
  women as managers, 275
  women's role in, 268–269

Minneman, John, 214
Minoan civilization, 3
Monserrat, S. I., 266, 270
Moran, R., 277
Morrison, Colin, 177
Motivation, 5, 150–151
  delegation and participation in,
    164–165
  of employees, 8
  equity in, 157–158
  expectations, 162–164
  goal setting, 161–162
  needs in, 152–157
  North American theories of, 151–168
  rewards in, 158–161
  satisfaction and, 157
  as universal vs. culture bound,
    165–168
  See also Rewards
Mouton, J. S., 174
Multi-party democracies, 59, 61
Multi-unit communication signals,
    195–196
Multidimensional scaling, 46
  affective autonomy, 46
  conservatism or embeddedness, 46
  egalitarianism, 46
  harmony, 46
  hierarchy, 46
  intellectual autonomy, 46
  mastery, 46

N

Nation-state, 56–57, 63
National culture, 20
  understanding subcultures, 50–51
National languages, 110
National variables, 20
Nationalization (forced divestment),
    70–71
Nature, relationship to, 26
Need theories, motivation and,
    152–157
Needs, attitudes, and norms, 20, 24

Negotiating norms
  in Brazil, 211–212
  in People's Republic of China,
    212–213
  in Russia, 214–215
Negotiating styles, 211
Negotiation process, 5, 206
  concessions and agreement, 208–211
  cross-national dimensions of, 193–194
  exchange of information, 207
  four phases of, 210
  in international contexts, 205
  persuasion, 207–208
  relationship building, 206–207
Nepal, 58
New economy, 9
Newenham-Kahindi, A., 186
Newly industrialized countries (NICs),
  130
Nixon, Richard, 200
Noise in communication system, 194
Nonverbal communication, 198
Norms, 25
North American Free Trade Agreement
  (NAFTA), 98–99
North/South divide, 130
Numeracy rates, 138–139

O

"Occupy" movement, 61, 63–64, 134,
  279
Oddou, G., 256
Olivas Lujan, M. R., 266, 270
Operations, interference in, 72
Organisation for Economic Co-operation
  and Development (OECD), 129
Organizational behavior, 3, 5
Organizational culture, expatriates
  adjustment to, 251–252
Organizational effectiveness,
  relationships to, 21
Organizational structure
  contracting arrangement, 232
  franchising arrangement, 232

Organizational structure (continued)
  international HRM choices,
    231–233
  international mergers, 233
  joint venture, 232–233
  licensing agreement, 232
  strategic alliances, 233
Organizations, national legal
  framework, 21
Orwa, B., 186

P

Parent country nationals (PCNs),
  219–224, 232
  benefits of, 220–221
  compensation and benefits, 238
  drawbacks of, 221–222
  ethnocentric staffing, 227
  international managers, 236
  See also Expatriates
Parkin, D., 274
Parochialism, 57–58
Participation, 176
Past-oriented society, 28
Path/goal clarification, 181–182
People with disabilities, 279
Per capital GDP, 132
Perceptual abilities, expatriate,
  249–250
Perceptual biases, 201–202
Personal space, 200–201
Persuasion, 207–208
Pesticides, 282
Peterson, M. F., 42, 46, 166–167
Phene, A., 88
Physiological needs, 152
Political contributions, 57
Political environment, 56–58
Political risk assessment and
  management, 72–79
  country characteristics, 74–75
  defensive risk management, 76–77
  factors affecting, 74
  forced divestment, 70–71

Political risk assessment and
    management *(continued)*
  industry and company characteristics,
      75–76
  interference in operations, 72
  sources of information, 73–74
  types of, 69–72
  unwelcome regulations, 71–72
Political systems, 5, 58–63
  colonies, 60
  constitutional monarchies, 59
  development and, 144–147
  dictatorships, 58–59
  managers and, 60
  multi-party democracies, 59, 61
  single-party systems, 59, 61
  sovereign systems, 58
Polycentric staffing, 227
Ponzi schemes, 17
Population dispersion, 138
Population growth, 136–138
Poverty, 127, 134
Power breakfast/lunch, 207
Power distance index, 30, 140, 187
Present-oriented society, 28
Private enterprise, 63
Private space, 27
Product life cycle, 228–229
Promotion, 240
Public space, 27
Punishment, as motivator, 160
Punnett, B. J., 97, 235, 266, 270
Purposive messages, 195
Pye, L., 213

R

Race, 5
Ramachandran, R., 266
Regional economic linkages, 15,
      98–99
Regulation. *See* Government
      regulation
Regulatory environment, 56–58
Reinforcement theory, 159

Relational abilities, 248
Relationship building, between
      negotiating parties, 206–207
Religion, 4–5, 20, 105, 116–123
  Buddhism, 118–120
  Christianity, 120–121
  defined, 117
  expression of, 117–118
  Hinduism, 121–122
  history and geography, 89–90
  Islam, 122–123
  major world religions, 118–132
  other beliefs, 123
Remittances, 231
Retirement, 240
Rewards
  how to use, 160
  in motivation, 158–161
  potential variations in, 161
  punishment vs., 160
  types of, 159
  when to use, 159–160
Ricks, D., 235
Risk assessment and management.
      See Political risk assessment and
      management
Rituals, 193
Rituals of Dinner, The (Visser), 193
Role clarity, 251
Role conflict, 251
Role discretion, 251
Role novelty, 251
Role-playing, 255
Ronen, S., 35
Rossman, M. L., 277
Royal Bank of Canada, 73
Rule of law vs. rule of man, 145
Russia, negotiating norms in,
      214–215

S

St. Lucia national program, 3–4
Schwartz, S. H., 42, 46–47, 166–167
Security need, 152

Self-actualization, 152
Self-efficacy, in expatriate experience, 246
Sensitivity training, 254
Shenkar, O., 35
Singapore, 9, 128
Single-party systems, 59, 61
Sinha, J. P. B., 184
Smith, P. B., 42, 46, 166–167
Smith and Peterson event management approach, 40–46
  co-workers, 41
  family, 41
  formal rules, 40
  friends, 41–42
  national scores, 43–45
  own experience, 41
  specialists, 41
  subordinates, 40–41
  superiors, 41
  unwritten rules, 40
  wide beliefs, 41
Social needs, 152
Social services, 134
Societal variables, 20
Society, government and, 64–65
South Korea, 84
Sovereign systems, 58
Space, 27
Spam, 194
Spatial relationships, in communication, 199–200
Spouses
  adjustment of, 250–251
  dual-career couples, 257–261
Sri Lanka, 86, 107
Staffing. *See* Employee groups; Human resource (staffing) choices
Stanford, Alan, 17
Stereotypes, 204–205
Strategic alliances, 37, 233
Stress management, in expatriate experience, 247–248
Strodtbeck, F., 25. *See also* Kluckhohn and Strodtbeck's value orientation model

Subcultures, 50–51
Subjugation to nature, 26
Subprime lending crisis, 7, 62, 64, 71
Substitution ability, in expatriate experience, 248
Successful Professional Women of the Americas: From Polar Winds to Tropical Breezes (Punnett et al.), 140
Suppliers, 8
Survival and self-expression, 38–39
Synergy, 51
Szalay, L., 202

T

Taliban, 58
Tallman, S., 88
Task significance, 156
Tata, 125
Tax laws, 69, 240
Technological developments, globalization, 7
Terpstra, V., 15, 22, 107, 109
Terrorism, 64, 75, 85, 131
Theory x/theory y (Herzberg), 173–174
Theory z leadership style, 184
Third country nationals (TCNs), 219, 224–226
  benefits of, 224–225
  compensation and benefits, 239–240
  drawbacks of, 225–226
  international managers, 237
  women workers, 268
Third world countries, 130. *See also* Developing countries
Thomas, A., 6
Time orientation, 26
Trade, 95
Traditional/secular-rational values, 38
Trait theory of leadership, 171–172
Transformational leadership, 179–181

Transitional economies, 130–131
Translation, 113–114
Transparency International's
    Corruption Perceptions Index,
    147, 280
Triandis, H., 202
Trompenaars, F., 46–47, 167
Tung, R. L., 234, 238, 256
Turkey, 82

U

Uncertainty avoidance index (UAI), 30,
    188–189
Underdeveloped countries, 129. *See
    also* Developing countries
United Nations, 56
  Center on Transnational Corporations,
    268
  Development Index, 127, 131,
    134
  Human Development Report,
    132
  Office of the High Representative for
    the Lease Developed Countries,
    Landlocked Developing
    Countries and the Small Island
    Developing States
    (UN-OHRLLS), 130
  Population Fund, 136
United States, 68–69, 82–83
  as free-market economy, 61
  women as managers, 273–274
United States Council for International
    Business, 129
United States Foreign Corrupt
    Practices Act, 281
Ury, W., 205
Utilitarian involvement vs. loyal
    involvement, 47

V

Values, 23–24
Visser, Margaret, 193

Vroom, V. H., 176
Vroom and Yetton decision tree, 176

W

Walumbwa, F. O., 186
Wang, P., 186
Wang, Z. M., 46
WASPS (white Anglo-Saxon
    Protestants), 85
Wealth, management and, 126
Western Europe, women in
    management, 274
Whorf, B. L., 106
Wint, A., 89
Women
  in Africa, 274
  barriers faced by, 266
  in Canada and United States, 273
  in developing countries, 139–140
  dual-career couples, 257–261
  equality of, 264–265, 271–272
  in European Union (EU), 270
  in Far East, 269
  gender gap report, 265
  as international managers, 275–278
  in Japan, 274–275
  in Latin America, 270–271
  as managers, 272–273
  in Middle East, 275
  in People's Republic of China, 275
  role in business, 264–271
  in Western Europe, 274
Workforce, 21
World Bank, 8, 62
World Bank Development Index,
    132
World Economic Forum, Global
    Gender Gap Index, 264
World Trade Organization (WTO),
    61
  Doha round, 6
  free trade, 7
  globalization, 9, 56
  Seattle meetings (1990s), 9

World values surveys, 38–40, 144
    survival and self-expression, 38–39
    traditional/secular-rational values,
        38
Wright, Lorna, 17

X

Xerox, 72–73

Y

Yang, F. Y., 213
Yang, K. S., 213
Yetton, P. H., 176

Z

Zahidi, Saadia, 265

About the Author

Betty Jane Punnett, a native of St. Vincent and the Grenadines, is Professor of International Business and Management at the Cave Hill Campus of the University of the West Indies. She went to Cave Hill in 1999, from the Mona Campus. Prior to Mona, she taught at the University of Windsor in Canada. She has lived and worked in the Caribbean, Canada, Europe, Asia, and the United States. Her major research interest is culture and management, and she is currently working on several research projects in this field, including a study of leadership and motivation in Africa and the African Diaspora in Canada, the Caribbean, and the United States. Professor Punnett holds a PhD in International Business from New York University, an MBA from Marist College, and a BA from McGill University. She has published over seventy academic papers in a wide array of international journals; she has also recently published the following books: *Management: A Developing Country Perspective* (2012 – Routledge), *The Handbook for International Management Research, Experiencing International Business and Management,* and *Successful Professional Women of the Americas.* A new edited book on managing in Africa is due to be published in 2013. She edited *Insights* for the Academy of International Business (AIB) for several years and has served with the Academy of Management and AIB in a variety of capacities.